More Praise for *Church Unique*

"*Church Unique* is a much-needed book. I find that too many of our churches preach the uniqueness of God's gifting and calling and then turn around and attempt to copy the ministry and calling of some other well-known church. While we can learn much from the best practices of other churches, it's a terrible mistake to try to become just like them. Will Mancini shows us a better path."

—Larry Osborne, author, *A Contrarian's Guide to Knowing God;* senior pastor, North Coast Church, San Diego, California

"When I finished *The Purpose Driven Church,* I wanted to lead a church like Saddleback. When I finished *Church Unique*, I wanted to discover God's one-of-a-kind fingerprint for my congregation. Will Mancini gave me an inspirational and courageous playbook to mobilize my mainline church for its own missional calling to follow Jesus Christ."

—Rev. Richard Kannwischer, senior pastor, First Presbyterian Church, San Antonio, Texas

"As chief vision chef, Will Mancini offers up a creative recipe that will satisfy a leader's hunger to create, cast, and implement a vision that is unique to his church."

—Aubrey Malphurs, senior professor of pastoral ministries, Dallas Theological Seminary; president, Malphurs Group; author, *Advanced Strategic Planning*

"Having personally coached leaders around the globe in the area of vision, I am very selective when I invite someone to coach us at Discovery Church. Will Mancini is one of the few. The process he leads and shares in *Church Unique* is extremely helpful whether you're just beginning or are a seasoned leader who's been through visioning processes in the past. If you have ever had that inner pause as a leader that makes you wonder if something is missing, this book may provide the key to greater clarity and new levels of ministry effectiveness."

—David Loveless, pastor, Discovery Church, Orlando, Florida

"The process outlined by Will Mancini has unleashed among our leaders a renewed joy and energy for clarifying, articulating, and advancing God's vision for us in our community. In my fifteen years as pastoral leader of Trinity Church I have never been more excited and hopeful about the future of our 134-year-*young* church!"

—Rev. Dr. Richard C. Noack, senior pastor, Trinity Klein Lutheran Church, Spring, Texas

"Will Mancini is a cutting-edge, innovative leader who forces other leaders to look within themselves and their churches, attempting to dig out the reality of who they are and what they are about. His ability and his life message need to be read and heard by the masses today."

—Ronnie Floyd, author and senior pastor, First Baptist Church Springdale and the Church at Pinnacle Hills, Springdale, Arkansas

"Will Mancini's expertise concerning visionary leadership and strategic thinking has been a huge guiding presence to my ministry. Anything Will writes should be read."

—David Saathoff, lead pastor, Bandera Road Community Church, San Antonio, Texas

"The process and principles of this book can be helpful at any stage in your organization's life. If I were starting my ministry all over again, the first thing I would do is follow the pathway outlined in this book. If you are feeling stuck, this book is for you. Most important, if you are experiencing rapid growth that demands a constant refocusing on your vision, get this book. Will Mancini has worked with Upward Unlimited for years, helping us to define and communicate our vision more clearly. Among the many fruits of the clarity we now enjoy is the confidence that we are passing on our vision and protecting our DNA for the next generation."

—Caz McCaslin, founder and president, Upward Unlimited

"Will Mancini has mastered a process of helping leaders understand God's vision for the church, discover their vision for ministry, and communicate that vision to those they lead. It is not another program or one-size-fits-all approach. It is a tested process of discovery and discipline that results in a clear vision for healthy ministry and dynamic churches.

The end result is a vision that is biblical, compelling, clear, transferable, practical, and unique. These principles will invigorate your leadership, motivate your team, and revolutionize your ministry."

—Willy Rice, senior pastor, Calvary Baptist Church, Clearwater, Florida

"Most vision books are for people without vision. Not this one. Will Mancini's *Church Unique* is carbonated clarity for your vision process. If you are just looking for a quick fix to cut and paste into the quagmire of wasted words known as your mission statement, then this is not the book for you. But if you are ready to awaken your church's dormant uniqueness and live in the vivid high-defintion picture that only your congregation can create, then stop reading this and turn directly to page 85. Will and his crew of carnivorous learners have given us a new hero's mantra: 'Save the church leader—save the world.'"

—The Wayfarer Team, "Awaken Redefinition"

"I know that the Church Unique concept works, because I experienced it firsthand. Through the process, our church leadership was able to unlock the special vision that sets our church apart and positioned us to reach people in new and exciting ways. Far too many congregations are frustrated with cookie-cutter theories that just don't work with their church culture. The Church Unique principles did just the opposite—they helped us articulate our purposes directly out of who we really are."

—Ryan Rush, senior pastor, Bannockburn Baptist Church, Austin, Texas; author, *Home on Time*

"Many of the church and leadership books I peruse follow the same cookie-cutter approach, but Will Mancini's *Church Unique* is different. The chapters moved me beyond 'this is well written' to 'how do I engage in this with my team, NOW?' When I wasn't wincing from the ways he nailed my ineffective vision efforts, I felt motivated to jump right in. The churches surrounding me (all too often including ours) are desperate for the path to a healthier future but all too often find well-written platitudes that provide momentary relief rather than lasting direction. *Church Unique* goes beyond the easy quick fix to deeply useful vision for a God-honoring future. *Church Unique* gives hope, regardless of the health of your congregation. A book to implement, not just buy. Worth the price for his section on 'thinkholes' into which ministries can sink without self-awareness."

—John Crosby, senior pastor, Christ Presbyterian Church, Edina, Minnasota

"You are holding in your hands a book that will cause you to rethink the way your church fulfills the Great Commission. Will Mancini has been a longtime friend and consultant to Castle Hills First Baptist Church. He has helped us understand the spiritual DNA that makes our church and mission to San Antonio so unique. He loves to help church leaders prevail over problems and obstacles. His understanding of the processes involved in bringing about change is extraordinary. This book can mentor you through difficult circumstances. It can guide you through the process of seizing initiative and opportunity. The principles you will discover in the pages of this book have been used, tested, and proven to be effective."

—R. James Shupp, senior pastor, Castle Hills First Baptist Church, San Antonio, Texas

"Every once in a while God brings unique people across your path to add significant value to your life and ministry. Will Mancini is one of those people in my life. At a critical time in the life of our church, Will came into our journey and helped us navigate through the challenging waters of remaining true to our vision in a rapidly changing context. We understand and communicate our mission today with incredible clarity, thanks in large part to Will. I highly recommend this book as someone who has reaped the enormous benefits of its content."

—Vance Pitman, senior pastor, Hope Baptist Church, Las Vegas, Nevada

"After walking the Vision Pathway years ago, we still consider it to have been one of the most important strategic steps in the history of our church. Most of what we do today has an imprint from the process. It has helped us to clarify our purpose and it continues to drive our ministry decisions. *Church Unique* carries my highest endorsement as a much-needed resource for church leaders."

—Tim Sims, executive pastor, Gateway Community Church, Houston, Texas

"In *Church Unique*, Will Mancini clearly articulates how churches are hindered when they follow the model of the day rather than grow to celebrate the organic, God-given shape and culture for them through a practical and dynamic 'visioneering' process that delivers. I've experienced it, I've seen the benefits, and I believe in it."

—Brian Audia, executive director, Surgance, Inc.

"Few people ever press the pause button in ministry to think. That's why I'm so excited about *Church Unique*. This book will force you to take multiple steps back and review the church DNA that God has given you. Then it will help you to rebuild who you are with more focus and intentionality. So if you want to really think through every aspect of your ministry and become the church God has called you to be, then dedicate yourself to this book."

—Billy Andrews, Southside Baptist Church, Warner Robins, Georgia

"Every time I am with Will Mancini, I walk away challenged to give my life to leading God's church. Will Mancini maximizes his engineering background, his theological training, and his church leadership experience to help churches move beyond the practice of imitation, beyond the worship of innovation to the exciting world of becoming their Church Unique. I believe Will's grand contribution is that he helps church leaders learn to think about how God designed their church for His unique purpose. Every church leader has a hunger to fulfill God's plan for his congregation, but the models and mantras that are meant to help can get in the way. Before you know it, you are up a Willow Creek without a Hybels.

Church Unique celebrates God's creative work in each of us and gives us confidence to embrace the corporate grace, collective soul, and divine mandate that makes our lives and our churches unique. Welcome to the inspiring season of living out your personal story and becoming uniquely you! The genius of *Church Unique* is found in the tools that help leaders move beyond understanding to integration. Read this book with a pen in your hand."

—Bruce Wesley, senior pastor, Clear Creek Community Church, League City, Texas

Church Unique

CHURCH UNIQUE

HOW MISSIONAL LEADERS CAST VISION, CAPTURE CULTURE, AND CREATE MOVEMENT

Will Mancini

A LEADERSHIP NETWORK PUBLICATION

JOSSEY-BASS
A Wiley Imprint
www.josseybass.com

Published by Jossey-Bass
A Wiley Imprint
989 Market Street, San Francisco, CA 94103-1741—www.josseybass.com

Jossey-Bass books and products are available through most bookstores. To contact Jossey-Bass directly call our Customer Care Department within the U.S. at 800-956-7739, outside the U.S. at 317-572-3986, or fax 317-572-4002.

Jossey-Bass also publishes its books in a variety of electronic formats. Some content that appears in print may not be available in electronic books.

Library of Congress Cataloging-in-Publication Data

Mancini, Will, date.
Church unique : how missional leaders cast vision, capture culture, and create movement / Will Mancini. — 1st ed.
p. cm.
Includes bibliographical references and index.
ISBN 978-0-7879-9683-3 (cloth)
1. Christian leadership. 2. Church growth. 3. Mission of the church. I. Title.
BV652.1.M358 2008
253—dc22

2007049552

Printed in the United States of America
FIRST EDITION
HB Printing 10 9 8 7 6 5 4 3 2

LEADERSHIP NETWORK TITLES

The Blogging Church: Sharing the Story of Your Church Through Blogs, by Brian Bailey and Terry Storch

Leading from the Second Chair: Serving Your Church, Fulfilling Your Role, and Realizing Your Dreams, by Mike Bonem and Roger Patterson

The Way of Jesus: A Journey of Freedom for Pilgrims and Wanderers, by Jonathan S. Campbell, with Jennifer Campbell

Leading the Team-Based Church: How Pastors and Church Staffs Can Grow Together into a Powerful Fellowship of Leaders, by George Cladis

Organic Church: Growing Faith Where Life Happens, by Neil Cole

Off-Road Disciplines: Spiritual Adventures of Missional Leaders, by Earl Creps

Building a Healthy Multi-Ethnic Church: Mandate, Commitments, and Practices of a Diverse Congregation, by Mark DeYmaz

The Tangible Kingdom: Creating Incarnational Community, by Hugh Halter and Matt Smay

Leading Congregational Change Workbook, by James H. Furr, Mike Bonem, and Jim Herrington

Leading Congregational Change: A Practical Guide for the Transformational Journey, by Jim Herrington, Mike Bonem, and James H. Furr

The Leader's Journey: Accepting the Call to Personal and Congregational Transformation, by Jim Herrington, Robert Creech, and Trisha Taylor

Culture Shift: Transforming Your Church from the Inside Out, by Robert Lewis and Wayne Cordeiro, with Warren Bird

Church Unique: How Missional Leaders Cast Vision, Capture Culture, and Create Movement, by Will Mancini

A New Kind of Christian: A Tale of Two Friends on a Spiritual Journey, by Brian D. McLaren

The Story We Find Ourselves In: Further Adventures of a New Kind of Christian, by Brian D. McLaren

Practicing Greatness: 7 Disciplines of Extraordinary Spiritual Leaders, by Reggie McNeal

The Present Future: Six Tough Questions for the Church, by Reggie McNeal

A Work of Heart: Understanding How God Shapes Spiritual Leaders, by Reggie McNeal

The Millennium Matrix: Reclaiming the Past, Reframing the Future of the Church, by M. Rex Miller

Shaped by God's Heart: The Passion and Practices of Missional Churches, by Milfred Minatrea

The Missional Leader: Equipping Your Church to Reach a Changing World, by Alan J. Roxburgh and Fred Romanuk

The Ascent of a Leader: How Ordinary Relationships Develop Extraordinary Character and Influence, by Bill Thrall, Bruce McNicol, and Ken McElrath

Beyond Megachurch Myths: What We Can Learn from America's Largest Churches, by Scott Thumma and Dave Travis

The Elephant in the Boardroom: Speaking the Unspoken About Pastoral Transitions, by Carolyn Weese and J. Russell Crabtree

CONTENTS

About Leadership Network xvii
Foreword xix
Introduction xxi

PART ONE
Recasting Vision

1. Unoriginal Sin: Neglecting Uniqueness 5
2. The Fall of Strategic Planning: Obscuring the Essence 17
3. The Iniquity of Church Growth: Caging the Kingdom 27
4. Lost Congregations: How Churches Adapt to the Vision Vacuum 40

PART TWO
Clarifying Vision

5. The Good News of Clarity: Why Believe in Vision Today? 51
6. Clarity Pre-Evangelism: Softening Your Heart for Clarity 61
7. The Alpha and Omega of Clarity: The Ultimate Source of Vision 69
8. Hear the Cloud of Witnesses: Learning from Vision Legacies 75
9. Discover Your Kingdom Concept: How to Ascertain Vision 83
10. Take a Closer Look: Navigating Your Discovery Process 99

PART THREE
Articulating Vision

11. See with New Eyes: Defining Your Vision Frame 111
12. Carry the Holy Orders: Mission as Missional Mandate 119
13. Feel the Common Heartbeat: Values as Missional Motives 128
14. Show Me the Way: Strategy as Missional Map 136

15. Talk the Walk: Measures as Missional Life Marks 151
16. Frame the Future: Preparing for a Vision Lifestyle 164
17. Speak with New Tongues: Articulating Vision Proper 178

PART FOUR
Advancing Vision

18. Wage War Against the Status Quo: From Articulation to Traction 197
19. Meet Long in the Upper Room: The Secret of Attunement 207
20. Transform the Future: Delivering Vision Daily 215

Parting Thoughts

21. Resurrect Your Uniqueness: If You Copy Someone Else's Vision, Who Will Accomplish Yours? 234

Appendix A Logos and Strategy Icon Examples 237
Appendix B Vision Path Examples 243
Notes 247
Bibliography 255
Acknowledgments 259
About the Author 261
Index 263

This book is dedicated to
Abigail
her daddy's treasure
T.G.W.W.

ABOUT LEADERSHIP NETWORK

SINCE 1984, Leadership Network has fostered church innovation and growth by diligently pursuing its far-reaching mission statement: to identify, connect, and help high-capacity Christian leaders multiply their impact.

Although Leadership Network's techniques adapt and change as the church faces new opportunities and challenges, the organization's work follows a consistent and proven pattern: Leadership Network brings together entrepreneurial leaders who are focused on similar ministry initiatives. The ensuing collaboration—often across denominational lines—creates a strong base from which individual leaders can better analyze and refine their own strategies. Peer-to-peer interaction, dialogue, and sharing inevitably accelerate participants' innovation and ideas. Leadership Network further enhances this process through developing and distributing highly targeted ministry tools and resources, including audio and video programs, special reports, e-publications, and online downloads.

With Leadership Network's assistance, today's Christian leaders are energized, equipped, inspired, and better able to multiply their own dynamic Kingdom-building initiatives.

Launched in 1996 in conjunction with Jossey-Bass (a Wiley imprint), Leadership Network Publications present thoroughly researched and innovative concepts from leading thinkers, practitioners, and pioneering churches. The series collectively draws from a range of disciplines, with individual titles offering perspective on one or more of five primary areas:

1. Enabling effective leadership
2. Encouraging life-changing service
3. Building authentic community
4. Creating Kingdom-centered impact
5. Engaging cultural and demographic realities

For additional information on the mission or activities of Leadership Network, please contact:

Leadership Network
(800) 765-5323
client.care@leadnet.org

FOREWORD

UNIQUENESS PERMEATES GOD'S PLAN. From galaxies to sandbanks, fossils to snowflakes, each element is unique. God's unrivaled creation soars with originality.

So do His children. Each of us is a fresh version of His creativity. No two of us are identical. Each person is a unique compilation of DNA, environment, and circumstances. No one replicates anyone.

Elements of nature: unique.

His children: unique.

Our Lord loves to do all things new. Why would we expect Him to act differently with His church? Will Mancini says we shouldn't. In this volume to hold, he urges us to see each congregation as a one-of-a-kind creation. Each band of followers is distinct from every other.

Each congregation plays the music a bit differently. Even if it plays the same piece as the group down the street, the music emerges uniquely because the musicians are not the same. Smart conductors discover the sound within their band and exploit it.

Wise church leaders do so as well. This book steers us away from the latest conference fads toward innate congregational strengths. If you are looking for a one-size-fits-all approach to a healthy church, try another book. If you are ready to roll up your sleeves and seek the uniqueness of God's presence in your fellowship, this is your tool.

Will Mancini skillfully engages virtually all of the great ideas and opinions that are being employed today. He methodically distills and reorders them in a way that makes vision more than a statement. In many ways, this book is the missing link to all the chatter regarding church strategy. It is a unique approach in a saturated discipline, a both-and approach yet still simple. If you think your church doesn't need this book, read Chapter Four. If you think you don't have time for such a book, read Chapter Nine. Will works through the mixed messages and synthesizes the compelling truths with the simplicity and clarity he demands from the churches he works with.

We speak from experience. The Auxano team has led our church—Oak Hills Church, San Antonio—through this process. Although we are still piecing things together, we see a clearer vision emerging. May you discover the same.

Max Lucado and Steve Dye
Oak Hills Church
San Antonio, Texas

INTRODUCTION

The differences between congregations are becoming greater with the passage of time. The safe assumption today is that no two are alike. Each congregation has its own culture.

—Lyle Schaller

THE MESSAGE OF THIS BOOK IS uniquely bound in my own story. I lead a small band of Christ followers who are deeply passionate about the health, growth, effectiveness, and faithfulness of the church. We call ourselves "Auxano," named from the Greek word that Luke used to describe the early church expansion and multiplication in Acts. We are a new breed of consultants, new enough to seriously dislike the term "consultant," so we call ourselves "navigators." In less than a decade, we have worked with an unusually large bandwidth of churches ranging from insanely creative church plants to the rocket-ride growth phenoms of suburban America, to struggling revitalization projects, to the large and vibrant evangelical mainlines. Unlike many classic consultants, we have adopted a team approach to how we learn, collaborate, and serve the local church. We acknowledge, as with many others who have written in the past decade, what a challenging yet optimistic time this is for the church in North America.

I mention the variety of our consulting work not to throw you a resume at first blush but to underscore the uniqueness of this book. What has enabled us to serve such a variety of effective churches while the tectonic plates of modernity and postmodernity shift and grind? You will find the answers in *Church Unique.* In these pages we uncover the thinking, the tools, the process experiences, and the stories that our team has accumulated as we play the roles of clarity evangelist, missional strategist, alignment specialist, and cultural architect, all in the diverse body of Christ and in these most challenging times. To say it another way, we:

- Help missional churches articulate strategy and develop process
- Exhort overprogrammed churches to bury their ministry treadmill

- Show traditional churches how to put on "missional training wheels"
- Expose unintentional dynamics in our churches that are perfectly designed to create the religious consumerism that every pastor battles
- Encourage all churches to carry the heartbeat of Jesus to the surrounding community with their Church Unique

It is with optimism, born from our shared experience, that we see the future of the church. Every day, local churches step either closer to or further away from becoming the movement that God designed them to be. The baggage of institutionalism either weighs heavier or is unpacked. The heartbeat of redemptive passion beats stronger or grows faint. We believe that "the future as movement" for the local church is intrinsically tied to two assumptions. First, a unique vision must "ooze" from the leader's life as well as the church's leadership community. Second, this vision must create a stunningly unique culture inside the church that is inclined and motivated to penetrate the culture outside the church. In other words, reaching the surrounding community should be innate, driven by the church's DNA rather than programming. Therefore, I write with one purpose: *to challenge you to find your Church Unique—that is, to live a vision that creates a stunningly unique, movement-oriented church.*

What This Book Is Not

A quick survey of church leadership material today reveals several dominant categories. *Church Unique* clearly distinguishes itself from them with an innovative approach.

School's Out!

Church Unique is not written from a primarily academic approach. There has been some excellent work researching and documenting the emerging church while challenging all churches to wake up to cultural change.* There have also been some effective "strategic planning" or "ministry

**Missional Church* by Guder and Barrett, *Emerging Churches* by Gibbs and Bolger, and *The Shaping of Things to Come* by Frost and Hirsch are three excellent works and a good place to start.

planning" tools produced by professor-practitioners (for example, *Advanced Strategic Planning* by my friend Aubrey Malphurs). *Church Unique* stands in contrast to these works. Yes, we must clarify the need for missional makeover in the local church, but who is showing us what it really looks like? Yes, we must have planning models to learn from, but who is helping local churches better define or redefine their DNA? This book speaks to these issues from the experience of our team of full-time navigators living in the pressure cooker of daily church leadership and change processes.

Questions About Questions?

Church Unique does not offer conclusions and extrapolations based on surveys or other empirical analysis. I walk the tightrope of a love-hate relationship on this point. On the one hand, I am profoundly grateful for researchers such as the Barna Group and Gallup Research, who serve the church with careful, integrity-based work that is indispensable. On the other hand, I am a little skeptical when someone writes a book on what the church is supposed to look like as a result of having mailed out a bunch of surveys. Books and consulting approaches from this methodology can be very helpful, but for me they create heartburn on two accounts: I have seen survey work distorted to fit preconceived expectations, and I have seen misapplication of survey results hurt the church through overanalysis. Allow me to illustrate. If I write a survey and send it out to three hundred "effective churches," I can relatively easily develop my framework for "ten habits of effective churches" or something of the like. If I then take this to your church, I will evaluate your work on the basis of this predetermined criteria. This process quickly leads to a scorecard of what you are doing well and what you are not doing well. Once I dole out your B pluses and C minuses, what one conclusion have I left with you? That you must work on your weaknesses, of course. The problem with this is simple. If your primary focus, or paradigm for effectiveness, is trying to enhance your limitations, you will end up worse off than when you started. You will be immensely more effective if your focus is on discovering and developing your strengths.

To this end, *Church Unique* starts by looking at your surrounding microculture and at what makes your church one of a kind. What is God's unique thumbprint for your church? What is different about your church's corporate grace and collective soul? What does your church do better than ten thousand others? This perspective honors God by taking into account what He has made and what He is up to. This represents a synthetical approach that logically must come prior to an analytical one. (Many of you learned to do Bible study the same way, starting with synthesis or tentative conclusions about the unity of a biblical book before interpreting the individual verses of the text.) Clearly, there is a time and context to do analysis, but beware if it is the overarching approach.

Biting the Silver Bullet?

Church Unique does not focus on a particular tactic of church leadership. Again, the books that do this can be very helpful. Examples are books on staffing, on how to be a good executive pastor, on how to do evangelism and raise funds, and so on. I commend books like these regularly, while recognizing two limitations. First, we are suffering in general from overly fragmented approaches to church (synthesis versus analysis again). So learning about tactics at best leaves us susceptible to a tack-on approach that inhibits us from integrating vision into the life of the church. At worst, it can overpromise the future by offering "the solution"—the silver bullet syndrome—because it may falsely represent the missing key to church effectiveness. Second, the tactical approach usually does not take into account any of the unique features of your church or the microculture surrounding your church.

Models or Model Makers?

Church Unique is not the story of one church's approach. Personally, I find "church biographies" to be enjoyable and inspirational reading. (For example, I've just read *Confessions of a Reformission Rev,* by Mark Driscoll. I appreciate his raw humor and refreshing insight as he tells the story of the Mars Hill Community.) As important as it is to swap our stories, there is one function that these books do not perform. Though telling you about their unique vision, they rarely give you insight and guidance for developing *your own vision*. Please understand that I do not say this to be critical, only practical.

In contrast to the "one-church's story," we show snapshots along the journey of many churches. These snapshots are not simply to illustrate, but to offer practical take-away value for you to contextualize your mission and focus your own strategic initiatives.

So what does *Church Unique* promise? It presents ideas on how to discern your "corporate grace" and surrounding microculture, as well as how to synthesize these into your unique Vision Pathway. More than that, it gives you a Vision Integration Model. This model is a framework for retrofitting all tactical learning to your unique vision. As we discuss *vision as lifestyle,* the ideas of church culture and vision integration will be important. You will not create contagious culture unless your unique vision seamlessly touches and manifests itself in every facet of body life!

A Lifestyle of Visionary Leadership

The contents of this book are an alternative to classic strategic planning. In place of a static planning document, I show you how you can develop a Vision Pathway that leads to a *lifestyle* of visionary leadership, over and against the concept of a vision *statement.* Table I.1 highlights some differences between classic strategic planning and *Church Unique's* Vision Pathway approach.

In a nutshell, this approach represents a counterpoint to an epidemic we are witnessing in the North American church that I would describe as a "vision vacuum." The symptoms of this condition have become so normalized that they may be hard to recognize. Leaders in the vortex of the vacuum clamor for the right tools, programs, and resources to propel their church forward in lieu of discovering better ways to direct leadership energy. The result is massive cloning and a glut of photocopied vision in the body of Christ. Even though this outbreak is real and widespread, I believe there is a clear and attainable remedy. What does it involve? A better way of leadership includes the disciplines of careful observation, vibrant imagination, and demanding collaboration that forge a *unique* vision based on what God is *uniquely* doing in each church's *unique* context. There was a time when a one-size-fits-all approach was viable. That time is no more. Until leaders not only embrace uniqueness but celebrate and leverage it, they will miss out on God's best for their ministry. The answer is having a vision that oozes, that is original, organic, zeroed in, and extravagant. When leaders start thinking clearly, engaging locally, focusing redemptively, and risking boldly, their church becomes an

Table I.1. Strategic Planning vs. Vision Pathway

Classic Strategic Planning	Church Unique's Vision Pathway
Vision as content	Vision as lifestyle
Mission as statement	Mission as missional mandate
Values as statement	Values as missional motives
Strategy as plan	Strategy as missional map
Measurement as goals	Measurement as missional life marks

Figure I.1. Preview of the Vision Pathway

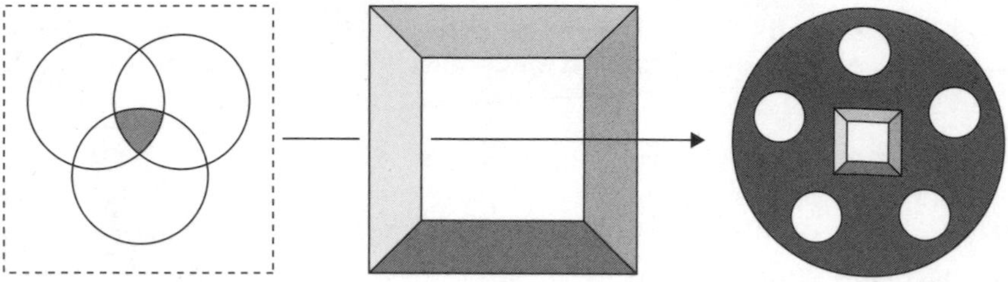

1
Discover
your
Kingdom Concept
(*Church Unique* Part 2)

2
Develop
your
Vision Frame
(*Church Unique* Part 3)

3
Deliver
your
Vision Daily
(*Church Unique* Part 4)

unstoppable force and an irresistible influence. It becomes a church that prevails not because it is "purpose-driven" but because it is *purposeful.*

Are you ready to discover and live a vision that creates a stunningly unique church culture? If so, *Church Unique* is your map. In this book we walk you through how you can discover, develop, and deliver your unique vision by creating your own Vision Pathway. The clarity and practical application you realize through this process will take you to new levels of effectiveness and to a lifestyle of visionary leadership.

Figure I.1 outlines the simple steps we follow in these pages to help you develop, discover, and deliver God's unique vision for your church.

Discovering Missional Vision

Part One, "Recasting Vision," exposes the nature of the vision vacuum in churches today. Where have two decades of the conference-craze era left us? What is the current usefulness of strategic planning in the church today? How do the emerging church and the recovery of the *missio Dei* challenge previous church-growth assumptions? These questions and more are explored. Part One explains how churches have lost their way and are in need finding their unique Vision Pathway.

Part Two, "Clarifying Vision," shifts decisively to the essential nature of clarity for church leaders today. Where does clarity come from? How can leaders better ascertain the future? How can the leader have 100 percent confidence in articulating the identity and direction of the church? As we answer these questions, I trust you will find some fresh perspectives that significantly enhance your understanding of vision and continue to develop your skills as a visionary. For leaders who resonate with the missional thinking and writing of the last decade, Part Two supplies a perspective that pushes you to solidify and mature the movement you are already leading as you discover your "Kingdom Concept," the simple, clear, "big idea" that defines how your church will glorify God and make disciples.

Part Three, "Articulating Vision," presents a model for articulating missional vision that includes developing your Vision Frame. The Vision Frame contains five components that define your church's DNA and creates the platform for all vision casting. The Vision Frame is expansive enough to include the church's evolving vocabulary that anticipates where God is taking you. Once a leadership team completes the grueling, yet rewarding, process of clarifying vision, what are the right words to capture your Kingdom Concept? Which terms unlock the understanding of strategy? What language engages the hearts of your people?

Part Four, "Advancing Vision," introduces you to a Vision Integration Model that helps you deliver vision daily. What practical steps help visionary leaders go to the next level? How can leaders raise up and align more stakeholders in the congregation? What do you do with those preciously frustrating saints who are anchored to yesterday? Is there a model for a central vision that redefines how the various departments and staff people can work together? Behind the Vision Integration Model is perhaps one of the most important assumptions of the book: *the success of advancing vision is directly proportional to the degree to which the vision is first aligned and integrated.* As we discuss vision as lifestyle, the ideas of church culture and vision integration are vital.

In other words, nourishing internal culture must precede expanding outside influence. Real change is inside-out.

Lyle Schaller, perhaps one of the most respected church consultants of the twentieth century, whose observations and work span five decades, supports this principle. Of his forty-some books, one of the most important observations about growth trends is this: "The crucial issue [for growth] is *not* the central theme of the strategy [for the church]. The crucial question is whether the congregation, including the configuration of the paid staff, is organized to be supportive of a clearly defined and widely supported central strategy."[1] In other words, the central strategy you choose is not as important as whether there is ownership and integration around whatever strategy you choose.

The Vision Integration Model gives you and your leadership team a common framework and shared understanding that most churches never have. It works for any denominational background, church size, and leadership style.

Finally, throughout the process of recasting vision, clarifying vision, articulating vision, and advancing vision, the chapters use the metaphor of redemption. This metaphor is used for two reasons. First, if the potential impact of creating a stunningly unique culture is so huge, salvation is a wonderful and stimulating analogy. Second, you will find the threefold pattern "lost, found, and transformed" thoroughly familiar in your personal experience and in the daily work of tending to people's hearts.

I remember, before I felt the urge toward vocational ministry in college, as a young high schooler hanging on every word my pastor said. (I attended a small Bible chapel in the Brandywine Valley of Southeastern Pennsylvania.) One day, as he preached, he said something that gripped my soul: "I always wanted to be a king maker and not a king." I honestly can't remember the sermon or the context of the statement. The words simply penetrated my mind and everything else vaporized. It wouldn't be until twenty years later that I recognized the prophetic resonance within my little heart. Having had the opportunity to lead a great model, I would rather work behind the scenes as a model maker. My greatest joy is seeing a leader for the first time articulate a stunningly unique model of ministry for his or her church. That is the passion behind *Church Unique*. My prayer is that God grant you a breathtaking view of His vision for your life and ministry as you interact with the pages of this book—laboring, loving, and living for Jesus Christ.

Church Unique

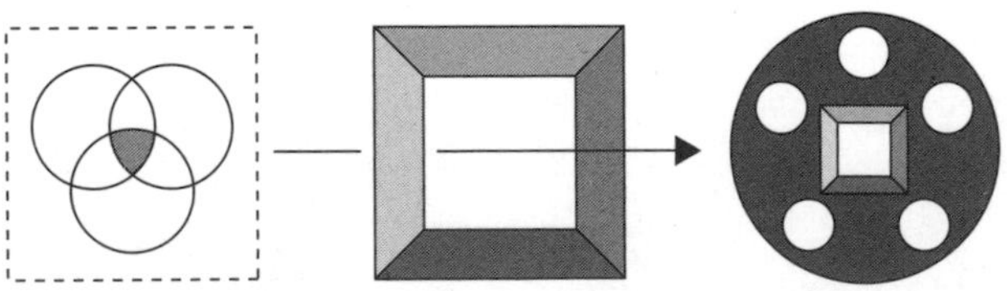

PART ONE

RECASTING VISION

A PUMPKIN FARMER WAS STROLLING through his rows of beautiful green leaves at the beginning of the season, as the acorn-size pumpkins were starting to add dots to the landscape. He glanced down and noticed a clear glass jar. Curiosity got the best of him, so he took the jar over to one of his pumpkin buds, threaded the small pumpkin on its vine inside the open jar, and left it sitting there in the field.

Months later, with the experiment long forgotten, the farmer was walking his land, greatly satisfied with the large beautiful pumpkins that covered the patch. He rediscovered the glass jar, totally intact, and was startled to see it completely filled up with the little pumpkin that grew inside. The thin glass barrier had defined the shape of the orange mass within. The pumpkin was only one-third of the size it should have been.

The problem for this little pumpkin is the same problem for most churches today. Rather than growing to their full potential from their unique DNA, they conform to the shape of an external mold or model. These "glass jars" create invisible barriers to growth and predetermine the shape of community for churches across the country.

Part One shows us the jars we must break so that we can celebrate the organic, God-given shape and culture for each local church—and, most important, *your* local church. Visionary leadership today seems to be about more "jar-sharing" than about DNA-discovering. Therefore, it's time to redeem vision by recasting it. In other words, *we need to rethink what it means to be visionary,* to see it in a different light. Once vision is assessed and reestablished, missional leaders can break the mold, one church at a time, by leading their people into God's unparalleled future for their church.

I

UNORIGINAL SIN

NEGLECTING UNIQUENESS

In the life of faith each person discovers all the elements of a unique and original adventure. We are prevented from following in one another's footsteps and are called to an incomparable association with Christ. The Bible makes it clear that every time there is a story of faith, it is completely original. God's creative genius is endless. He never, fatigued and unable to maintain the rigors of creativity, resorts to mass-producing copies.

—Eugene Peterson

JACOB, MY THIRTEEN-YEAR-OLD SON, recently enjoyed an energetic two-hour plane ride with his new friend Matthew. At some point in the get-to-know-you moments they swapped signatures. Evidently Matthew thought that Jacob's signature was a little boring. So every ten minutes I was interrupted by another napkin crossing the aisle for my review. Each napkin contained five new examples of carefully scripted signatures—Jacob Mancini. "Which one do you like best, Dad?" my son enthusiastically inquired. Changing the slant, restyling his J's, and mimicking the sophistication of a doctor's script, my son was enthralled with finding his right signature—an impressive one. With his mounting frustration, I searched for just the right words to free my son from his overanalysis. "The right signature," I confidently asserted, "is the one that comes most naturally."

Today I visited one of the largest churches in South Carolina: a downtown, red brick, white-columned, Southern Baptist church immersed in the distinct accents of Southeastern culture. Tomorrow I will spend a day at the first Protestant church established in the city of Houston, an elegant mainline nestled in the cultural center of the museum district and the world's largest medical center. This weekend I will be in a suburb of Phoenix, working with an Assemblies of God congregation whose pastor preaches to seven thousand while wearing a Hawaiian shirt. Each of these churches has its own signature—a way it does ministry most naturally. Every week I am confronted with brute force that local churches are *unmistakably unique and incomparably different.* God doesn't mass-produce His church.

Infinite Uniqueness

Let's not dismiss the infinite creativity of our ingenious Lord when it comes to the thumbprint of the local church. How much does God delight in creative uniqueness? Consider the snowflake. No two snowflakes that have ever fallen in the history of existence are identical. How is that possible? It is God's handiwork; each complex snow crystal has an almost infinite number of discernible crystal variations. As these extremely sensitive flakes blow about in the wind, the ever-changing conditions lead them to grow in different patterns. The final design is a reflection of these growth conditions.[1]

Consider what God does when fifteen people come together in His name. How much uniqueness is in those fifteen individuals? How about a church of a hundred people, or a thousand? Is it possible that the uniqueness of these groups far outweighs the uniqueness of a small water crystal blowing in the winter wind? Wouldn't each church, however small, carry a unique collective soul, because each church is a different subset of one-of-a-kind saints? Doesn't each locale present its own growth conditions that affect the pattern and development of God's people? If every snowflake that was ever created in the universe differs, is it so hard to conceive that every one of the more than three hundred thousand churches in North America is unique?

These questions drive us to the essence of recasting vision. The starting point for vision—for thinking about our church's future—is not deciding where we want to go or exploring what is working for other churches but understanding *how we are unique.*

Uniqueness = Culture

What is the uniqueness I am referring to? It is not simply about worship style or programs offered; it is something more significant yet subtler at the same time. It is something that is often overlooked: a culture that is unique to a particular church. Culture is the combined effect of the interacting values, thoughts, attitudes, and actions that define the life of your church. By nature, it is a little difficult to define because the term represents a broad, intangible concept. George Barna offers an expanded definition as "the complex intermingling of knowledge, beliefs, values, assumptions, symbols, traditions, habits, relationships, rewards, language, morals, rules, and laws that provide meaning and identity to a group of people."[2]

Robert Lewis and Wayne Cordeiro describe this complex intermingling of culture as "the most important social reality in your church. Though invisible to the untrained eye, its power is undeniable. Culture gives color and flavor to everything your church is and does."[3] Another common definition of culture is the "unspoken rules of how things get done." As each church expresses its life and ministry slightly differently, the outcomes are ultimately influenced by its culture.

There are as many illustrations of culture as there are groups of people, whether a nation, company, church, club, or high school. For three years, I participated in a local Indian Guides chapter with my two sons. The program, sponsored by the YMCA, builds a small community of fathers and sons around personal achievements in an outdoor context. The culture is nourished by tribe meetings, awards system ceremonies, and special clothing. Each week, we grabbed our patch covered leather vests and headdresses. Every campout, we couldn't wait to watch the medicine man jump over the raging campfire. Everything we did was laced with Indian language, starting with our very names. Because my two boys were Straight Arrow and Red Eagle, I thought it would be cool to be Running Wind. (Eagles and arrows both need wind.) Overspiritualizing my name got me in trouble with some other dads who interpret "wind" a little differently! When you boil down Indian Guides, it is all about stepping into the microculture that multiplies the values, thoughts, attitudes, and actions of Native American culture. The experiences we shared have transformed my skill and appreciation for observing and respecting nature. A walk through the woods is now an expanded experience.

Just like Indian Guides, your church has its own culture. But without such obvious features as headdresses and teepees, your church's culture and how it characterizes its own uniqueness can be difficult to discern. This is especially true for the inside observer because the culture itself is so all encompassing and intangible at the same time. Again, Lewis and Cordeiro speak to this issue: "Church culture is foundational to the life and witness of every church. *Unfortunately too many church leaders fail to recognize or understand the implications of this reality*"[4] (italics mine). In Part Two, we walk through specific steps to discern culture in the process of articulating vision. But for now, let's remove some of the enigma of culture by considering sources of uniqueness for a church. For the questions posed here I add short illustrations from my consulting experiences:

- *Leaders:* What are the unique strengths of the leader(s) in your church? Think of the unique strengths of biblical leaders—the faith of Abraham, the humility of Moses, the courage of Joshua, and the vision of Nehemiah. For example, when I think of David Saathoff at Bandera Road Community Church in San Antonio, Texas, I think of a leader with an unusual ability to replicate the value of lost people into other leaders' lives.
- *Gifts:* If each person has unique spiritual gifts in your church, what does the collective gift mix look like? When I worked with a church plant in the San Diego area, I was struck by the significant presence of the gift of mercy that permeated the core team.
- *Heritage:* What kind of heritage do your people share? Is it multifaceted, or do they share many family ties? What does a common ethnicity say about your church's DNA? A traditional Baptist church in the Dallas area with around five hundred members in attendance had more family ties than any church I have encountered. They were also facing significant decline. Are these blood connections a liability or a possibility for a new home-based evangelism strategy?
- *Experiences:* What shared experiences do your people have in common? When I consulted with a church outside of Ft. Lauderdale, the leaders realized for the first time that most of their people came to Christ after the age of forty; this was a result of a season of brokenness in their lives. They began to see themselves as wounded healers, with a special ability to touch one segment of the adult population.
- *Tradition:* How does the denominational background, or lack thereof, have an impact on your uniqueness? At First Presbyterian Church of Houston, the "thoughtfulness" of the confessional heritage seeped its way into every aspect of their vision and began to focus their outreach strategies.
- *Values:* What values drive decision making in your church? What unique convictions do your people share? A megachurch pastor once interrupted a strategy session I was leading for an "urgent" care need that I did not think was that important. Later we

articulated their crown-jewel value as "Each individual matters." It wasn't until then that I began to appreciate how this five-thousand-member church adapts, unlike other megachurches, to live out this core value.

- *Personality:* If you were to describe what makes your church distinct from every other church, what would you say? I work with two Methodist churches on opposite ends of the spectrum in the same city. First Church of Pasadena emphasizes awe and reverence, while Gateway Community emphasizes authenticity and approachability.
- *Evangelism:* How do your people talk about the Great Commission? How does your church nuance it? Bannockburn Baptist in Austin decided they were not going to measure the Great Commission one person at a time, but rather one family at a time. Their tagline is "Inspiring Generations."
- *Recovery:* What sins and sin patterns have your people been delivered from? What patterns of worldliness are they most tempted by? (Consider how the epistles deal with concerns unique to varying locales.) One church has identified its corporate grace as helping people with sexual brokenness.
- *Motivation:* Is there a deeply motivational rubric behind how your church sees its mission (for example, community, service, prayer, or worship)? When Chuck Swindoll planted Stonebriar Community Church in Frisco, Texas, they articulated their mission around the big idea of "joy."

The list could go on, but this begins to show the intricacy of any church's originality. Few churches understand their own uniqueness or even think about it systematically.

Lost on the Way to Your Own DNA

This chapter's title, "Unoriginal Sin," refers to the common habit of neglecting what makes a congregation unique and gravitating toward adopting programs and mind-sets that work elsewhere. Leaders today have not clearly discerned the uniqueness of their church. Like a child who playfully delights in the falling snow, oblivious to the intricate beauty of each flake, church leaders are missing out on the special beauty of what is right in front of them. Somehow, they have lost the way to discovering their own DNA.

"Thinkholes"

The most important question is, Why do leaders miss the matchless thumbprint of their identity in the local expression of Christ's body? I see six common hazards that stand out across the landscape of church life. Because all of them affect thinking, I have called them "thinkholes." A thinkhole represents the quicksand-like dynamic where, at certain times and places, vibrant thinking gets sucked beneath the surface to suffocate and disappear from view. Can this strange term represent a common reality? Absolutely. Vacuums of thinking can be found all around us. In American culture, 50 percent of adults will never read a book in their life yet log hours of daily "amusement" ("a" = without and "muse" = thought) through television.[5] This simple instance illustrates a silent epidemic at work all around us. The reality is that most people don't think; they only rearrange their prejudices. Real thinking can be disruptive to the status quo and requires a great deal of courage.

Along the great race of leadership, thinkholes are the obstacles, barriers, and danger zones that keep us from thoughtful self-knowledge. Let's examine six kinds of thinkhole that blanket the church landscape.

MINISTRY TREADMILLS. The first thinkhole is the *ministry treadmill.* The treadmill is set in motion when the busyness of ministry creates a progressively irreversible hurriedness in the leader's life. The sheer immediacy of each next event or ministry demand prevents the leader from taking the time required for discerning the culture and defining the DNA of the church.

Most leaders in this environment find it impossible to devote even one day a month for a seven-month process to explore their church's culture. This process is exactly what I recommended to one pastor, who enthusiastically embraced our approach. Even so, he insisted that the process continue with one exception—that we complete it in ninety days or less. I knew that the best journey would require more time, but I agreed to start in the hope he would change his mind. Twelve months later, having sensed God's work in our midst, the pastor apologized to me in front of his executive leadership team and thanked me for my patience. For this pastor, the process was the most significant marker in his ministry lifetime, but his need for speed almost jeopardized developing the vision of the church.

The need to hit the brakes on the ministry treadmill is highlighted by George Barna in the updated edition of his book *The Power of Vision.* He states that for success in visioning, "the process necessarily *extracts a significant cost* from the vision seekers. *Devotion to the process* of discovering the vision is the most important component of all the activities associated with God's vision" (italics mine).[6] His word choice is telling; most leaders are not willing to extract the significant cost of time. Today's demands can choke out needed dialogue for tomorrow. When this occurs, our multiplied activity prevents us from living with a clearer identity.

COMPETENCY TRAP. The second thinkhole is the *competency trap*. As ministry leaders experience success over time, that very success can become a liability. The gold medals of yesterday's accomplishments become the iron teeth around the leader's ankle. A subtle presumption develops ("I know how to do this thing") that eclipses active listening and reflective observation—important habits required to discern a church's DNA.

The next time you are in a learning environment, notice who is taking notes and asking questions. It is not uncommon that the most accomplished people in the room are the least receptive to new learning. This is why young leaders often intuit culture so well; they have less of an experience base to pollute their perceptions and assumptions about what works.

The competency trap is easy to identify in two scenarios. The first is when a leader transitions to a new church. He or she naturally brings along the ministry patterns and programs that previously defined success. But what the leader can't bring along is the other church's culture. Because it is easier to duplicate familiar programs than to incarnate new ones, the leader overlooks the DNA discovery process. The second scenario occurs when an experienced leader is navigating a major transition, such as relocation or bringing on new staff. Often the leader races faster around the familiar pathways of yesterday rather than discovering new pathways of effectiveness. This "dig in your heals" approach turns leaders into talkers instead of listeners. Presumption prevents the breakthrough to self-knowledge that would otherwise open the door to new levels of leadership.

NEEDS-BASED SLIPPERY SLOPE. On the *needs-based slippery slope*, leaders are constantly trying to meet people's needs and expectations within the church. Whether the needs ring of religious consumerism or are legitimate concerns of life and death, the slippery slope works the same. With the leaders' cruise control set to "react," thoughtful leadership becomes unnecessary because there is always a persistent parade of needs to be answered. The vision of the church is reduced to making people happy. The reality is that such a church is probably missing out on fulfilling its unique calling and role in the community by trying to be all things to all members. Sliding down the needs-based slope is perhaps the most "spiritual" way of avoiding the hard work of self-discovery.

Even Jesus did not meet all of the physical needs in his sphere of influence. Yet in John 17:4 he is able to pray to the Father, "I have brought you glory by completing all of the work you gave me to do." Though Jesus did not meet *every* need, he met all the needs he was created and called to meet. Just like the person of Jesus, the local church as the body of Christ must understand what it is created and called to do. Jesus exercised tremendous *discernment to know* and *courage to go* where God was directing. Local church leaders must go and do likewise, carefully differentiating the voice of God from the squeaky wheels of unmet needs.

It is interesting to note that a church mired in this thinkhole works best when there is a crisis, because the crisis itself imparts an amazing (and often unprecedented) sense of clarity and unity around an obvious need. But this type of clarity is fleeting. Unfortunately, leaders can't see this pattern and slide back into the thinkhole once the crisis is over.

CULTURAL WHIRLPOOLS. The fourth and fifth thinkholes are found in the *cultural whirlpool*. The acceleration of cultural change in North America in the previous century brought revolutions of new information that spin faster and faster. The changes were brought about by quantum advances in technology and communication—from the automobile to FM radio to television to the Internet.[7] Change is not bad in and of itself; change puts the leader at a disadvantage when trying to keep up. Last week I heard a forty-two-year-old pastor gripe in his sermon about not being "up to speed" with his iPod. (Yet just ten years earlier, the same leader planted an innovative church.) Life is no longer perceived through a viewfinder of still pictures that advance with each generation, but through a kaleidoscope that is turning daily. Change happens faster than ever.

The *local* church is obviously and inextricably bound to these shifts in the cultural whirlpool. These realities of change, including the shift from modernity to postmodernity, have been so well covered by many books that I'll decline even a cursory treatment. One illustration, however, is offered in order to connect changes of culture to the challenge of discerning a church's DNA.

Change has created great variation in the fabric of North American culture. Demographers refer to the increasing number of population lifestyle segments in striving to capture these differences. To the classic demographic labeling of the young urban professional (yuppie) in the mid-1980s, marketers have added more finely tuned listings each year (humorously, of course):

Muppy: middle-aged urban professional

Dinky: dual income, no kids yet

Glams: graying, leisured, affluent, married

Sitcom: single income, two children, oppressive mortgage

Sadfab: single and desperate for a baby

The net effect is that the cultural realities around us become less like a large steel plate and more like hundreds of droplets of mercury, that are hard to pick up and examine.

Fifteen years ago, most people would raise their hand in response to the question, "Can you state with 100 percent confidence the name of the CBS network news anchor?" In most groups who are asked the same question today, few if any raise their hand. Cable and satellite TV have introduced so many viewing options that our country is less unified in its television viewing experience. In fact, a family of four may have a television in each room with four channels playing simultaneously.

Suppose you want to communicate to this family of four. It would be much easier if, conceptually speaking, they lived their lives on the same channel. But since mom, dad, sophomore Ted, and his little sister Susi channel surf in their own oceans, it's much harder to share a common vocabulary. The challenge for church leaders is exactly the same. The pastor on Sunday morning no longer speaks to a monolithic culture with shared experiences and anchor points, like the connection to a Ted Koppel or a Dan Rather. Because a crowd of people under the same roof can come from so many cultural milieus, it is increasingly difficult to discern and then lead from a common DNA.

The increasing pace of change in the cultural whirlpool leaves leaders with two temptations that distract them from thinking clearly about their church's identity. The first is *BuzzChurch*. This means to define the DNA around innovation itself. These leaders enjoy the adrenaline rush of having to do continuous cultural exegesis for ministry. The resulting vision is the need to be constantly cutting-edge. In the race to be relevant, it's all too possible to miss the deeper essence that God wants to nurture. The irony is that this cultural whirlpool is actually an addiction to new thinking.

Current conference offerings that come to mind with this temptation are Fellowship Church's annual C3 Conference on creativity and a new Buzz Conference hosted by National Community Church. The ad for the conference asks, "Is your church buzzworthy?" I believe it is critical for the church to be creative and I love the cultural savvy of "buzzmakers" such as Ed Young Jr. of Fellowship Church and Craig Groeshel of Life Church.tv, but these conferences can attract folks who are creative for creativity's sake, and not for the sake of their church's unique calling.

The second temptation is *StuckChurch*. For every leader who surfs the waves of cultural change, there are a hundred who are stuck in a whirlpool vortex—and they feel they can't keep their head above water. This response is a second kind of thinkhole in the cultural whirlpool. The changes around them outpace their energy and discipline for new learning. Rather than rolling up their sleeves to think about their culture, they just grow too tired for the task. What do they do to justify their position? They simply define their vision in terms of glorifying and propagating the past.

I was facilitating a deacons' meeting for a church in Virginia several years ago. It was clear that the church needed to switch its traditional and contemporary service times. With thousands of younger families moving into the area, our research showed that these folks would be more receptive to a contemporary service at 11:00 A.M. rather than 8:30 A.M. Bob, a man in his seventies, looked at me with quite a scowl for most of the meeting. Toward the end of the night, I chose to engage his nonverbal hostility. He was a traditional service attender, so I probed his resistance to the change. "Bob, are you not awake at 8:30 on Sunday mornings?" I asked. "I'm awake at 6:00 A.M. every day," he quickly asserted. After a few more questions I made my last inquisitive plea: "Bob, if an eight-year-old girl who did not know Jesus, your Savior, might hear the gospel at the 11:00 A.M. service because we moved the traditional service to 8:30 (which you are wide awake for!), would you be for the change?" "No," Bob replied. A dead silence came over the room. Finally, Bob broke it with the sad heart of a man stuck in the past: "I have been attending church at 11:00 A.M. since I was eight years old."

Amazingly, the deacons that night chose StuckChurch by sticking with Bob and not the recommendation of their senior pastor to change the service times. As with thousands of other churches, change is resisted and leaders are pulled under by the whirlpool of cultural change.

THE CONFERENCE MAZE. In the *conference maze,* leaders rely solely on training events to instill direction and vision for their church. Many pastors in the last two decades have built a model of ministry by borrowing one, and in doing so they create a "glass jar" church. This is not surprising when you consider the conference offerings and their glut of photocopied vision prepackaged for import. At the forefront of this maze-craze are Willow Creek Community Church and Saddleback Community Church, followed by dozens of other newer megachurches, including

North Point Church, Fellowship Church, Grainger Community Church. I want to state up front that I am a raving fan of Bill Hybels and Rick Warren as leaders. They have accomplished untold good for the kingdom by helping a generation of leaders reimagine ways of accomplishing the Great Commission. But lurking in the wake of their conference ministry is the growing virus of unoriginal sin. They would be the first to warn you not to copy their models, but they sell their own DNA-saturated curriculum to thousands of churches. Have you ever been to one of these conferences? The resource rooms look like a half-kicked anthill with hundreds of leaders clamoring for books and plug-and-play programs.

The dramatic irony is that what happens at the conference is the exact opposite of what propelled the host church to be effective in the first place. Each of these leaders endured a process of self-understanding and original thinking that helped in articulating a stunningly unique model of ministry. But after discovering their Church Unique, these leaders no longer taught the same way they learned. Rather than helping churches with *process,* they sell them a *product.* Why don't the mavens of conferencing offer another kind of learning experience? Maybe it has to do with the fact that such a process requires a lot of relationship, creativity, and energy, whereas a product requires only a credit card.

Where does the conference maze lead us? I was talking to a pastor of a six-hundred-member Bible church in the San Francisco Bay Area. He confessed that after the last conference they went to his staff was more confused than ever. The conference maze brought only confusion, not clarity. When I walk into a church, it usually takes five minutes to identify the last conference the staff attended. I recently visited a four-thousand-member Baptist church and knew they had been to a Saddleback conference when I saw the banners hanging in the foyer. Last week, at one of the largest evangelical Lutheran churches in the country, I knew they had recently attended a conference at North Point when I picked up a new brochure in their foyer.

The success of these megamodels creates a great temptation for others to copy them. In that moment, leaders walk into a thinkhole. I am not against studying best practices; I'm just against *not thinking* in the process! Unfortunately, the quantity of conference offerings has only increased the complexity of the maze (along with the promise of better cheese should you navigate your way through it).

DENOMINATIONAL RUT. The final thinkhole is the *denominational rut.* Denominations by and large still continue to resource congregations with little appreciation for local uniqueness. Their structures have not adapted to the cultural whirlpools mentioned earlier. Despite good motivation, they get stuck maintaining the structures of yesteryear, unable to outfit the strongest churches in the pack. Therefore a church can't look to its denominational leadership for help in discerning what makes it an original. It is sad to me that denominations have not been able to adapt. If they could, I would urge them to come alongside their best churches to help them express a unique DNA within their unique denominational heritage.

A powerful observation by Lyle Schaller solidifies the point raised in the opening epigraph of the Introduction: "The differences between congregations are becoming greater with the passage of time. The safe assumption today is that no two are alike. Each congregation has its own culture. . . . *The local community setting has moved ahead of the denominational heritage as a factor in creating the distinctive congregational culture*"[8] (italics mine). If denominational leaders aren't savvy to these "contours of locality," what help can they give their local church?

If you have influence in your denomination, or are a denomination leader, I urge you to reread Lyle's quote. Retooling is not easy, and our times beg bold denominational leaders to take action.

What thinkholes are dotting the landscape in your church? Which dynamics tend to pull you away from discovering your Church Unique? Use the summary chart in Table 1.1 to review and discuss them with your team of leaders. Remember that God's journey for you today reflects an incomparable association with Jesus Christ that is completely original.

Table 1.1. "Thinkholes" Summary

Thinkholes	How We Neglect Uniqueness	The "Thinking" Problem	Thinkhole Practices
Ministry treadmill	Busyness eliminates time for reflection	No time to think	Add more programs
Competency trap	Presumption decreases appetite for learning	No need to think	Work harder
Needs-based slippery slope	Consumerism removes the need for discernment	Needs are all we think about	Make people happy
Cultural whirlpool: BuzzChurch	Innovation short-circuits self-awareness	Addicted to new thinking	Be cutting-edge
Cultural whirlpool: StuckChurch	Change outpaces the discipline for learning	Too tired to think	Glorify the past
The conference maze	Success increases the temptation to copycat	Let's borrow their thinking	Model best practice
Denominational rut	Resources disregard local uniqueness	No one helps us think	Protect theology

2

THE FALL OF STRATEGIC PLANNING

OBSCURING THE ESSENCE

Changes that appear turbulent to organizations that rely heavily on planning may appear normal to, even welcomed by, those who prefer a more visionary or learning approach. Put more boldly, if you have no vision but only formal plans, then every unpredicted change in the environment makes you feel like the sky is falling.

—Henry Mintzberg

REMEMBER THE OLD BOARD GAME CHUTES AND LADDERS? Players compete to get to the top of the game board. The way is marked with both hazards (chutes that make you slide backward) and helps (ladders that zoom you ahead). The simple strategy is to avoid all the chutes and try to land on the ladders. One time, I was playing with some young children who didn't really know the object of the game. Because of their fascination with sliding on the playground, they thought it was just as much fun to slide down the chute on the board game as it was to climb up the ladder!

The image of sliding backward, unaware of the demise, is a fitting one for church leaders who pursue strategic planning. While attempting to step ahead and bring the church to a new level of effectiveness, they are really slipping backward and making it harder to win. The strategic plan may actually obscure the concept of Church Unique and fail to guide the church to a better future.

A pastor friend once told me that the fastest way to get out of a hole is to stop digging. Ironically, there are times when the tools we work with are so mismatched to our current challenges that we only exacerbate the problems we are trying to solve. In such a case, we must abandon the wrong tools in order to pick up the right ones. For those of you who resolve to discover your Church Unique, this chapter is written to warn you that strategic planning is no longer the preferred tool for leading the church into the future. For many pastors and well-meaning layleaders, it's time to put down the shovel.

Falling down the Chute

The practice of strategic planning developed in the 1960s and was used broadly by organizational leaders through the 1970s and 1980s. Strategic planning is the process of determining the overall direction of the organization and then "breaking down" that broader direction into objectives that are then divided into smaller, more measurable action steps or goals. Though the practice has continued in the last two decades, the "returns" from engaging the planning process have been elusive.

Application of strategic planning, despite its limitations, remains prevalent in the leadership practices of thousands of churches across the country. These churches spend many dollars and hours on strategic planning, with marginal results. Despite plentiful criticism from worn-out laypeople and disillusioned church staff, little or nothing has been written to the church audience to address the problem. Furthermore, there is little support for pastors to combat insistence on a strategic plan from well-meaning elders and deacons—especially the corporate gladiators of the 1960s, 1970s, and 1980s. Unfortunately, for a church with a few decades of history an entire generation of retired businesspeople keeps the application of this planning method alive and well in the leadership ranks of our churches.

Case Study A: "Losing Ground"

To illustrate the problem of strategic planning, I will use the words of a well-meaning layleader. In the wake of a twelve-month strategic planning process, this leader put together the "status of the church" report. Here is the last paragraph of his report:

> What are the implications of this study? On the surface [the church] appears to be a vibrant, committed, giving, mission-minded church on an excellent, well kept and adequate campus. The calendar and schedule are full, there is an excellent hard working staff backed by

> managerial and support staff. There are plenty of educational, worship, and mission opportunities, and giving to the church has remained high and consistent. The attendance numbers and the near static growth in membership present, however, an unanswered question. *Why with the staff, programs, giving, and opportunities has the church tended to lose ground rather than gain ground and what can and should be done about it?* [italics mine]

Can you hear the frustration in this man's report? Everything seems to be in place and everyone is plenty busy. Despite a huge investment of time and money, including the work of an outside consultant, the strategic planning process has left them "losing ground." The most thoughtful leaders are still standing around scratching their heads.

Case Study B: "What Do We Do Next?"

I have been in conversation with a historically strong church in one of our country's banner evangelical cities. The church recently completed an eighteen-month strategic planning process that produced a Ministry Master Plan. Why, after completing this process, were they calling on Auxano as group of vision navigators? Simply put, they didn't know what to do. That is, they did not know how the contents of a strategic planning document should intersect with the realities of existing church life. How is this possible? The answer becomes clear as we unpack the fallacies of strategic planning. Before doing so, let's scan the contents of the Ministry Master Plan itself. The resulting document contains:

- A "purpose statement," "mission statement," and "vision statement," each between forty and seventy words
- An eight-point bullet list of "ministry characteristics," each bullet containing long descriptive phrases
- A six-point "core values" list, each with a sentence of description
- A ten-point "passions" list with paragraph explanations and biblical justification
- Three sets of "strategic objectives," including "overarching objectives," "targeted objectives," and "supporting objectives"
- Five overarching objectives containing twenty action steps
- Three targeted objectives containing thirteen action steps
- Three supporting objectives containing nine actions steps
- Ten pages with the content organized around eighty-four pieces of content

The report is certainly a testimony to a lot of time from a lot of people. But what are we to make of this complex document? Why, with all of this information, are leaders wondering what to do next?

Despite the thoughtfulness of this strategic planning document, it neither inspires people to become a Church Unique nor provides practical, daily guidance for leaders. Why? Let's start by examining two very different approaches for any vision or planning document.[1] The approaches can be defined by a subtle change in emphasis: Are we talking about the organization to people, or talking to people about the organization?

First, are we talking about the organization to the people? The ministry plan with ten pages and eighty-four pieces of content emphasizes explanation and justification of all the activity in the organization. The volume, complexity, and structure of the report are overwhelming to most ministry professionals, not to mention volunteers. To state the limitation of the classic strategic plan in one sentence, it misses the human element. Remember those large, multifold travel maps? I travel a lot and enjoy being with churches across the country. But if I had to pull out one of those cumbersome, old-school maps every time I jumped into my Hertz, I would go insane. Which side is up? What part of the map do I look at? Which ramp do I take? The map would probably end up in the back seat—never to be unfolded again.

An alternate approach asks, *Are we talking to people about the organization?* The priority here is not the plan itself but the church leader, volunteer, or attender for whom the report is actually intended. In this case, the document leans toward simplicity in order to bring clarity. Using the map analogy again, this is like getting directions from Mapquest. I enter my starting point and my destination and get step-by-step driving directions with a highlighted map showing me exactly where to go. Simple, clear, and easy to understand. Undoubtedly, both kinds of map may be accurate, but only one gives me clear and specific guidance as to how to get to my destination without an overload of data.

These two case studies represent thousands of stories from similar vision teams and long-range planning committees in churches across our land.

Three Fallacies

As we continue to recast vision, I want to take a moment to debunk strategic planning. I do this only to inspire better visioning. To be clear, though I'm offering a strong critique of strategic planning, I am in no way discouraging the process of "future thinking" or planning in general. I'm asking leaders to reconsider how they execute and express their planning work. To do so, we will explore three key fallacies of classic strategic planning. Keep in mind that the remedy for these fallacies is given in Part Two and Part Three.

Fallacy One: The Vision Shredder

Have you ever put the wrong document in a paper shredder? There's no way to get it back. You just can't put the strips back together; no amount of time and tape will fix it. A similar thing happens to vision when you develop a strategic plan. The assumption is that more information will produce clearer direction, but just the opposite is true. I call this the "fallacy of complexity." Too much information shreds the big picture into so many small pieces that the vision is hopelessly lost. More information equals less clarity.

We live in an information revolution. This revolution pushes the limits of our humanity by delivering an ocean's worth of information to us daily—giving us "knowledge fatigue." Imagine our world: knowledge doubles every year, more than one million Websites are created each day, and some 65 percent of preschoolers today will work in jobs that don't yet exist. The bottom line is that people do not need more information; they need more meaning from the right information. Leaders of today must learn how to deliver meaning by distilling what they say.

To illustrate this point, consider an historic event designed to memorialize the soldiers who lost their lives in the American Revolutionary War. The year of the memorial was 1863, and the event planner secured one of the greatest orators of the day to be the keynote speaker. His name was Edward Everett. That day, Everett spoke for two hours and delivered an address that consisted of 13,607 words. The president, Abraham Lincoln also spoke that day. He got on and off the platform so fast that the photographer didn't have time to take his picture. The Gettysburg Address was 286 words in length. This perfect distillation and articulation hit the bull's-eye of the nation's heart. Today his words still echo in the lives of millions of Americans. Fewer words had further reach.

NO IDEA ABOUT THE BIG IDEA. To state the fallacy of complexity more academically, we would say that analysis does not lead to synthesis. In other words, the ability to break the whole into parts does not inherently help us keep the whole in mind. For example, a mayor thinks and communicates synthetically motivating city residents to raise money for a new bridge. But an engineer thinks and communicates analytically in order to make the bridge a reality. Both types of thinking—analysis and synthesis—are essential, but they have completely different functions. Analysis breaks the whole into parts (how many steps are required to build the bridge?). Synthesis builds the parts into a whole (why should a bridge exist in the first place?). The fallacy of complexity erroneously assumes that if we deal with the details long enough, the big idea will continue to emerge. This would be like the mayor trying to generate enthusiasm for bridge construction by showing math formulas for bridge design. Inevitably, enthusiasm dies as the city folk are buried by irrelevant and boring information. Likewise, in most church settings the details of the strategic plan eclipse the big idea or the all-encompassing vision that people have not yet captured.

FROM FOX TO HEDGEHOG. One might push back in objection, to say that a good strategic plan synthesizes and clarifies the mission or vision of the organization as a singular idea. Even though this is theoretically true, in reality it never happens. Two things muddy the waters of clarity in almost every strategic plan. First, too much information obscures the big idea that may in fact be there. Second, there may be several competing, mutually exclusive big ideas. In either case, the secret is learning to say more by saying less. Andy Stanley writes: "Too much information may, in fact, have a canceling effect—that is, multiple ideas or concepts can actually compete with each other for the listeners' attention and retention . . . and with every additional thought you introduce, you diminish the effectiveness of the prior ideas you may have presented."[2] In fact, research conducted by an advertising firm has shown that "whenever there were at least four different fifteen-second commercials in a two-and-a-half minute commercial time-out, the effectiveness of any one fifteen-second ad sinks to almost zero."[3]

In our Case Study B cited earlier, there are actually three competing statements: a mission statement, a vision statement, and a purpose statement. Only one of these statements is necessary, and if it is stated well it will need fifteen to twenty-five words, not forty to seventy. By having all three of these terribly long, redundant statements, we severely diminish the opportunity for anyone to carry and communicate the vision contagiously.

Jim Collins's use of "the fox and the hedgehog" fable from an ancient Greek poet illustrates the fallacy of complexity. The poet Archilochus wrote, "The fox knows many things, but the hedgehog knows one big thing." In *Good to Great*, Collins demonstrates that great organizations live and breathe from a hedgehog concept. They are ruthlessly clear about the *one thing* at which they can be the best in the world. Organizations that act like foxes, chasing after too much too often, never achieve a singular focus. They stay stuck being "good."[4]

Fallacy Two: The Silo Builder

Church leaders know what organizational silos look like. What defines success for staff members? The answer is, "Butts in seats in my ministry area!" Many churches use "nickels and noses" as the *only* measure for success. This primary measure of worship service attendance is translated down into the ministry departments. The result is a golf-team mentality where team success is measured by adding up individual scores at the end of the day. Quiet competition simmers underneath the calm surface of most staff meetings, with individual ministries trying to outdrive the others.

When a strategic planning process is introduced into an environment where real teamwork is already challenged, the plan itself becomes a silo builder that reinforces the concrete walls between ministry areas. This is the second fallacy of strategic planning, the "fallacy of accountability." As multiple goals are developed for each separate ministry area, the expectation is that staff and volunteers will experience better coordination, with clearer responsibilities. The false assumption behind this practice is that more goals help people work better together. Exactly the opposite is true. More goals typically create a more fragmented approach, as each leader focuses solely on his or her responsibilities and outcomes. In an effort to establish positive steps of *accountability within ministry areas*, the church misses out on *synergy among all ministry areas.*

What the church really needs is a strategy that helps members function more like a football team than a golf team. A football team shares one score, which is based on coordination of highly diverse functions—there may be forty-six individuals with forty-six performance indicators, but there are not forty-six goals. The singular goal is to get the ball into the end zone.

A strategic plan can easily divide a team by giving each player an individual goalpost. How exactly does this happen? Let's refer back to the Ministry Master Plan briefly outlined earlier in this chapter. There were three kinds of objectives, with a total of forty-two action steps or goals. Here is why the plan inhibits synergy:

- *Too many goals threaten to make any one goal unclear.* Would we rather have forty-two goals that no one remembers or one goal that forms the ever-present gauge on your "dashboard of ministry"?

- *Too many goals weaken the connection between the goals and the larger vision.* Do we want workers who are excited about the big picture as they do their daily "bite-sized" tasks? Imagine your volunteers as brick makers. Do you want every brick maker focused on bricks-per-hour efficiency, or brick yield loss, or brick compression strength, or mortar viscosity, and so on, at the risk of not envisioning the beautiful cathedral he is building?
- *Too many goals make it harder for people to have shared goals.* How can our leaders all point in the same direction on cue, as we navigate ministry together (like the choreography of a school of fish darting through the water)? How do our goals inadvertently create competition for the same limited resources?
- *Too many goals inhibit good decision making on the front line of ministry.* Do we have a lot of goals because we are trying to compensate for lack of trust and communication? Are we releasing competent people on the front line of ministry, or are we dictating decisions from the boardroom?

Time and time again, I see more goals equaling more confusion. Well-intentioned pastors and planners think they are building a ladder to greater achievement. What they really are building is a chute that flushes synergy down the drain.

Fallacy Three: Leadership Blinders

It has been said that all leaders live under the same sky, but not all view the same horizon. Some leaders see a wider horizon and keep their eye on the emerging skyline. Continual learning contributes to their sense of adventure and their ability to steer their organization. Others, however, unknowingly wear blinders. The shifting horizons don't signal new opportunities because they are unanticipated and out of view.

The third limitation of strategic planning is how it keeps blinders on leadership. I call it the "fallacy of predictability." The assumption is that the near future will resemble the recent past. But rapid cultural change has meddled with this assumption. Change now happens so fast that the planning processes of yesteryear are obsolete. Unfortunately, not even the future is what it used to be. Innovation expert Jim Carroll paints a compelling picture:

> Clearly you need different skills to take you into a future that is becoming far more complex, challenging and different by the minute. How can you keep operating the way you do—with the same culture,

> structure, rules and methodologies, when the rate of change that envelopes your organization is so dramatic and so darned fast? We live in an era of unprecedented and relentless change. The emergence of China as a super-power; hyper-innovation and business market turmoil; constant career change and rapid scientific advances. Competition is changing overnight, and product lifecycles often last for just a few months. Permanence has been torn asunder. We are in a time that demands a new agility and flexibility: and everyone must have the skill and insight to prepare for a future that is rushing at them faster than ever before.[5]

Despite the realities of relentless change, the strategic planning process in churches still presents five-, ten-, and even twenty-year plans. How ludicrous! With permanence "torn asunder," we can't extrapolate the present reality as we used too. The ten-year plan becomes an exercise in fantasy, not vision.

Planning assumes predictability in much the same way that a hiker counts on a map to navigate. There are fixed points in the future that can be anticipated, because the mountain pathways and earth-shaped landmarks stay relatively fixed over time. Their presence is predictable. But imagine the scenario of a sailor on the open water. There are few geographic landmarks, and no landmass to provide an ever-present constant. In fact, shifting winds, changing currents, and impending squalls require an entirely new set of skills and tools. Navigating a liquid surface necessitates ceaseless observation and adaptation to the surrounding environment. How should we begin to adapt our perspective on planning in today's environment? Reggie McNeal offers a guiding light. Leaders must focus more on *preparation* than on *planning*. Planning relies on predictability. But preparation helps leaders stay clear amid uncertainty. Planning assumes continuity; preparation equips leaders to be flexible enough to seize opportunity.[6] It forces them to pray, learn, and discern what God is doing—all aspects of understanding God's unique vision for the church. After all, isn't it God who does the planning (Jer. 29:11)?

Is your church's relationship to the future arthritic or adaptive? If you are engaged in a strategic planning process, be cautioned. It might be forcing leaders to wear blinders to the changing world around them. It might also be strengthening unhealthy silos that rob the church of precious energy every day. Finally, it might be running your vision through someone's mental paper shredder, never to be recovered again.

Consider reviewing Table 2.1 with your team. What fruits have planning processes yielded for you in the past? On the basis of your previous experience, which fallacies have affected you the most? Which have affected your church the most?

Table 2.1. Strategic Planning Fallacies Summary

The Fallacy of:	The Wrong Assumption	The Strategic Plan Backfires as a:	The Real Need
Complexity	More information will provide clearer direction	Vision shredder	Clarity
Accountability	More goals will help us work better together	Silo builder	Synergy
Predictability	The near future will resemble the recent past	Leadership blinder	Adaptability

3

THE INIQUITY OF CHURCH GROWTH

CAGING THE KINGDOM

It is clear that emphasizing the growth of the churches divides the camp. It is really a divisive topic. How strange when all are presumably disciples of the Lord.

—Donald McGavran, letter to his wife, Sept. 8, 1961

JOHANN FRIEDRICH BOTTGER WAS A GERMAN alchemist who lived between 1682 and 1719. Although Bottger made bold claims, including the ability to make gold, his talents are noted in history by the discovery of the porcelain-making process. The first facility to manufacture this "white gold" was set up in Dresden in 1709. Before long, the Royal Porcelain Manufacture gained a worldwide reputation, with its distinctive pure-white-and-cobalt blue design. Ironically, Bottger's achievements as an alchemist brought an unexpected consequence. Because of his boasts and early success, August the Strong imprisoned Bottger in order to protect this marvelous new invention and moved the alchemist's operation to his castle fortress in Meissen. There Bottger was held prisoner so his genius could stay in close proximity to and total control of the king.

Two notes are worth highlighting about Bottger's life. The first is that you can't deny his success even though some of his claims are undeniably exaggerated. After all, true gold was never made. Secondly, he was, rather ironically, held captive thanks to his greatest success.

As we turn our attention to the two little words "church" and "growth," we encounter two realities mirrored by Bottger's story. The first is the mixed reaction of church leaders over the past four decades to the success of the church growth movement. Despite its accomplishments, the question still looms: Are the greatest purveyors of church growth geniuses or charlatans? Voices stand on both sides. In 1961, the movement's founder, Donald McGavran, wrote his wife, as we've seen, "It is clear that emphasizing the growth of churches divides the camp." In 2005, Paul Engel and Gary McIntosh wrote, "For nearly half a century proponents and detractors of the Church Growth Movement have presented their viewpoints in various forms. . . . Research has determined that there are five main positions."[1] If you boil down the positions, it seems that two groups come to the forefront: those that emphasize what the church growth movement accomplished and those that emphasize what it overpromised.

I want to add to the conversation while keeping in mind the importance of visionary leadership. As we recast vision in Part One, my primary concern is rooted in the fact that church growth specialists have always thrown around the *vision* word. This begs the question: Are legitimate critiques of the movement therefore also valid criticism of being visionary? My answer is a vehement no. Yet I am very concerned, as younger leaders move past the church growth paradigm, that they not abandon the development of their minds and hearts for visionary kingdom building.

With such polarity of opinion about church growth, I want to explore the connection to visionary leadership today by looking at both sides of the equation. On the one hand, the movement has made an unquestionable contribution to church history. In this sense, there is true visionary work represented by it. On the other hand, and as with Bottger's legacy, it seems the greatest hazard for church growth proponents is being held captive by their own success. I suggest that it is not the principles of church growth that deserve the sharpest critique but the hearts of leaders who are imprisoned by too narrow a definition of numerical growth. Visionary leaders today must be wary of such a trap. By defining the primary limitation of church growth, we clearly separate problems associated with the movement from the need to live as a visionary outside of the movement. As a first step, let's first turn our thoughts toward a definition of church growth.

Zooming Out on "Church Growth"

To better understand how teachings on church growth have evolved, let's scan the popular perspectives of church growth and leadership in the latter half of the twentieth century. Figure 3.1 shows four components

Figure 3.1. Popular Perspectives of the Church, 1960–2010

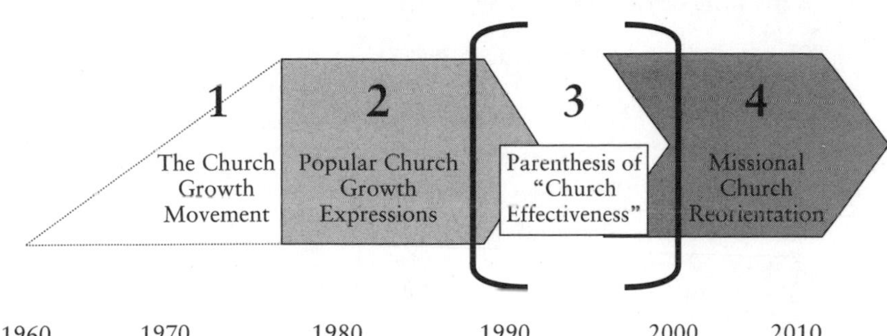

or stages. In reality, these stages overlap, but allow my clean lines to present a simple model. I trust you will find this diagram quickly situates any of the books on church leadership you have read. Let's review each stage.

Stage One: The Church Growth Movement

The formal start of the movement traces back to the life of Donald McGavran, a third-generation missionary born in 1897. After three decades of missionary labor, primarily in India, McGavran published *The Bridges of God* in 1955. (In 1956, it was the most widely read book on mission theory.) At this point, two important aspects of McGavran's life are noteworthy. First, he was no ivory-tower thinker. His insights were born out of a deep passion and demonstrated sweat for the Great Commission. Second, he was a voracious learner. For example, he was driven to understand why churches in one village grew 200 percent while churches down the road grew only 10 percent. His passion and learning eventually opened doors for him to teach back in the United States—at a time in life when most kingdom players retire. In 1965, he was invited to become the founding dean at Fuller's School of World Mission. In 1970, he published what is considered to be his magnum opus, *Understanding Church Growth*. It is noteworthy that until 1970 much of McGavran's work and teaching was targeted toward international missions. But more and more pastors from North America were expressing interest in his growth principles, so in 1972 the seminary offered a course for pastors cotaught by Peter Wagner, a professor and former missionary. The following decade brought the strongest days of the movement, with organizations, publications, and influential leaders waving the banner.

McGavran's teaching was driven by trying to answer four basic questions in his ministry:[2]

What are the causes of church growth?

What are the barriers to it?

What are the factors that can make the Christian faith a movement among some populations?

What principles of church growth are reproducible?

One popular principle espoused by McGavran was the homogeneous principle—the idea that "the gospel spreads more naturally among people through their language and the indigenous forms of their culture, than through alien languages and cultural forms." Another example of his teaching shows the emphasis on people groups: the idea that "apostolic ministry is more effective when we target people groups than when we target political units of geographic areas."[3] Principles such as these became the staples of pastoral training in our seminaries for decades.

The movement proper began to lose steam, starting with McGavran's death in 1990. Though the words *church growth* would continue to multiply in popular usage, the continuity of a singular "movement voice" waned by the turn of the century.

Stage Two: Popular Church Growth Expressions

With the success of the church growth movement came an explosion of popular church growth expressions, including seminary classes, seminar offerings, books, periodicals, and consulting approaches. You might know a name or two who received their doctor of ministry degree from Fuller at the height of the era. The impressive list of alumni includes Elmer Towns, Kent Hunter, John Vaughan, John Maxwell, Rick Warren, Bob Logan, Bill Sullivan, Leith Anderson, Paul Ford, and Eddie Gibbs. By the late 1970s, the movement had expanded to the point that everyone talked about church growth whether they espoused the specific teachings of McGavran or not. Here are just a few of the books using the words *church* and *growth* either in the title or subtitle, between 1978 and 2000:

Design for Church Growth, by Charles Chaney (1978)

Church Alive! A Fresh Look at Church Growth, by Francis Cotterell (1981)

Leading Your Church to Growth, by Peter Wagner (1984)

Balanced Church Growth, by Ebbie C. Smith (1984)

44 Ways to Increase Church Attendance, by Lyle E. Schaller (1988)

Beyond Church Growth, by Robert Logan (1989)

The Bonsai Theory of Church Growth, by Ken Hemphill (1991)

How to Break Growth Barriers, by Carl George (1993)

Kingdom Principles for Church Growth, by Gene Mims (1994)

The Purpose Driven Church, by Rick Warren (1995)

The Church Growth Handbook, by William Easum (1996)

Book of Church Growth, by Thom Rainer (1998)

The Every Church Guide to Growth, by Elmer Towns (1998)

Not only were books proliferating under the church growth banner but entire disciplines became associated with the category. Most notable are survey researchers (George Gallup and George Barna), church marketing (a new industry that created a dozen companies with a national platform), and application of business management to the church (strategic planning).

As the category broadened, criticism grew. It included a preoccupation with "numbers," inappropriately overlaying "business practices" on the church without theological critique, and observations that most growth was primarily "transfer growth" from neighboring churches and not true "conversion growth."

But it was hard to tell when criticism was valid or even warranted because much of it didn't have a clear target. Church growth became a large and nebulous category. Gary McIntosh writes, "The conceptual broadening of the term *church growth* to embrace more and more subspecializations of ministry and more and more organizations has created to a large extent a popular misunderstanding and wrongful criticism of the Church Growth Movement."[4] Examples of subspecialization are church planting, small groups, spiritual warfare, conflict management, change management, marketing, strategic planning, and fundraising. Nevertheless, the movement multiplied. Even though the 1970s represented the strongest decade for the movement proper (stage one in Figure 3.1), the 1980s represented the height of church growth's popular expression (stage two).

Stage 3: The Parenthesis of "Church Effectiveness"

As the influence of both the formal movement and popular expressions of church growth reached a climax, innovative practitioners began avoiding church growth language, giving rise to the third stage. Ed Stetzer and David Putnam speak to the transition away from growth in this statement: "The movement was filled with methodological mania. Every book promised if you did what they said, your church would grow. Unfortunately, they told you to do different things. Soon pastors were frustrated. They wondered to which guru they should listen."[5] Savvy pastor-leaders began writing about "church health," bringing the corrective tone of *quality* to the impulse toward quantity. The cover flap of Rick Warren's *Purpose Driven Church* read, "The issue is church health, not growth!" Warren declared, "If your church is healthy, growth will occur naturally."[6] Christian Schwartz's popular consulting approach, Natural Church Development, also emphasized health over growth. Stetzer and Putnam even refer to a "church health movement."[7]

A simple Web search, however, reveals more books written on ministry effectiveness than any other topic, including church health. Because there was never an organized movement, I think it is best to view this as a parenthesis, by which I mean to emphasize that effectiveness teaching has no centralized leader or organization as its source, and that its emphasis was relatively short-lived. Some books that mark this window:

> *Maximizing Your Effectiveness,* by Aubrey Malphurs (1995)
>
> *Effective Evangelistic Churches,* by Thom Ranier (1996)
>
> *The Twelve Keys to an Effective Church,* by Kennon Callahan (1997)
>
> *The Habits of Highly Effective Churches,* by George Barna (2001)
>
> *Seven Practices of Effective Ministry,* by Andy Stanley, Reggie Joiner, and Lane Jones (2004)

A massive backdrop was emerging for this effectiveness emphasis of stage three as a result of large-scale cultural shifts. This is indicated by the gap or break between the parentheses in Figure 3.1.

The shifts have been described as the end of modernity and the dawn of postmodernity.* Within this shift we have and are experiencing the close of "the era of Christendom" and the rise of a "post-Christian era."

---

*Again, I am assuming the reader's understanding; see *The Missional Church* by Darrell Guder and Lois Barrett. Guder writes in his introduction: "In Great Britain during 1983 by the publication of Bishop Lesslie Newbigin's short monograph *The Other Side of 1984: Questions for the Church* the concerns raised by the bishop were certainly not new. But as a missionary statesman and leader who had returned after decades in India to minister in Britain, Newbigin analyzed with penetrating clarity the challenge presented by the changing context of Western society. In a word, what had once been a Christendom society was now clearly post-Christian, and in many ways anti-Christian. Newbigin brought into public discussion a theological consensus that had long been forming among missiologists and theologians. He then focused that consensus on the concrete reality of Western society as it has taken shape in this century. His conclusions have mobilized Christian thinkers and leaders on both sides of the Atlantic" (p. 3).

In the era of Christendom, the rise of the church influence in the West gave the Judeo-Christian worldview a level of cultural prominence.* In the post-Christian era, there is no starting point and no embedded influence toward Judeo-Christian values, latent within the culture. Practitioners in this transition increasingly realize the problems of church as usual (the primary indicators being the continued decline of church attendance and the validation that those professing Christianity reflect little difference in life-change factors from those who reject Jesus[8]).

Stage Four: Missional Church Reorientation

As the post-Christian era dawns, a new perspective, stage four, has developed and is accelerating fast. I call it a reorientation because it has emerged from the ashes of Christendom as a new paradigm—not a mere improvement over what preceded it. The idea of the missional church has single-handedly captured the imagination of church leaders of all backgrounds and denominations. Take your pick: from the boomer power pastors of suburbia to the preaching punks of "emergia" and the collared intellectuals of "liturgia," everyone wants to be missional. But what does it mean? Essentially it is a way of thinking that challenges the church to re-form and reforge its self-understanding (theologically, spiritually, and socially) so that it can relearn how to live and proclaim the gospel in the world. Perhaps the best motto of the reorientation is the imperative to "be the church." Church is not something you do or a place you go to, but *what you are.*

The missional church concept was being formulated in the ranks of academics decades before it hit the street. The pull-back of this academic rubber band finally released in 1998 with publication of *The Missional Church*. Its author, Darrell Guder, asserts, "The basic thesis of this book

---

*A short recounting of my dinner conversation tonight with Judy, a woman in her late seventies, illustrates the point. We were at dinner learning about the Protestant Reformation. I thought she was an evangelical, but during dinner I learned that she is not. She explained her dislike of Jesus' teaching in that he claims to be "the way, the truth, and the life" in John 15. She is put off by Jesus' assertion of being the "only way." The remarkable thing is that she also shares a deep interest for Scripture and has attended church regularly her entire life. My point is that although Judy is not a believer, she grew up in the cultural environment of Christendom. Jesus is not Lord of her life, but she would be offended to be considered not Christian. The point of distinguishing the post-Christian era is the reality that people like Judy for the most part will not exist. By and large, people who don't follow Christ will find little interest in church.

is that the answer to the crisis in the North American church will not be found at the level of method and problem solving. We share the conviction of a growing consensus of Christians in North America that the problem is much more deeply rooted. It has to do with who we are and what we are for. . . . Either we are defined by mission, or we reduce the scope of the gospel and the mandate of the church. Thus, our challenge today is to move from church with mission to missional church."[9] Since these words were penned, many have jumped on the missional bandwagon—I believe, for good reason.

FROM DOING TO BEING. The missional reorientation represents an important shift in focus from methodology to identity. Within the first three stages of Figure 3.1, most of the church's questions dealt ultimately with how-tos of evangelism. Assuming the influence of Christendom, methodology questions ask, "What can we do to reach more people?" In contrast, the church's question of identity in the disorientation of the post-Christian era asks, "Now that our influence is gone, how do we reshape our self-understanding so we can be like Christ in the world?" Again, this reflects a shift in emphasis away from doing toward being.

The theological launch pad for this emphasis on a re-formed identity of the church is the identity of God Himself. Guder quotes one of the seminal works by David Bosch: the missional church "is put in the context of the doctrine of the Trinity, not of ecclesiology or soteriology. The classical doctrine of the *missio Dei* as God the Father sending the Son, and God the Father and the Son sending the Spirit [is] expanded to include yet another 'movement': Father, Son, and Holy Spirit sending the church in the world."[10] Therefore the church's new identity is a reclarification of its "sentness." Sending is not something you do, but being sent is something you are.

ATTRACTIONAL VS. INCARNATIONAL. There are plentiful implications of this stage four reorientation. One of the most common is the move away from an "attractional" mind-set to an "incarnational" one.[11] Attractional means that the church's basic strategy for reaching the lost revolves around getting "seekers" or the "unchurched" into the church building. Once inside, the opportunity to present the gospel defines the primary opportunity for evangelism. This paradigm reflects the common assumption for most popular church growth expressions. In contrast, the incarnational emphasis of the missional mindset focuses on living and sharing the gospel "where life happens." (Just as for Jesus, who "walked across the street" between heaven and earth by putting on "flesh"—to incarnate.) The importance is placed on the church "disassembling" itself for the primary work of evangelism in the nooks and crannies of everyday life. In the attractional mode, big church buildings are important, and the church gathered is the consummation of evangelism. In the incarnational mode, fluid and flexible communities of faith are important; the church scattered is consummation of evangelism. The rallying cry against the attractional model is that the church should be measured by its sending capacity, not its seating capacity.

LOST PEOPLE: PROSPECTS, OR THE PEOPLE JESUS MISSES MOST? To further illustrate the distinction, a church's language about the people it wants to reach quickly exposes an attractional or incarnational mind-set. Southern Baptists have traditionally referred to potential members as "prospects." This sales term does little to edify the relational development with unbelievers outside of church walls. Rather, it defines success as "selling" the church and getting people to join, that is, getting them inside the church building. Years ago, Bill Hybels of Willow Creek Community Church articulated a core value of "Lost people matter to God, therefore they matter to us." I have always appreciated Hybels's evangelistic fervor, but this articulation connotes an attractional mind-set. The value is a propositional statement, not a gesture of affection. As a hard, impersonal fact it underscores their primary strategy to get people to the "seeker service." Recently, Willow Creek completed a capital campaign for more than $100 million to expand their facility to this end. But the heartbeat of the missional church has found different language to carry a renewed identity of being sent. A growing church plant outside of Phoenix calls unbelievers "the precious." This term cuts to the heart. It sends people out on the constant journey to know, to help, and to love precious people every day. Or take the approach of Jim Henderson, a megachurch pastor of evangelism who got fed up with typical methods. He suggests that the emphasis in the parables of the lost coin and sheep is not on what the sheep and coin feel but what God the Father feels. Rather than referring to unbelievers as lost people, he adapted his language to say "the people Jesus misses most."[12] The shift in language assumes that followers of Christ will likewise have people they miss most. The difference in word choice may seem subtle, but it moves the idea of evangelizing from something we do—church-inspired and project-oriented—to something we embody—personally inspired and life-oriented. These small shifts in terminology represent quantum shifts in identity, because they lead Christ followers to be the church and not just go to church.

Unwrapping the Bad Rap

Having put church growth in context, what are the iniquities of the church growth movement that make it inadequate for today? If you listen to the critiques, I believe you'll find that the answer lies in not what the movement taught per se, but in the questions that the movement was trying to solve. As Donald McGavran and his followers developed church growth methodology, it seems that they were doing important kingdom work, *given their set of problems and presuppositions*. Their problems started by trying to understand dramatic variations in evangelism effectiveness on the mission fields of India and ended with trying to reverse declining church attendance in North America. Their presuppositions were bound within Christendom; they worked when Christianity was a viable, latent force within Western culture. They were not dealing with the postmodern shift that we face today. Rather, they were trying to figure out better evangelism *methodology* within the paradigm of accepted Christianity. Keep in mind that McGavran's earliest thinking, which I've previously referenced, was chiseled from his missionary work in India as early as the 1920s. Approximately fifty years after McGavran's influence began, it became clear that change was imminent. One of the most significant events in identifying the shift to a post-Christian era came in 1983 with publication of Bishop Newbigin's *The Other Side of 1984: Questions for the Church.*[13] This short monograph recognized the changes that were occurring and initiated conversation about the future of the church.

Now if the set of problems and presuppositions change (to new ones we are now facing), does this make the conclusions of the church growth era wrong? No, it just makes them less applicable. For example, do I rag on my grandfather if he can't figure out how to wind-up his quartz watch? Of course not. Instead, I gently tell him that the darn watch doesn't need to wind up anymore.

People often make bullet lists of positive and negative contributions of the church growth movement, but I propose a critique that I hope is as useful as it is simple. First, let's salute Donald McGavran as a man who labored for the gospel before the dawn of the post-Christian era. Dare I say that this missionary had some brilliant observations? Second, let's identify the real problem more clearly.

Church Growth vs. Growth Idolatry

Much of the bad rap for church growth stems from the concern over a preoccupation with numbers. The idea is that too much focus on quantity—getting people through the doors of the church—dilutes some other emphasis on quality (however the church chooses to define it, for example as spiritual growth or theological depth). But does an inordinate focus on church attendance come from the growth principles themselves, or from something deeper within the leader's heart? Is it possible that the real culprit is not the movement per se but a "growth idolatry" lurking in the leader's life? Growth idolatry is the unconscious belief, *on the soul level,* that things are not OK with me if *my* church is not growing. I have struggled with this sin, and I know many other leaders do too.

An idol is anything we add to Jesus in order to make life work. The irony is that in the call to preach the gospel many ministers fail to apply the gospel personally in ways that free their heart from a performance trap. This performance, of course, is measured most easily by church attendance, so the temptation to compare is always as close as our heartbeat. For some, the competition nurtured through sports fanaticism or market indicators magnifies the intensity of having to grow. When it's time to attend a pastor's gathering, deep emotions are connected to how the church is doing. If it's growing, we can't wait to find subtle ways to tell our ministry colleagues. If it's not, we hope no one asks (or we just don't attend the group). One of my closest friends in ministry confessed to me that the worst year of his life was the first year his church did not grow. Addicted to a track record of 15 percent attendance growth over ten years, he saw the first year of attendance plateau, hitting him like the black plague.

Show Me the Bigger Box!

The result of growth idolatry is the default vision of the "bigger box" church. The ever-present vision for campus expansion and larger buildings is the epitome of the attractional model. Are there other ways to expand the kingdom? Yes, but growth idolatry strongly persuades us that kingdom growth must mean numerical growth of our local church. So I ask, who really wanted the bigger box: the church growth principle? the people in the church? the pastor? As Larry Osborne of North Coast Church always says, "People like it small, but leaders like it big." Thus we return to Bottger's ironic dilemma of being imprisoned because of his own success. The problem in applying some good methods to grow is that they work. When they do, we open a door to the possibility of becoming a slave to the growth in attendance at our church. Howard Hendricks understood this when he exhorted us as young pastors, "I am not fearful for your failure; I am fearful for your success."

I see growth idolatry reflected most often in three scenarios. The first is when churches exhibit little financial generosity outside of their local ministry. One pastor I know has a vision of planting thousands of churches in his lifetime. But with each year of success and more resources to invest in planting, the mother church seems to grow ever stingier. The second is when churches get their bigger building but don't know what to do next. I did a funeral with a pastor in St. Louis years ago. As we drove from the gravesite, he confessed that after moving into their $10 million facility, he was completely at a loss when it came to the church's vision. Instead of discovering his Church Unique and clarifying a new vision, growth idolatry had demanded the bigger box. The third scenario is rapid expansion of the multisite movement. Although multisite is a strategic option for many, it can serve the growth idolatry of some who would be better off planting churches than leveraging one teacher across other local venues.

A poignant statement in the vein of growth idolatry was made by Gordon MacDonald. He posed the issue years ago at the Willow Creek Summit in this way: "I have wondered if our evangelical fervor to change the world is not driven in some part by the inability to change ourselves." Pointing the drive of more impact back to a brokenness within, God used his question to help me see my own idolatry that day. Reggie McNeal offers another reflection on the same problem: "Unfortunately it [the church growth movement] fell victim to an idolatry as old as the Tower of Babel, the belief that we are the architects of the work of God. As a result we have the best churches men can build, but are still waiting for the church that only God can get the credit for."[14]

Visionary Leadership Transcends the Church Growth Movement

The ultimate take-away from this chapter comes from the question asked earlier: Is the importance for developing visionary leadership necessarily tied to the heyday of church growth? Popular church growth practitioners threw around the vision word all the time. But the art of vision didn't originate within it and is in no way bound by it. For now, I hope that you can separate out any critiques of church growth from the practice of being visionary. In summary, I would suggest:

- The church growth movement was a visionary movement that offered helpful principles within the context of the era of Christendom.

- It's hard to critique the movement because eventually so many popular methodologies used the language of church growth that its definition was significantly blurred.
- The primary culprit of popular church growth methodology—the iniquity of church growth—is not the teaching in and of itself but the tendency to nurture growth idolatry in the pastor's heart.
- The need for visionary leadership must be separated from both nuanced critiques of the church growth movement generally and from the root problems of growth idolatry.

The next two parts of this book continue to place the practice of visionary leadership in a sphere that transcends the church growth teaching of the past fifty years. At this point, it suffices to acknowledge Jesus as the greatest visionary who ever lived. Whose footsteps ever showed a clearer sense of origin, mission, and destiny? If we aspire to follow him, let's not falter in our vision work because of a short season in church history marked by growth idolatry.

We thank the Lord that *He* promised to build *His* church. The Lord is the builder; we are not. The Lord is the owner; we are not. The power of Hades will not prevail against Jesus our Savior and our Visionary.

4

LOST CONGREGATIONS

HOW CHURCHES ADAPT TO THE VISION VACUUM

When people can't see what God is up to,
they stumble all over themselves.

—Proverbs 29:18, *The Message*

NESTLED IN THE SUBURBS OF SAN JOSE, California, is an interesting tourist attraction: an estate built by the heir of the Winchester rifle fortune. In 1884, a wealthy widow named Sarah L. Winchester began a thirty-eight-year construction project guided by a superstitious fear. Evidently, Mrs. Winchester was convinced by a medium that continuous building would appease the evil spirits of those killed by the famous "gun that won the West" and help her attain eternal life. So Sarah kept carpenters' hammers pounding twenty-four hours a day. The Victorian mansion came to be filled with so many unexplained oddities that it is now known as the Winchester Mystery House. Even though it has 160 rooms, three elevators, forty staircases, and forty-seven fireplaces, its size alone does not account for the architectural marvel—what does so is the bizarre purposelessness of the design. Stairs lead into the ceiling; windows decorate the floor, and doors open into blank walls! Random features reflect excessive creativity, energy, and expense, from exquisite hand inlaid parquet floors to Tiffany art glass windows. Busyness, not blueprints, defined success.

The Winchester Mystery House is an accurate picture of what a church looks like in the absence of vision; there is lots of activity with little progress or purpose. Interesting programs and exquisite sermons do not necessarily lead to a meaningful whole. Structure exists for *structure itself* and not for *life*. But poking fun at church structure is too easy. So let's shift gears to a deeper issue: the life of the churchgoer.

The Heart of the Matter

When Nehemiah gazed at the broken walls of Jerusalem, it wasn't the physical devastation alone that broke his heart. The stony rubble signified that God's people were not being protected and released to carry out God's mission in the world. In the Mystery Church, the result is the same. The cost of overconstruction (instead of broken walls) leaves us with awkward ministries, structures, and philosophy. But what's really at stake? The hearts of people and the mission of Christ hang in the balance. Where there is no vision, the people perish (Prov. 29:18).

Let's do a closer heart examination. What really happens in the soul of a congregant when left in a church's vision vacuum over time? Consider:

- What is left to excite the heart of our church attenders?
- What then fuels the dreams of our people?
- What nourishes the identity of those who call our church home?

The simple answer is *something does,* even when vision is absent. People need vision and they need hope. Their very souls seek some conduit for meaning. So, if the visionary leaders are not providing and nourishing it, where do people find meaning?

Soul Fast Food

I have observed four substitutes for a well-balanced diet of vision that I call "soul fast food." They fuel our most faithful people; it is how they get their hope for a better future. Unfortunately, they are also four sources of a malnourished membership identity. Remember that these are the people we count on each week to make church happen. Like children of parents too busy to cook, our congregants grab this fast food as they intersect with church life.

French Fried "Places"

The places of our God moments matter. But space itself has addictive features, just like your favorite fries. (Which is why I make a beeline to In and

Out Burger when I fly to California.) These are spots where we encounter God, whether it be the carpeted stairs near the altar, the ultrahip café where we get fed via live feed, or the intricately beautiful stained glass of the sanctuary. Again, these places are important, and they should be. But in the absence of a vision that transcends our favorite nooks and crannies, the space itself becomes the vision supplement. The primary use of the term *church* to connote place compounds the issue. Don't believe me? Just throw the word *relocation* into the next church business meeting.

Consider Teresa. I did a wedding for a friend last year and Teresa was the wedding coordinator. As I got to know her, I learned that she stopped going to a church that she attended for years. Her church (Abundant Life Methodist) had navigated two transitions in a one year period: a relocation and a change of name to Gateway Community Church. As the name change suggests, the features of the new facility resembled a community center more than a church. When I asked why she stopped attending, her eyes welled up. She emoted for fifteen minutes about the sacred moments at the altar's prayer rail in the old facility. She even mentioned how she pressed her nose "into the wood" of the rail Sunday after Sunday. Teresa's bottom line was clear: "How could the church relocate its facility and not provide the prayer rails?" Rearranging the church furniture literally derailed her journey.

Time out. I know some of you are thinking, Aren't those times at the prayer rail precious and exactly what ministry is all about? Yes they are—absolutely. The meaning of place reflects God's design, starting with the Garden and ending with the New Jerusalem. But space is essential, not central, in the economy of vision. In other words, space ought not define our deepest connection *to* and association *with* a church. Jesus highlights this with the woman at the well: "true worshipers will worship the Father in spirit and truth" in contrast to location, "neither on this mountain nor in Jerusalem" (John 4:21–23).

THE POWER OF PLACE. It is important not to underestimate the gravitational pull of the brick-and-mortar church on the hearts of our people *and on us* as spiritual leaders. Church buildings and sacred place can create an aura of prestige and entitlement that takes spiritual leaders off mission. Did you know what the sale of indulgences funded in Martin Luther's era? It paid for the Catholic Church's building projects. St. Peter's Basilica is thought to be the largest church building in Christianity. It covers an area of 5.7 acres and has a capacity of more than sixty thousand people. Emperor Constantine initially had it built on the site where the apostle Peter was buried. In the mid-1400s, Pope Nicholas V began a reconstruction project. A formidable undertaking, it took 120 years, the succession of several popes, and the services of many famous artists and architects (Michelangelo and Raphael, for example) before it was finally completed. In 1514, Pope Leo X authorized an indulgence to fund the building project. It was this indulgence that led to Martin Luther's protest.

VISION QUACKS. One expression of our preoccupation with place is the rise (and now plateau) of the capital campaign consulting industry. The business of capital campaign or stewardship consulting picked up speed in the late 1960s. The aim of the campaign is to guide the leadership of the church through a season where greater giving can be realized from congregants and designated toward special projects, usually church facilities. Today, amid other forms of church consulting, these "money guys" are the big boys on the block.

What message do these "experts" bring? "Pastor, we know you need help raising funds for the building you need to have. We're here to help you do it." With bold claims, the industry has exploited fear of loss and the promise of gain in the mind of the pastor who never had a fundraising class in seminary. One reason this industry has grown is the ease of selling laypeople with the principle of spending money to make money.

Pastors who go through the process give these consultants mixed reviews. Some are grateful, some frustrated, but most feel the relationship left something to be desired. Why? There are many reasons. The most significant, I believe, has to do with an approach that eclipses missional vision and ignores your Church Unique. At the end of the campaign, or after a big new building is built, it is entirely possible that the building itself becomes the cheap substitute for real vision. The dramatic irony is that the industry spends a lot of time talking about vision. But while animated fly-bys, 3-D building models, and umpteen brochures are heralding the promise of the new church building, people are being robbed of a more substantial articulation of the church's future. The result is anorexic vision.

As a further point of clarification, each of the junk food categories in this chapter is not bad in and of itself. They all malnourish, because they are used inappropriately as a substitute. This clarification is important because the next potential source of malnourishment is *you*.

Big Mac "Personalities"

Spiritual leaders matter to our people. I hope you have hundreds of people who think you hung the moon, because of your walk with Jesus. But 90 percent of pastors I meet would never want *their* personality to be the umbilical cord connecting their members' identity to the church. Charisma is not vision. It is a vehicle to deliver the vision. The under-shepherd is not a substitute for the Good Shepherd.

Yet year after year, pastoral transition results in attendance attrition. Numbers yo-yo around pulpit presence. For many churchgoers, connection to their church is connection to the pastor. We have a common question in surveys we design: "To whom do you feel most connected at the church?" Options range from "friends and family who brought me" to "members of my small group" to "the pastors and/or staff." We regularly see numbers ranging from 15 to 35 percent of people who feel most connected to the paid staff. What really amazes me, in further support of this point, are those really bad staffing situations. Even when a clearly unproductive or unethical minister leaves the church, scores of people follow. In the absence of vision, people in our churches will cling to *something,* even our least capable staff.

Leaders who understand this principle encourage me. In recent years, I have worked with men like Max Lucado and Chuck Swindoll. Their fame creates a raging current of people who define their identity around a gifted teacher. Yet both of these men have not only worked hard to keep vision central; they have sacrificed easy attendance by removing their face from the church brand. They are both trying to build healthy disciple-making organizations, not high-volume drive-thrus.

Supersized "Programs"

Programs are important, and good methodologies for doing ministry should come and go. But most of them come and stay; like sour milk, they stay way past their expiration date. For years, church leaders have struggled with how to dismount a dead horse. Why? When the program exists in a vision vacuum, the how of doing the program displaces the why in the *heart of the program's leaders.* That is, mastering the how is what makes the volunteer *feel* important. Remember Joel Barker's teaching on paradigms decades ago? A scholar and futurist, he popularized the concept of paradigm shifts and the importance of vision to drive change within an organization. One of his useful nuggets is that when the paradigm shifts, the value of thinking in the old paradigm drops to zero.[1] This is exactly what happens when church people resist change in a program. They simply don't want their *personal value* to drop to zero (who does?). Therefore the program itself nurtures their identity.

A classic example is how people brought up in Sunday school naturally resisted the small-group movement. A Sunday school leader who resists this change is really resisting the loss of validity and credibility received over time as an influencer within the Sunday school way of doing things. The introduction of a new way, such as more discussion, less lecture, and a different atmosphere, threatens the person's importance. It changes the rules of the game after he or she has mastered the old rules.

Today most pastors can identify a program or ministry that needs to be cut, but they are unwilling to have the conversation. Take your pick from A to Z, from Adopt-a-pet outreach to the Zebra-spotting small group. (Give me a break; I wouldn't want to mention a program we would *never* cut, such as Awana, BSF, Beth Moore Bible Study, Adult Handbells, Financial Peace University, Monday Night Visitation, Men's Fraternity, Stephen's Ministry, Griefshare, FAITH, Class 401, MOPS, EE, or Mr. Smith's Sunday school lecture.) It is such a sore spot it's hard to even write about. Pastors look at me with eyes almost begging for a script on how to talk with rogue leaders. The problem is not the volunteer but the vision. We need the vision to raise our sight to see the why behind the program to begin with. Without seeing the more compelling why, we cultivate masters of how. Their hearts find more meaning in working efficiently on yesterday's methods than in working effectively into the future, So, to place and personality we add programs as the third source of a malnourished membership identity.

Apple Pie "People"

Of course the church is about people. So why would I connect people to the poor nourishment of the fast-food American church? Perhaps the greatest substitute for healthy membership identity is the group of people at church—whether ten or a hundred—who "know my name." At the risk of bashing biblical community, please hear me out. I am not slamming community itself. I am identifying "community without a cause" as both unbiblical and a common source of identity for the churchgoer. This reality is easily tested in two scenarios. First, just recommend a change in service times. People protest because you are essentially reshuffling the cards in the relational deck. Second, just ask an Adult Bible Fellowship or a small group to multiply. All hell breaks loose because people don't want you to mess with their relationships. These familiar friends, albeit essential to church life, have become *central* to the person's identity. Now, I admit that I am walking close to thin ice; so you won't hear me saying that relationships are not important. I am simply acknowledging how commonly the "us four and no more" mentality traps the hearts of our people.

Granite Etching vs. Sand Writing

The real nourishment of your people should come from the vision of your Church Unique. Then the enduring purpose of the church reflected locally can replace the substitutes of place, personality, programs, and people. Does that sound too good to be true? It shouldn't.

Jim Collins used a yin-yang symbol in his classic book *Built to Last,* to illustrate an important and related point. He said that enduring organizations have two dominant characteristics that are complementary opposites. The first is a strong conviction about core ideals that never change; these are purpose and values. The second is a clear understanding that everything else *must* change in order to preserve the core. Collins describes this as "a relentless drive to stimulate progress."[2] If you take a hundred-year time frame, for example, organizations would not exist if they did not stimulate progress by changing methods, processes, structures, leadership, and technology. The fascinating observation is that by discerning the core ideology and distinguishing it from what is noncore, a leader can free people to embrace change by connecting their identity to the core ideology. This allows people to feel important despite the fact that the methods or technology or structure may be changing. In other words, if people are nourished by unchanging vision, they are more agreeable when the rules change with tactics. Collins says it takes clarity and discipline to understand which things in the organization belong to which category.

For example, if a watchmaker has a core ideal of "keeping accurate time," he or she hopefully would be on the look out for new ways to keep better time. This occurred when quartz technology replaced the springs and gears of a mechanical timepiece. Decades ago, however, Swiss watchmakers missed the opportunity and lost their dominant position in the global market. How did they miss it? They lost sight of the distinction between unchanging-core (accurate time) and must-change methods (quartz or gears and springs). Refusing to embrace new technology, they behaved as though gears and springs were their core purpose instead of accurate time. Henry Ford said that if he gave people what they asked for, it would have been a faster horse. A century later, we enjoy the core ideal of "faster transportation" at 70 mph because of new inventions that reinforce the enduring value of "faster."

Going back to our Sunday school example, we might identify authentic, growing relationships as a core value and Sunday school (meeting on campus for sixty minutes in a primarily lecture format) as a noncore method. In the 1950s, Sunday school might have been an effective method for living out the value of authentic, growing relationships. But as the fabric of community life changes, Sunday school may no longer protect and preserve this value. If so, then it is time to change the method of preserving the core value. So what happens when a change of method is introduced, such as home-based small groups? It depends. If people are emotionally attached to the method, they will resist change. If they are emotionally connected to the core value, however, they will not only embrace change but might insist on it.

The yin-yang of "never change" and "must change" becomes a helpful framework to evaluate the hearts of our church folk. Before moving on, let's swap metaphors to one that is more Jesus-friendly: granite and sand. Every leader needs to etch some things in granite (never-change core) and write some things in sand (must-change methods). The problem is that when we fail to *clarify* and *nurture* the things written in granite, our people get too attached to the things written in sand. This is how our four P's (place, personality, programs, and people) fit in. These are sand, not granite. As the fluid and flexible stuff of the kingdom they not only *should* change but *must* change. So why is change management so hard in church? Because we don't see the stuff of sand in light of the stuff of granite. In the absence of vision, the stuff of sand becomes the vision. In the absence of granite, sand is all we can grasp.

But what if our people were so captivated by the granite etching that it set us free to play with sand drawings? This is the point I don't want you to miss at the close of Part One. The leader's role is not just to communicate in both granite and sand but to show how the two components work together. The leader should help people embrace change by nurturing an emotional connection to the unchanging core vision. The leader should then preserve and champion the core vision by showing people how to constantly adapt. Isn't this what we are all longing for? Should pastoral transition stop the mission in its tracks? Or should the church look for a new visionary on the basis of the unique movement already under way? Can we change or stop a program like Awana on Wednesday night without leaving two dozen volunteers hopelessly disheartened? Or can we experiment with a new children's ministry idea with excitement and enthusiasm because of a deeper shared vision?

Make no mistake: our change management problems today are vision problems first and people problems second. Many leaders want their people to run a missional marathon but unknowingly feed them junk food, leaving them malnourished and unprepared for the future.

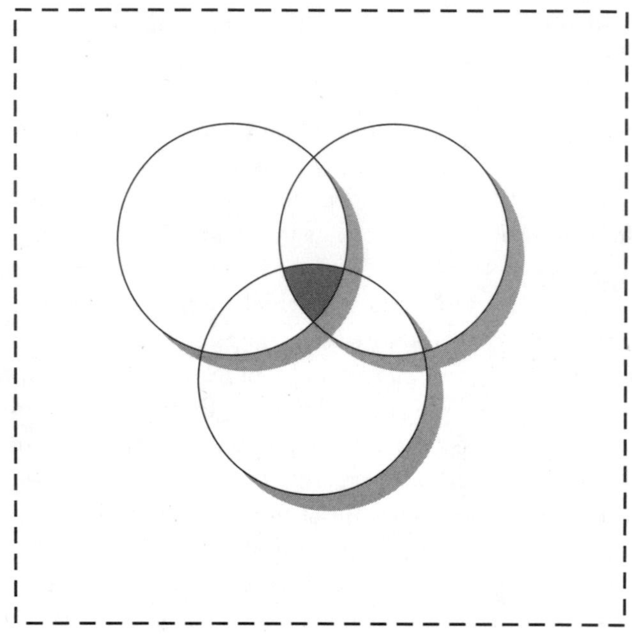

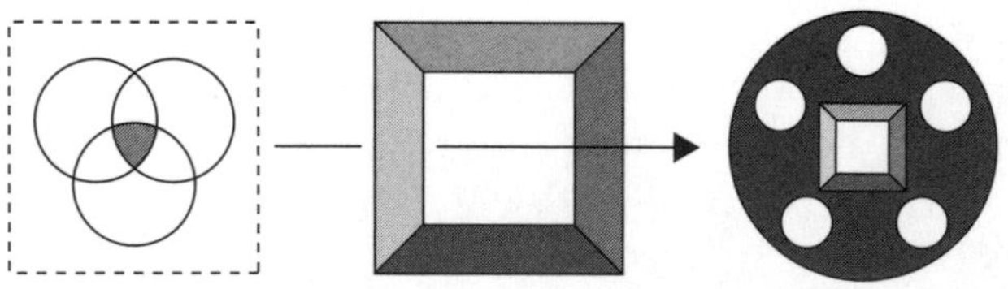

PART TWO

CLARIFYING VISION

A MAN WENT FOR A WALK on a hot summer day and passed by three workers who were making bricks. "What are you doing?" he asked them. The first worker sighed as he looked up, "What does it look like? I'm making bricks!" The second worker turned around and asserted, "We're building a really big wall." The third worker happily exclaimed, "I'm building a cathedral, and it's going to be one of the most beautiful cathedrals of all time!"

Part Two explores why these workers answer this same question differently. Why, under the strenuous conditions of manual labor, does one worker stay emotionally connected to the big picture? Why does the vision live in his heart and mind and not in the others'?

Part One dealt with leadership practices that constrict vision and set the stage for our need to "recast it." If the cathedral in the story of the three workers was a copy from another in the next town, they would be much less inspired to build it (Chapter One). If the three men carried their strategic planning notebooks to work, they would be weighed down with details of "bricks-per-hour" efficiency and mortar viscosity (Chapter Two). Finally, a supervisor driven to build his own ego would certainly have drained any internal motivation from even the third worker (Chapter Three).

Part Two shows a better way. How do you ascertain what God wants you to do and find true clarity? Once you know your unique vision, what's the best way to communicate it?

How do you attune hearts to a common vision and compel people to live extravagantly for Jesus Christ?

I wish you could see the delight on leaders' faces, and hear the ah-ha's as a team crystallizes their Church Unique with stunning clarity. I am not sure there is a more exhilarating moment in leadership.

5

THE GOOD NEWS OF CLARITY

WHY BELIEVE IN VISION TODAY?

Clarity is the preoccupation of the effective leader.
If you do nothing else as a leader, be clear.

— Marcus Buckingham

I WAS CAPTURED BY A MOMENT OF CLARITY thanks to the insistence of a "blue shirt" at Best Buy. As an old gamer, I'm addicted to playing Halo (one of the most played video game of all time) with my three kids, Jacob (CROSS-figh2er), Joel (praying sn1per), and Abby (sonic 4ngel). Years ago, I dropped the extra bucks to upgrade to the Xbox 360, including fifty dollars per wireless controller per kid. A blue shirt asked me what kind of cables I used to connect the game console to my HDTV. Then he began to push the seventy five dollar Monster brand cables. A little skeptical, I decided not to make the purchase. Three months later, with the promise of greater clarity haunting me, I bought the most expensive wires I have ever seen—thick enough to drive a Mac truck over. Thinking I had been duped, I furrowed my brow as I pushed the last gold-plated connector into my television.

What happened next was unbelievable. When the Xbox booted up, it was like experiencing Halo for the very first time! To my amazement, the familiar game play environments of Relic Island and Beaver Creek glowed with new detail, new precision, and a new reality. Seeing something familiar with more clarity is an amazing experience. The same entertainment epiphanies occur hundreds of times each day at stores like Best Buy. Consumers stare in the aisles, awed by the next evolution of high definition.

For me, the upgraded cables unlocked a clearer understanding of what was already there. The video game's designer had already created the detail. I just couldn't see it. The role of today's leaders is to do the same: clarify what is already there and help people perceive what has gone unnoticed.

High-Definition Leadership

Let's take a close look at the concept of clarity before applying it to leadership. Our vernacular applies "clarity" in a jillion ways. We speak of clearing our throat, clearing the football field, and clearing the air. We shop on the clearance rack, hope to be legally clear of charge, receive security clearances, and clear the narrow bridge with our car. We long for clear days, clearer colors on our laptop, and clearer sound with noise-canceling headphones. Teenagers long for clear faces.

What is clarity really about? A synthesis of definitions brings clarity to the concept of clarity: it means being free from anything that obscures, blocks, pollutes, or darkens. Being clear as a leader means being simple, understandable, and exact. The leader helps others see and understand reality better. Leaders constantly bring the most important things to light: current reality and future possibility, what God says about it and what we need to do about it.

Clarity is good news because it untaints misuse of vision. In discussing the church growth movement, I acknowledged that for some the concept of vision has been polluted. I also urged you to keep the problem of growth idolatry and misuse of management practices in the church separate from the purity and necessity of leading with biblical vision. One way to do so is to zero in on the priority of clarity for leaders. Are we clear—simple, understandable, and exact—about the mission of Jesus in the world? It may help some readers to substitute the word *clarity* for *vision*.

Let me reassert that missional leaders cannot let the previous arrogant use of vision hinder the skills development required for clarity. Yes, having vision has been used to bolster egos, justify presumptions, and drive ministry projects in unhealthy ways. But vision that is born from clarity can be an antidote for such arrogance, much as having a clear estimation of self constitutes the foundation for humility. From here on out, when you read "clarify vision," I would like you to keep in mind the implicit ideas that:

- Clarifying vision is about looking to the past as much as the future.
- Clarifying vision requires careful consideration of strengths and limitations.
- Clarifying vision is as much about identity as it is methodology.
- Clarifying vision is always about what God is already doing.

Clear vision is anchored vision. When a missional leader talks about the future, it is based on a clarity that is *past and present* and *Word- and Spirit-dependent.*

Catalyzing Movement with Clarity First

Clarity is good news because it is so catalytic. A chemical catalyst by nature speeds up the reaction between compounds in a way that preserves the natural dynamics of a reaction. In other words, a catalyst never forces something unnaturally. Rather, it frees up organic movement. In this way, clarity becomes critical for shaping culture. It does not force ideas, values, attitudes, and actions onto people but allows them to be naturally captured. It speeds up the process of enculturation. People belong sooner and participate faster. Barriers and "initiation energy" are removed, freeing people to become stakeholders in the cause-based community of Jesus. Let's consider the catalytic dynamics that occur when a leader takes the time to start with clarity first.

Clarity Makes Uniqueness Undeniable

The leader's role requires stewarding what God has uniquely given, and being in tune with what God is uniquely doing. The first step for a leader is to draw attention to this uniqueness, to make it obvious, make it attractive, and show how remarkable it is. Only then can the leader leverage the uniqueness and play to the collective strength of his or her church. There is no appreciation of uniqueness without clarity first.

Clarity Makes Direction Unquestionable

Followers cannot travel an unmarked path. The leader's compass can't be broken; the trumpet blast can't be uncertain. Does your church have many missions, or just one? Does your ministry team exist for a purpose or not? If you can state it, don't just tell me what it is; be so clear about it that the very articulation will generate a gravitational pull. To make the way definable and obvious, you must have clarity first.

Clarity Makes Enthusiasm Transferable

When a leader leads, there is always an exchange of enthusiasm. Many times this comes with clarity—the moment when a follower gets it. The very experience of capturing a clear idea or mission makes people want to share it. But the ease of sharing it is directly proportional to clarity. When passion and a clear idea are wed, the passion can more easily spread. Cascading contagion requires clarity first.

Clarity Makes Work Meaningful

Work can easily become routine—dull, hollow, and void of significance. The role of the leader is to make sure that brick-making churchgoers always see the great cathedral their bricks are ultimately building. Clarity can lift the mind's eye to a greater reality. There can be no cultivation of meaning without clarity first.

Clarity Makes Synergy Possible

Collaboration is lost to sideways energy every day in the local church. Why? The three reasons I see most are mistrust, personal ego, and lack of strategic clarity. I have observed that lack of strategic clarity is the most prevalent of the three. Leaders rarely clarify what working together really looks like. Breaking ministry silos requires clarity first.

Clarity Makes Success Definable

Everyone wants to be a winner. But in too many churches, people don't know how to win. What does scoring a touchdown together look like? Where is a scorecard I can carry that lets me know whether or not I am making a difference? Painting the picture of victory and unleashing people's drive for achievement requires clarity first.

Clarity Makes Focus Sustainable

Henry Ford said that the great weakness of all human beings is trying to do too many things at once. How does a leader or organization learn to say no to the good things that are the enemy to the best? Where will they get the best missional returns, given limited resources? They must have a conviction forged from clarity about what matters most. If the secret to concentration is elimination, you can't do it without clarity first.

Clarity Makes Leadership Credible

The silver bullet syndrome has left many leaders impotent. Firing one disconnected idea after the next, year after year, leaves church members cautious at best and disillusioned at worst. Real visionary leadership is not about just having a bunch of creative ideas; it is about having creativity within a clarity that builds momentum over time. From this clarity the consistency and passion of a leader is more credible because followers are able to internalize what matters most in the church. Leaders earn more confidence with clarity first.

Clarity Makes Uncertainty Approachable

To fear the future is to be human. It can paralyze people and deter them from living with courage and investing into kingdom initiatives. Even though the biblical leader can talk about ultimate certainties, he cannot talk about intermediate certainties. Questions such as "What will happen to my children?" or "How many people will the church plant reach next year?" retain uncertainties. The leader can combat uncertainty with a clarity that inspires hope and expectation. Marcus Buckingham comments, "By far the most effective way to turn fear into confidence is to be clear; to define the future in such vivid terms, through your actions, words, images, pictures, heroes, and scores that we can all see where you, and thus we, are headed."[1] To lead by rallying people around a better future, albeit unknown, requires clarity first.

New Levels Bring New Devils

If clarity is so beneficial, why do we find it in short supply with most leaders? Every leader must contend with clarity gaps and complexity factors. Clarity gaps are the logical areas where obscurity and confusion enter the leader's communication world. Complexity factors literally wage war against the leader's practice of clarity by making it difficult to maintain focus. When it comes to clarity, new levels bring new devils. The higher the leader goes, the harder the leader must work to stay clear.

Clarity Gaps

There are four clarity gaps that can obscure vision and create confusion in the leader:

Clarity gap number one is between a leader's perception and reality. This gap is caused by clouded perception. Simply put, leaders must be savvy to their surroundings, both the environment and the people. Can you accurately describe the cultural nuances of your city or community? How do people who drive by your church perceive it? Do you know the morale of your congregation? Do you know how your leadership team feels today? Bridging gap number one requires relational connectivity and the disciplines of observation and listening.

Clarity gap number two is between what the leader is thinking and what the leader is saying. This gap is caused by ambiguity in the mind. Some leaders are intellectual giants who cannot be articulate. Other leaders captivate an audience without cataloguing their thoughts. Have you distilled and simplified your most important thoughts? Have you reflected deeply about the specific location God has called you to reach? Have you carefully considered the words and metaphors that capture your ideas most vividly? How has Scripture and the direction of the Holy Spirit shaped your thinking year after year? What really is the most important thing you need to say to your people? Is there any static at all between what you are saying and what you are thinking? Bridging gap number two requires a highly cultivated process of thinking and spiritual reflection. Journaling or formal writing often helps the leader process thoughts better.

Clarity gap number three is between the leader's words and how followers receive the leader's words. Like a dropped cell call, this is caused by various sources of disconnection and static between people, even if the leader is communicating clearly. What are your followers thinking about before you speak? What are their deepest concerns, fears, hopes, and aspirations? How will their hearts receive your words and metaphors? How often do you need to be with them? How often do you need to speak to them? How do they feel about you today? How many ways will they need to hear your ideas?

Clarity gap number four is between the followers' understanding and the words they use to communicate their understanding. Keep in mind that this gap is not a function of the leader himself. Unfortunately our followers are not motivated to constantly check the alignment between what they think and how well it is being communicated. Therefore the leader must initiate bridging this gap. What hinders your followers' opportunity to say what they think? Are they always free to share how they feel? Is there adequate trust to communicate with vulnerability? Who can help you interpret what your followers are saying? Which followers are best at articulating what they think and therefore summarizing what others are thinking? Bridging gaps three and four takes phenomenal patience coupled with pursuit of feedback. It requires constant creativity, understanding how various people learn, and knowing when to restate ideas for comprehension and repeat them for memory. It requires humility.

My purpose in reviewing gaps is not to get bogged down in communication theory but to raise the bar on how quickly clarity can evaporate within the leader's constellation of relationships. Like the bars that indicate signal strength on a cell phone, every leader has signal strength levels that distinguish perceiving, thinking, and communicating with others. The effective leader must spend extra time bridging these gaps by practicing clarity.

Complexity Factors

Complexity is simplicity's evil twin. If the gaps we face aren't bad enough, every leader must also wrestle with factors of complexity. There are three big ones every church leader battles.

Table 5.1. Bridging the Clarity Gaps

Clarity Gaps	Bridging Behaviors
The leader's perception vs. reality	Relational connectivity, discipline of observing, discipline to listen
The leader's thinking vs. what the leader is saying	Cultivated process of thinking and spiritual reflection
The leader's words vs. how followers receive the leader's words	Patience with pursuit of feedback, creativity, understanding how people learn, humility
The follower's understanding vs. how followers communicate their understanding	Patience with pursuit of feedback, creativity, understanding how people learn, humility

THE NEBULOUS NATURE OF THINGS SPIRITUAL. Spiritual leaders traffic in an unseen world. The stuff of God is conceptually vast, and the matters of Spirit include fruit you can't pick off a tree. Imagine the difference in explaining the game of checkers and chess. Chess is more complex, and so is church work. After all, the Bible is a complex revelation of redemptive history. Even a small church of ninety people represents an organism with exponentially extensive patterns of communication. In the same way that it takes more words to explain the game of baseball than it does the game of golf, it takes more words to explain the purpose of the church than that of most other businesses. This is why Andy Stanley beats the drum of "clarify the win" when highlighting the importance of clarity at every level—for every ministry and every team in the church.[2]

THE RISING FLOOD OF OVERINFORMATION. Tidal waves of information surge against our brain each day and leave us standing in deeper waters of knowledge, most of which is meaningless trivia. Because the people we are communicating with are also trying to keep their head above water in the information age, we must be aware of how to communicate with a competitive advantage. Who really cares what you have to say? Why would I want to listen to you when I can access almost everything you are going to tell me with a few clicks on Google? A couple of Harvard guys wrote the book *The Attention Economy,* convinced that overinformation is the defining problem today. The thrust of the book is that winners today are those who capture attention first—those who are best at breaking people's perception threshold. It's convincing enough for me to want to back up the familiar sequence of Romans 10: "How can they hear, if we don't first get their attention?" I will suggest practical steps in getting attention in Chapter Fifteen. But for now, know that the landscape is hostile toward maintaining clarity.

THE MULTIPLIED OPPORTUNITY OF SUCCESS. Many churches struggle with clarity because their effectiveness bears more fruit. In other words, with success come more options. Ironically, these new options can dilute the very success that brought them. The key then is to uncover which opportunities are really distractions in disguise so they can be avoided or turned down. The ongoing irony is that more focus brings even more success, making it then again harder to maintain clear focus. Only those who sustain a single-minded resolve can continue to reap the hundredfold fruit. The reality is that *focus expands.* The focus that brought early success is the same focus that will bring you exponential success. Reflect on this short segment by Rob Bell from a 2006 Catalyst podcast (Episode 6) as he answers the question on focus, "How do you say no to great opportunities?"

> I think a pastor has to be protected from the opportunities because they are endless. I don't care how big your church is; you have endless opportunity. If your life and energy are spent living in response to the opportunities that come your way, then someone else has dictated your mission; you are essentially at the whim of whatever invitations comes across your desk next. I first and foremost search deep and spend lots of time asking, "God, what is it you have given us to do this season?" And that drives everything. So we wait for a clear vision to emerge and then go after it and say "no" to everything else. . . . Everything serves the very, very few, simple, intentional, focused things that are the best of the best of the best that God has put on our hearts to do; and we do those well. I say no to 99.9 percent of everything that comes my way. The good is the enemy of the best; no I would actually say the *great* is enemy of the best. Especially to all you listeners out there who have incredible gifts and talents and end up doing five, six, twenty-two, or a thousand and four really good things. Yet there is one or two things that are great that don't get done or get done with half the energy. It's not good; it's not a life.

Leaders must constantly fight the good fight of clarity to overcome complexity. When God blesses the ministry, the discipline to say no determines whether the battle is won or lost. This is true for both the church as a whole and the individual leader.

Howard Hendricks illustrated this less-is-more dynamic with a simple funnel diagram (see Figure 5.1). Over time you accumulate more education, more experiences, more relationships, and more resources, all of which multiply your opportunities. The increasing number of possibilities line the top of your life's funnel as the myriad things you *can do*. The key, however, is to move down the funnel to the bottom "x"—the thing that

Figure 5.1. The Clarity Funnel

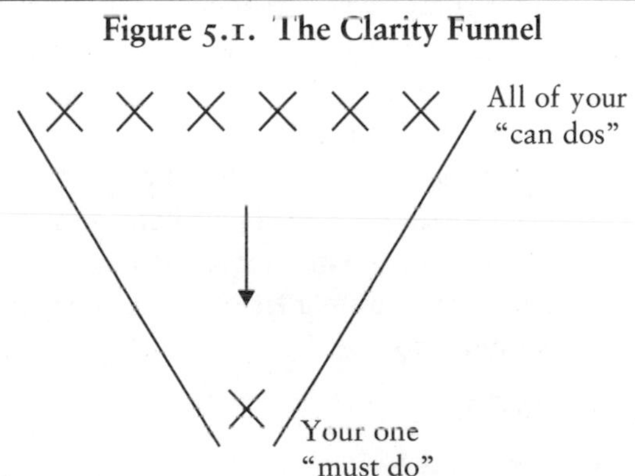

you *must do* for God. Of course, the difficulty is saying no to opportunities in order to move down the funnel. Hendricks would end his teaching moment with the words, "The secret to concentration is elimination." Your church has a funnel too, and the same principle applies. An example illustrates this point.

Two churches were started in the same growing suburb of Houston in the early 1990s. A large lake divides the area the churches serve, so they are in two different communities, yet only four miles apart. The church on the north side reached a plateau of twelve hundred in attendance years ago, while the other on the south side continued to grow and is currently over thirty-six hundred in attendance. Why has one church reached three times as many people given so many similarities in their history and local culture? Focus. The south-side church has fought the complexity of success by offering two primary venues: a service on Sunday and spiritual formation groups. They have chosen over time to either *not start* or *do away with* dozens of programmatic types of ministry. The church on the north side has more program offerings such as women's ministries and singles ministries that reflect the complexity of meeting too many needs in the absence of a clear, focused vision. The irony is that with fewer resources and less staff than the south side church, they try to serve one-third of the people with three times as many programs. This church is stuck doing all of the things it can do for God rather than the one thing it must do.

My life testifies to what I call "working the funnel." Many people ask how I came to be a consultant. The most difficult part was leaving really good opportunities all along the way. With each step, it felt like a huge risk. For me, these included leaving a budding career as a chemical engineer, then exiting my executive experience in a marketing and advertising firm, and ultimately stepping out of an incredible opportunity I had as a pastor. My clarity funnel journey led me to realize that what I wanted to do most—expository preaching—was not my gift. A mentor finally told me I was a better leader than I was a teacher, and the trajectory of my calling began to turn. It took me at least three years to grapple with the death of my vision to grab hold of God's. Today I see my must do for God as bringing clarity to the leaders I serve.

Having discussed the benefits and barriers of clarity, I now turn attention to how clarity is achieved. For the high-definition leader, the process is more difficult than buying Monster cables at Best Buy. The first step toward finding clarity is the subject of our next chapter. It's time to discover your church's must do.

6

CLARITY PRE-EVANGELISM

SOFTENING YOUR HEART FOR CLARITY

We were meant to live for so much more . . . maybe we've been living with our eyes half open.

—Switchfoot, *Meant to Live*

I CUT MY TEETH ON EVANGELISM through the ministry of Campus Crusade for Christ while at Penn State. The ministry trained me well, and over the course of three years I articulated my faith weekly with both warm and cold contacts. In my zeal to win people for Christ, I carefully honed my skills by anticipating every possible response and pushback to the gospel. Armed with orange booklets and memory verse ammunition, I walked the dorm halls like a Roman soldier ready to rescue my fellow students from the kingdom of darkness.

It didn't take long to learn that people can't be argued into the Kingdom of Light. Befuddled at first, I didn't understand why such sound logic and careful reasoning did not pull more people across the line of faith. At some point, I was introduced to the concept of pre-evangelism and lifestyle approaches of sharing my faith. It was refreshing to embrace what now seems so obvious. In the battle for souls, the intellect will go only so far; the heart must be captivated by a love beyond reason.

Likewise, it is easy for leaders to acknowledge the benefits of clarity in the mind, but not in the heart. Many want clarity, but few find it. Listen again to two quotes from the last chapter. Marcus Buckingham called clarity the "preoccupation" of effective leaders. Rob Bell said, "I first and foremost search deep and spend lots of time asking" and waiting. Where does this resolve come from? I believe it comes from a conversion-like experience in the life of the leader to embrace the clarity-first principle. Most leaders spend their lives driving decisions, directing resources, and deploying people without the vantage point of substantial clarity.

Repent, for Clarity Is at Hand

So what inhibits the conversion to embrace clarity first? The process of finding clarity challenges the leader's heart. Specifically, there are four imperatives that speak to the need for "leadership repentance." As we have fun with this redemptive metaphor, don't miss the fact that I am speaking to real emotional blocks that most of us have. Before we jump into these imperatives, I want to explain why it is important for your heart to change.

Navigating the Tunnel of Chaos

Finding clarity requires navigating a tunnel of chaos. This is the point where deeper confusion is experienced first, before clarity can emerge. The tunnel may take hours, days, or months and it may involve much time in prayer, conversation, questioning, reflection, confession, and challenge, all with a spirit of relentless transparency. My father, who flew supersonic jets, once shared that in order to gain altitude you sometimes must first descend. Likewise, to achieve heights of clarity first requires descent into greater cloudiness. The heart must be prepared for this journey, because it will bring blood, sweat, and tears for those who embark on it. The way requires listening when one would rather talk. It involves recalibrating perceptions that we presume are correct. It may require dying to the fact that we do not possess a giftedness we try to project.

Simplicity on the Other Side: Four Imperatives

The resolve required to navigate the tunnel cannot be overestimated. A helpful insight is brought by the mind of Oliver Wendell Holmes. Consider carefully his words: "I would not give a fig for simplicity on this side of complexity, but I would give my life for simplicity on the other side of complexity." He asserts that there are two kinds of simplicity, or clarity. The first is meaningless simplicity. Without facing the factors of complexity and walking through the tunnel of chaos, the leader marches in place to a simplicity that is, well, simplistic. It is trite and valueless. That's why so many leaders give in to photocopied vision—it's so easy! Like a worthless fig, it just sits there, pretty words on paper never birthed from passion, therefore never giving birth.

The second kind of simplicity is worth giving your life for. There is magic in getting to the other side of complexity. Only there is life redefined and re-released. The other side is a utopia that leaders rarely find. Leonardo da Vinci said, "Simplicity is the ultimate sophistication." James Michener hints of the beautiful place where the pursuit of excellence and clarity in life is so focused that it leaves others wondering if we are at work or at play.

But many leaders get stuck in between. Somewhere between simplistic answers and ultimate freedom, they bog down in complexity. There are two reasons. The first is that they don't know anything better. These leaders don't feel stuck, because they are living with a lot of *good* ministry—good ministry that is the enemy to the *best* that the church ultimately can become. Clinging to what is good, they cannot reach for great because they can't see it. The second reason is that the tunnel of chaos is too unbearable. To borrow a phrase from St. John of the Cross, leaders must experience a "cloud of unknowing" that brings feelings of incompetence. If any process causes us to second-guess how we operate, it's emotionally challenging, and most leaders prefer not to go there.

That is the purpose of this chapter on clarity pre-evangelism: to push you to go there and enter the tunnel. It is designed to challenge your heart and prepare you for clarity. What is required for a breakthrough to discover a Church Unique? The four imperatives that follow point the way. Each shows how the leader should "repent" in order to successfully walk through complexity and find clarity.

IMPERATIVE ONE: FRAME IT FIRST. *State your vision framework before you frame your vision statement.*

Leaders first need to *repent from "stabbing at the future."* Every leader I know has some vocabulary for describing what he or she is trying to do. Most of the time, however, it is not a complete framework for how to think. In other words, the vision language does not answer the irreducible minimum questions of leadership. For example, you need more than a mission statement and more than a values statement (and more than both). The five-part framework I introduce later, the Vision Frame, gives you an understanding of the necessary components.

There are two reasons this is difficult at the heart level. The first is that the leader may see himself as the expert and may not see the need for building a real framework. The problem is that there have been enough books on vision to make a pastor feel like an expert. Unfortunately, most have received an inoculation that prevents them from catching the real thing, the virus of a personally realized vision.

The second reason is that the leader does not have the patience to allow *the team* to understand the framework before he or she actually articulates the vision. Think of it as the scaffolding that is put up before a building is constructed. Even though it is temporary, the scaffolding is essential to construction if you plan on rising more than one story. I usually visit a church staff between six and nine times in a given year. Each time, I make the people run the drills of practicing the framework so the team develops and deepens its understanding of the Vision Pathway.

IMPERATIVE TWO: LISTEN TILL YOU GLISTEN. *Discern the future by seeing more clearly what you already have.*

Leaders must *repent from neglecting the obvious.* Then they must turn their attention to exercising the definition of genius as the ability to *scrutinize the obvious.*[1] I worked with a young pastor who took the helm of a grand, historic church. In the visioning process, I took pictures of a few the historic plaques on the grounds. When I displayed them to the team, he leaned over and whispered in my ear, "Wow, I have never even read them!" He had been the pastor for three years.

Listening is nonnegotiable on multiple levels: from listening to people both inside and outside of the church to discerning the call of the Spirit. When it comes to a visionary's walk with God, listening must become lifestyle.

IMPERATIVE THREE: TEAM THE HORSES. *Go farther by pulling together.*

Leaders must also *repent from doing it themselves.* The church has suffered too long from the benevolent dictators who issue vision from on high. It is noteworthy that in the Apostle Paul's writing no less than thirteen times people are called "fellow worker" (the Greek is *synergos*).[2] Jesus' legacy is reflected in his life investment in the Twelve.

The beauty of clarity is how it is discovered together. The crucible of community isn't easy, but with collaboration the yield of fruit is ten times greater and ten times sweeter. Those who are gifted in creativity and visioning are also good at joining complementary perspectives. One such group is a team of creative communicators in South Carolina called

Wayfarer. The engine behind their productivity is their core value of "We before me." There has never been a time when twelve to fifteen people in the visioning process did not produce something far better than any one person could. When it comes to clarity, Ken Blanchard stated it perfectly in this short phrase: "None of us is as smart as all of us."[3]

Collaboration 101: in working with teams, we do three things to enhance collaboration. The first is to free participants to wear different hats in transparent dialogue. The four hats or roles that must be engaged by team members are the initiator, the challenger (classically called the devil's advocate), the processor, and the supporter. Though everyone tends toward a groove or default mode of operating, we encourage each person to experiment and feel free with all of the roles. One tool to help in keeping this dynamic in front of your team is the collaboration cube (www.collaborationcube.com).

The second aspect of collaboration is to develop a healthy respect for personality and temperaments different from our own. Many in ministry have been exposed to fun, short personality assessments (examples: the DiSC Profile, a popular personality assessment tool; or the four animals, lion, beaver, otter, and golden retriever). Generally a deep appreciation of these differences has not been developed in most groups. We recommend selecting a respected personality and temperament assessment tool, and we encourage teams to revisit the results monthly or quarterly.* For real team building and personal growth to occur, group members must be able to reference the learning in daily, informal interactions.

Finally, we define success at the outset in terms of a collaborative result; we call it the 100–80 rule. The standard for commitment to a decision is *not* that 80 percent of the team feels 100 percent good about the proposed idea. This often leaves some of the group feeling disenfranchised. Rather, we define success in reaching an agreed on decision as 100 percent of the group feeling 80 percent good. This means that each individual may experience a 20 percent loss from his or her own decision if left to it. The key is for the team to agree from the start that once everyone feels 80 percent good, the result is unmistakably better. One note of clarification: these ground rules for collaboration work best with smaller teams, ideally no larger than twelve, or fifteen at most.

---

*We use the Insights Discovery Profile, with results that our clients find extremely valuable. For more information, email: insights@visiontogrow.com.

IMPERATIVE FOUR: WORK OUTSIDE IN. *Discover an angel by inviting a stranger.*

W. Edwards Deming is considered one of the fathers of modern management. He taught that "profound knowledge comes from the outside."[4] Most of our lives are spent with a relatively small group of people—family, friends, and colleagues—that make up our primary networks. After a while, these close networks no longer bring profoundly new information or perspective into our lives. But an outsider can. A quantum leap can come from uncommon sources.

Here the leaders must *repent the myth of objectivity.* This is the belief that the leader can look at a situation or organization with little bias and no predetermined filter. It just can't happen. Once the leader has been around for thirty days, he can no longer claim neutrality. He is stuck in the trees no matter how badly he wants to see the forest. To distill the big picture with crystal clarity, the "strategic outsider" is a critical element.

In Exodus 18, we see this dynamic at work. Jethro, Moses' father-in-law, watches him during a typical day at work. He notices some serious problems that Moses can't see. As a result, he recommends a radical restructuring of Israel's organization, a change that will bring more *shalom*—peace and wholeness for God's people. Moses wisely listens and implements his advice.

The greatest performers in any arena are so because they demand coaching. Is Tiger Woods the best in his game because he doesn't need coaching, or because he has more coaches? His parents persuaded a local golf pro to start coaching him at age four. Years later, what do you think he was doing the night before he won his first Masters Tournament in 1997? You guessed it: talking to his coach. Which car needs more tinkering under the hood: the everyday Chevy or a high-performance NASCAR vehicle?

I am constantly amazed at how helpful the strategic outsider can be to the local church. I leave you two quotes from pastors who have used a vision navigator. While talking to a group of pastors, Chuck Swindoll described our process by saying, "They helped us see who we really were, not who we thought we were, because they brought a perspective from the outside." Willy Rice, who pastors Calvary Baptist Church in Clearwater, Florida, writes that their navigator was "God's instrument to sharpen our vision, shape our strategy, and bring clarity to the mission that God had already given us." I urge you to seek this objective, outside perspective whether you use a trusted friend (outside the scope of your daily activity) or a trained consultant.

Clarity Requires Humility

I would like to pause and ask you to reflect on your heart. There is one common thread that weaves the four imperatives: humility. Scan each again in Table 6.1.

"Frame it first" requires humility because it drives the leader to learn more about what a good visioning process looks like rather than assuming he or she already knows. "Listen till you glisten" requires humility because it forces leaders to take in with a patience that suspends the bias for action, for moving out. "Team the horses" requires humility because when working with others the process is invariably slower and messy; this can tempt the leader to take the reins too early. "Work outside in" requires humility because leaders are threatened with the notion that outside help is a sign of weakness. They think to themselves, "This is what I get paid for." Their own competence blocks the pipeline of objectivity and fresh perspectives that can often bring an epiphany of clarity.

Jesus embedded the core virtue of humility into the life of his disciples in numerous pages of Scripture. He leaves us with a picture that egotism and arrogance are blemishes on the face of a kingdom leader. The words of an ancient Chinese philosopher are apt in capturing this humility:

> A leader is best when people are hardly aware of his existence, not so good when people praise his government, less good when people stand in fear, worst when people are contemptuous. Fail to honor people,

Table 6.1. Four Imperatives to Prepare for Clarity

Imperative	Principle	Repent from . . .
Frame it first	State your framework before framing your statement	Stabbing at the future
Listen till you glisten	Discern the future by seeing what you already have	Neglecting the obvious
Team the horses	Go further with collaboration	Doing it yourself
Work outside in	Discover an angel by inviting a stranger	Thinking you are objective

> and they will fail to honor you. But of a good leader, who speaks little, when his task is accomplished, his work done, the people say, "We did it ourselves!"

In scanning the four imperatives, which have you tended to overlook? Take the list to your team and discuss them together. Which one is it most important to apply in the next three months?

7

THE ALPHA AND OMEGA OF CLARITY

THE ULTIMATE SOURCE OF VISION

I'm A to Z, the First and the Final,
Beginning and Conclusion.

—Jesus Christ at the end of time, *The Message*, Rev. 22:13

IN 1993, THE TECHNOLOGY WE KNOW as GPS (global positioning system) become operational. It took the government $12 billion and several decades to design and launch the network of twenty-four satellites operated by the U.S. Air Force from five ground stations across the world. Today GPS touches everyday life with built-in navigation in our cars and boats. Whether you're finding a restaurant on family vacation, hunting in the middle of nowhere, or just fascinated to plot your location while flying Continental, a hand-sized GPS can specify your longitude and latitude anywhere in the world within several feet. With every square yard of the earth's surface mapped, the GPS is the ultimate clarity tool for navigation.

The clarity that comes from this little handheld device does not find its source from within. The receiver is dependent on a large, sophisticated network of satellites orbiting the globe. In fact, the GPS must receive at least four signals from four satellites to fix a "transcendent" point of reference.

Like the GPS system, the leader's role in providing navigation must rely on a source that transcends his or her point of view. For the kingdom leader, the ultimate source of clarity is God's perspective as revealed in Scripture. Only from God's Word can we accurately understand our origin, mission, and destiny. We are not seeking a perspective at three thousand feet or thirty thousand, but an infinite vantage point from outside time and space—God's positioning system. To put our immediate pursuit of vision into perspective, it is imperative that we hit the pause button to take a fresh look at the panoramic view of redemptive history.

Between the Bookends of Utopia

The ultimate context of the sixty-six books of Scripture is four little chapters. The first two books in Genesis (Gen. 1–2) and the last two books in Revelation (Rev. 21–22) give meaning to everything in between. We see something unique in these chapters as they afford a peek into utopia. Only here do we see the world as God intended, in pristine condition, untainted by sin. The snapshot of life in these chapters depicts the perfect origin and the perfect destination in redemptive history. It begins in the Garden of Eden and ends in the city of New Jerusalem (Figure 7.1)—locations that are the utopian bookends of existence. It's no wonder that utopia is the most written-about subject in human existence. The Creator's original vision has locked it within our souls.

What is significant in these places of faultless beauty? Two features that stand out are humankind's *relational* capacity and *ruling* capacity as aspects of *imago Dei*—creation of man in God's image. From the Pentateuch to the Apocalypse, we see God's desire for relationship expressed by having "people for his own possession."* Through creation, He forms a perfect place where man is able to relate and rule with Him in perfect harmony. Living in perfect union with God, man is charged "to subdue and have dominion" over the creation. With this, Adam exercises a God-given authority to responsibly manage the world that has been placed under his care—a theme that also weaves its way from the perfect garden to eternity in heaven.

---

*This terminology is a wonderful concept and word study. Bookends to consider are Deuteronomy 7:6, "For you are a people holy to the Lord your God. The Lord your God has chosen you out of all the peoples on the face of the earth to be his people, his treasured possession"; and Revelation 21:3, "And I heard a loud voice from the throne saying, 'Now the dwelling of God is with men, and he will live with them. They will be his people, and God himself will be with them and be their God.'"

Figure 7.1. From the Garden of Eden to New Jerusalem

Eden: Garden Utopia mankind relates and rules	"Thy Kingdom come" God shows leaders better intermediate futures → mankind *rescues* with God while relating and ruling	New Jerusalem: City Utopia mankind relates and rules

The Rescuers

After the Fall, mankind is entrusted with a new responsibility reflecting his God-like capacity. In addition to relating and ruling, mankind is invited to join God's work in *rescuing*. The here and now is a place of brokenness between the bookends of utopia. So God intervenes *through people* to bring real restoring activity that hints at the grand finale to come. Why does God leave us, His people, though destined for glory, in this very unglorious world? The answer is that He wants us to experience this redemptive mission. He offers the opportunity to get dirt under our fingernails in the mind-blowing project of a universal makeover. Mission becomes the link—the invitation—between perfect origin and perfect destination. So all around our terribly imperfect planet we see this mission breaking forth as kingdom—God's rule on earth in and through His followers. Only God redeems, but mankind is His means. Or as Robert Coleman said it, "Men are His method."[1]

The first place we witness this dynamic is subtle, in the Hebrew narrative of Genesis chapter 3. Although Adam and Eve rebel, God makes a promise that an offspring of Eve will someday "bruise the head of the serpent," the first reference to Christ's work on the cross. Adam then responds to this promise in a faithful and heroic act. The first act of faith is the induction of mankind into the role of rescuer. Adam names his female companion for the first time as *Eve*. "Eve" in the Hebrew sounds like the word for "life-giver." By calling Eve "the mother of the living," Adam expresses faith in God's promise that they will be the trunk of a successful family tree. Most important, it acknowledges that the certain curse of death, though real, does not define his ultimate reality through nonexistence or a hopeless eternity. Rather it signals a new mission in the midst of death—becoming a redemptive agent in the death-reversing work of God to restore His kingdom.

Ever since Eden, God's remnant rescuers have been at work. This remnant has been as miniscule as Noah and as fragile as Abraham leaving for land unknown. The remnant has maintained national identity through Israel, whose rescuing banner was "blessed to be a blessing." It then escalated under God's sovereign design to become the church, transcending ethnic and geographic boundaries like never before. In the church age, Paul pronounces this rescuing role most explicitly when he writes, "Therefore, if anyone is in Christ, he is a new creation; the old has gone, the new has come! All this is from God, who reconciled us to himself through Christ and gave us the ministry of reconciliation" (2 Cor. 5:17–18). So with the resurrected Christ empowering his body—the church today—Jesus plays point position in the kingdom, a holy juggernaut forging toward the perfect ending with the rally cry to make disciples and seek and save the lost.

Better Intermediate Futures

Here we are—you and I living between utopias. For some of us (generally referred to as leaders), there is a clear realization that things are not as they should be. Marked by a holy discontent, leaders rise to take action. Moved to make a difference, leaders see a better possibility, a vision of a preferred future. As each leader relates, rules, and rescues with God in this messy world, God reveals to him or her a *better intermediate future* to pursue. That is, God sparks in their hearts new ideas, new aspirations, and new mental pictures of what could be. It may be the vision to start a battered wives shelter, plant a church in downtown San Francisco, reach kids with the gospel using basketball, adopt an unreached people group, or start an orphanage in Kenya. Whatever it may be, this vision of a better future is really an *intermediate* future, because it is one vision expression among many throughout history—as a domino in the middle of the procession, tilting toward the next one in line. It plays a minor yet important part in moving toward God's future utopia. So in light of God's grand vision already recorded in Scripture, any smaller vision of a better intermediate future is not new at all. It is, in a sense, already His. Therefore, our visions of a better future come from Him as orchestrated steppingstones to get us to His ultimate one.

The book of Nehemiah gives a powerful example of this dynamic. The book begins with a dramatic scene: Nehemiah hears the report of Jerusalem's devastation—the walls of the city have been razed (1:1–3). The need is clear, and the news of a devastated city shatters Nehemiah's heart. He begs the God of heaven for mercy, and he asks for personal success—the first explicit indicator of his calling to meet this urgent need in Jerusalem (1:5–12). God answers his prayer by granting good favor with King Artaxerxes. The king offers gracious assistance to which Nehemiah responds immediately. His quick reply demonstrates his vision. Nehemiah has carefully considered the rebuilding project, including time requirements, political ramifications, and resource strategies (2:5–8). As the drama unfolds amid strong opposition, we see the glimpses of Nehemiah's conviction (2:9–10), personal action (2:12–16), and effective mobilization (2:17–18). His leadership demonstrates dazzling success by rebuilding the city in fifty-two days.

In less than two months, we see Nehemiah's vision realized. Yet in the overall record of redemptive history it is just one step toward a better *intermediate* future. Immediately following Nehemiah's work, other leaders emerge, among them law enforcement (gatekeepers), worship leaders, religious leaders (Levites), and city officials. The fifty-two day mobilization phase set a context for leaders to emerge and with their own vision; they then created subsequent better *intermediate* futures. For example, the leadership of Ezra surfaces in chapter 8. Ezra was already a scribe, but there is no doubt that Nehemiah's leadership was a springboard to Ezra's effectiveness in leading the people to revival through focused teaching on the Law. As stated earlier, Nehemiah's vision is a lone domino in a much bigger sequence of visionary rescuers. When Nehemiah's domino fell, it influenced many others, including Ezra's.

Put in the ultimate perspective, Nehemiah's building project is a faint echo of a glorious New Jerusalem to come. Nehemiah's Jerusalem was built from the ground up and made of stone. The New Jerusalem will descend from heaven and radiate like "a most rare jewel, like a jasper, clear as crystal" (Rev. 21:11). In the final analysis, Nehemiah's vision is one derived from the Eternal Visioneer.

God's Vision, or Ours? *Both*

What's special about God's vision is how it becomes ours and lives as ours. We can never forget God as the source of vision; but we also cannot strip it of personal, visceral, and concrete reality in the leader's life. We live in real places that intricately nuance the story of restoration—the good and the bad, for the infinitely beautiful is mirrored by distortions infinitely horrific. We live in it. Unique expressions of sin, pain, and brokenness ripple through our specific stories and locales. At some point, a defining moment occurs; a particular call from God collides with a concrete need in our little corner of the world. The result is an atomic energy release, filling the leader's heart with compassion and the leader's conscious with conviction. A new vision is forged. Frederick Buechner described it as the place "where your deep gladness and the world's deep hunger meet." In this intersection, the vision is both God's and ours, for the work of the Spirit moves us so completely that the distinction of ownership blurs in our intimacy with Jesus. Emotionally, our vision can and should feel like the biggest thing in the world; but from an eternal perspective, it is pretty small. Yet it glimmers with significance because it helps form the mosaic of redemptive history. It is a critically important link in a long chain of legacies stretching to God's happily ever after.

In placing our pursuit of vision in the context of Scripture, a singular application emerges. As you work to discover your Church Unique and articulate a missional vision, the pursuit of God must come first. Jesus, the Alpha and Omega, is the source of ultimate clarity. Consider how Dwight Smith describes people with vision: "There is an itch about something that must be done that animates their lives. They cannot let it go! It is important to emphasize that such a vision does not come from trying to have one. In all of these people, it simply comes! God has so demonstrated Himself that they are filled with a picture of something that must be done."[2] In a similar fashion, Oswald Chambers describes vision as the "the big compelling of God." The emphasis in these statements is a vital, active relationship with God and a mind saturated with his Word. We must be living in tune with Him to discover what He wants us to do. The purpose of this book is not to instruct you in the spiritual disciplines related to this kind of relationship,* but to emphasize that the necessity of pursuing the God who makes us visionaries cannot be overstated.

*Two books in this Leadership Network Jossey-Bass series that are excellent treatments of this personal side to leadership development are *Practicing Greatness,* by Reggie McNeal; and *Off-Road Disciplines,* by Earl G. Creps.

8

HEAR THE CLOUD OF WITNESSES

LEARNING FROM VISION LEGACIES

I'd like you to step forward over here. Peruse some of the faces from the past. You've walked past them many times, but I don't think you've really looked at them. They're not that different from you, are they? Same haircuts. Full of hormones, just like you. Invincible, just like you feel. The world is their oyster. They believe they're destined for great things, just like many of you, their eyes are full of hope, just like you. Did they wait until it was too late to make from their lives even one iota of what they were capable? Because, you see gentlemen, these boys are now fertilizing daffodils. But if you listen real close, you can hear them whisper their legacy to you. Go on, lean in. Listen, you hear it?—Carpe—hear it?—Carpe, carpe diem, seize the day boys, make your lives extraordinary.

—John Keating, lead character in the film *Dead Poet's Society*

WHILE WRITING ON RETREAT IN SANTA FE, I received a call from one of the few people I allow to interrupt my solitude. My children affectionately call their mom's mother "Mama Lava." When Mama Lava called me, she was ecstatic. A long-time genealogy buff, she is brilliant at peppering any conversation with tidbits of family history. Always ready to make the next family tree breakthrough, this time the discovery was big. At the four hundredth anniversary of the settlement at Jamestown, a friend of hers sent a deposit of new historical data. On reviewing it, she found the name

"Firth"—my middle name and my mother's maiden name. I could feel her heart beat fast through the cell phone signal as she reported that this original Firth was a true gentleman in the first American settlement and part owner with those who funded the voyage itself.

The older I get, the more I appreciate the discipline and enthusiasm that Mama Lava has in "roots discovery." By connecting dots with the past, we bring new meaning to the present and walk into the future with a stronger sense of identity.

Missional leaders have something to learn from Mama Lava, for visionary leadership is the art of protecting the past as we champion the future. Bold aspirations must be rooted in the values and visions that have come before. Your vision at its best is always both a derivation and a dependent domino. In the last chapter, we discussed vision as derivation, with its source in the infinite imagination of God as proto-visionary and prime mover. In this chapter, we expand on the concept that vision is a dependent domino because your vision doesn't birth without someone else's vision knocking yours over. For you to be alive and in touch with God's work in the world, you were necessarily touched by the vision of others who came before. Subsequently, as your vision advances it hopefully touches many others—and new dominos fall.

This chapter is about listening more carefully to the ones who have gone before us. What can we learn about their vision? How does their vision intersect with what God is calling *us* to do? At first blush, this may seem to contradict the daring and forward-facing resolve of the visionary leader. I assure you it does not. As we assess the vision that has gone before, we pull back the slingshot for our own. Many emerging leaders have practiced this in worship settings with the recovery of an "ancient-future" experience. But this has been largely relegated to the practice of worship and is still blooming in the art of leadership.

"Tapping" Visionaries Before Us and Around Us

The review of redemptive history in the previous chapter nurtures appreciation for the visions of others who have gone before and those who have touched our lives. To paraphrase the author of Hebrews chapter 12, this involves tuning into "the cloud of witness" that surrounds us as if we were distance runners in an Olympic stadium. Here we are exhorted to run the race with endurance, focus, and freedom. With gold medalists of faith watching on, the presence of our predecessors can stir deep resolve and bring fresh inspiration. If we listen closely, we can hear them whispering to us. But what are they saying, and how can they help us?

Whispering Legacies

Predecessors, mentors, peers, and co-laborers across the globe work in response to the same revealed Scripture to usher in a better intermediate future on their own street corner. This reality begs the question: "How does past and present vision connect with what God is calling us to do?" Three dynamics are worth highlighting as whispering legacies that simultaneously motivate us, anchor us, and sharpen us. Here are a few tidbits from my own journey.

A WHISPERING LEGACY WILL MOTIVATE US. I discovered the joy of reading biographies years ago. I can still remember one of my first: Hudson Taylor. Living on the college campus at Penn State, I can remember feeling moved in my core as I entered his journey as a pioneer missionary to China. Somehow, I became bolder and more thoughtful as Taylor's approach (unconventional during his lifetime) modeled an incarnational heartbeat that adapted to the Chinese culture.

In those same years, I remember walking to the dining hall with Ric, an upper classman and my spiritual mentor. After blowing some steam after a lousy day on campus, I finally asked, "How was your day?" What Ric said caught me off guard. He responded nonchalantly, "You know, I am just trying to figure out how I can change the world today from our little corner at Penn State." After receiving this mild rebuke, my worldview expanded that day—and I have never completely recovered from it. Whether past or present, visionary leaders around us can generate amazing motivation that we must tap into.

A WHISPERING LEGACY WILL HUMBLE US. Not only does seeing our role in the bigger picture invigorate us, it anchors us. It is from this vantage point that we dream boldly yet not take ourselves too seriously. For many leaders, there is a fine line between courage and arrogance.

From here on, I want to urge you to hammer out the unique vision that God has given your church. This act is inherently daring, and you must not shrink back. I see young leaders pull back all of the time in false humility. For many, the broken models of leadership and demonstrations of egotism send their proverbial pendulum swinging in a nonaggressive direction. Their apostolic heartbeat is repressed.

So how do you nurture holy risk taking, without risking overconfidence? By entering into—I mean really digesting—the vision of others. Humility grows because as we see God working through other visionaries, it reminds us very simply of God's central role and our instrumental role.

It sounds the bell that if we don't want to participate in God's rescuing activity He will find others who will.

The Nehemiah experience retold earlier has been a bedrock vision for me in this way. God has impressed on my life a calling to help the broader church that could easily go to my head. But when I see a leader such as Nehemiah helping God's people twenty-five hundred years ago in a significant, catalytic way, I see my part as being a single water molecule in the waterfall of redemptive history. He was faithful in stewarding his gifts for a season. I must be faithful in stewarding my gifts during my short time at bat. Nehemiah helps me dream big without puffing up.

A WHISPERING LEGACY WILL SHARPEN US. This process of being sharpened is crucially important in uncovering our unique vision. Like an artist searching for just the right color on his palette, a leader can better understand the nuances of his vision by looking at the "palette of visions" around him.

One way I relate to this is to recall the experiences I had in preaching class at seminary. I had three classes over the course of two years, during which I struggled to find my own personality in the preaching event. I listened to tapes of Hadden Robinson, the classic expositor, and Rick Warren, the topical life-coach, and marveled at the contrast. I paid careful attention to my professors, admiring Reg Grant for his ability to weave a dominant metaphor through an entire message and Ramesh Richard for his unforced creativity with alliteration and poetry. Like an emerging chef looking to create my own recipe, I tasted and ruminated on every dish in site. About three years later, I began to feel comfortable with my signature dish—my own voice.

The same is true with understanding God's vision for your church. Although vision doesn't come directly through observing the vision of others, the process of discernment is significantly enhanced when we do. As a vision coach myself, I search high and low for opportunities to sharpen my own vision. Last summer, I took a week to read as much Lyle Schaller in one sitting as I could. I flew to a place of solitude, carrying a suitcase with more than twenty of his books, a sampling from each decade of the last five in which he has written. I didn't want to just acquire knowledge; I wanted to get to know a man who has walked before me with a similar calling and vision. I wanted to see how his perspectives, convictions, and understanding emerged over decades as a church consultant.

Recently, I hopped on a plane to enjoy a two-hour lunch with Howard Hendricks, another living legacy from whose fountain I continually drink. I said thank you to "Prof" by listing the five most important things I learned from him, and he graciously responded to follow-up question

I presented for each. Athough his vision for Christian education impressed thousands of students from a distance, I appreciate the imprint that Prof made on me up close. Both Schaller and Hendricks sharpen my vision in profound ways, because of the vision they embody.

Leading with a Vision Detector

When I was kid, my folks bought a house on property close to the battle line at the historic Brandywine Battlefield, in Southeastern Pennsylvania. I can remember strange people scouring our backyard acreage with elaborate metal detectors, hunting for muskets, coins, and other Revolutionary War paraphernalia.

In like fashion, leaders should walk around with vision detectors. That is, leaders should look for the artifacts of vision every day within their specific ministry contexts. The purpose of this chapter is to raise the importance of this practice: ongoing discovery of uncovering and appreciating the visionary contributions of past and present. As we do, we prepare for our own unique vision to take shape. In some cases, your unique vision is tied intricately to the history of your church. In other cases, the vision is a blank slate, fresh tracks where no one has previously traveled. In both scenarios, you will want to be constantly on the look out for vision artifacts. Here are just a few of the ones I constantly look for when I work with leaders in churches across the country.

ARTIFACT NUMBER ONE: UNCOVER THE CREATION STORY. All vision has a creation story—the events and the passion that birth the idea of a better future. All visionaries can identify some point of origin. If you are looking for this, you will be amazed at how much meaning you can squeeze out of it. The problem is that most creation stories remain in rough form, half-buried in the conscious of the organization with few people who can recall the unique "big bang" that got things started. In this case, the leaders must carefully uncover every creation story in the lineage of the people they are influencing. Here are two creation story tidbits.

As I got to know Lee McFarland, senior pastor of Radiant Church outside of Phoenix, he recounted his journey of leaving an executive role at Microsoft as director of worldwide operations. "I had 16,000 shares of Microsoft stock that were not yet vested. If I left to start the church, I would have to leave the shares behind. At first I felt a little angry toward God, because I knew He was calling me to leave and start Radiant. Finally, I just decided to pray—and I prayed that God would give our church one soul for every share that I was leaving behind." The church started with

147 in attendance in September 1997. Just eight years later, it was ranked as one of the fastest-growing churches in the country.

Caz McCaslin is the founder of Upward, a global ministry dedicated to "introducing children to Jesus Christ by creating opportunities to serve through sports." Year after year as Caz grew his local, church-based basketball league, he finally ran out of room. But the kids didn't stop showing up. One year when he had twenty-seven kids on a waiting list, Caz swelled with pride. But days later, he was struck by a holy urgency: "What if those twenty-seven kids never get a chance to hear the gospel?" Caz thought the answer was to build a bigger gym. But a good friend challenged his thinking: "You don't need a bigger gym, Caz; you need *a thousand* gyms." So he put his process in a book, challenged churches to "win the race to a child's heart," and built a first-class service organization. Ten years later, the ministry serves half a million kids and continues to rapidly expand.

The leader must master the details of the creation story—those that are specifically his, and those that are a part of the organization he is leading. The creation story should be honed for a thirty-second elevator ride or thirty-minute presentation—and everywhere in between. Caz now flies all over the country to share the creation story of Upward and motivate groups of leaders who are starting new programs.

ARTIFACT NUMBER TWO: COLLECT THE HIDDEN GEMS OF VISION VOCABULARY. In the articulation of past vision, there are key terms and phrases that live large with meaning. I call these the "words within the walls," and the leader can intentionally tune into them. Think of these ideas as gems that we need to find and collect to put in a jewel case for others to see and enjoy. Oftentimes these vision nuggets stay undiscovered at worst or unpolished at best. Consequently, they are *undernoticed* and *undercelebrated*.

When Rich Kannwischer took the helm of First Presbyterian Church in San Antonio, he followed a pastor of longstanding vision and respect both inside and outside the church, Louis Abendon. After a year of acclamation, Rich began the journey to articulate a new vision. In the process of discerning the hidden vision vocabulary, the first phrase that surfaced was a verse from Isaiah 40:8. Louis quoted it often in worship and after every Scripture reading: "The grass withers and the flower fades, but the word of our God will stand forever." When it came time to refine the church's missional mandate, they considered capturing the echo of these words within the walls with the missional mandate of "inviting one another into life together that stands forever." Another phrase the leadership team uncovered was, "Everyone loves the cardinals, but who will feed the sparrows?" This statement was repeated over and over to carry the church's heartbeat for social justice in the city. It was eventually embedded in the core value expressed as "spontaneous compassion." By first looking backward and polishing these vision gems, Rich is able to cherish the past as he champions a new future.

ARTIFACT NUMBER THREE: FIND THE "HALL OF FAME" MEMORABILIA. A friend's father, now in his seventies, sold his house and most of his possessions and moved into a one-bedroom apartment in an assisted living complex. If you engage him in conversations about his life, he will pull out a plastic shoebox filled with the memorabilia that represents the best of his life. Your first reaction is, "How sad; his entire life is in a shoebox." But if you listen as he tells you with emotion the tale behind each photo, each newspaper clipping, each tattered letter, each Navy medal, the vial of mercury, the patent papers (related to his career), and the copy of the U.S. Constitution, you understand so much more about the man than you would just by walking into his home.

Behind the pictures on the wall, the stained glass windows, and the sound system of your church home are the "shoebox" stories from the people who have forged the character of your church. What are the hall of fame memorabilia in your church's history? From them, what stories speak to your church's uniqueness?

At Oak Hills Church in San Antonio, where Max Lucado ministers, they live out their tagline, "A home for every heart." While they share stories that exemplify the best of Oak Hills, the theme of *grace* is found woven through. Each story nuances an indiscriminate dynamic where love and support collide to bring about personal transformation. Taking time to share the stories made the leadership of the church keenly aware that *redemptive grace* is a deep value and demonstrated part of their personality.

Here is a challenge: in the next thirty days take a vision detector with you everywhere. Don't just ask people in your church; ask leaders from any sphere of influence. Here are questions you can ask:

- Creation story: What circumstances led you to start the company? When did you know God was calling you to be a leader? What led this ministry to be birthed in the first place?
- Vision vocabulary: When you talk about the identity of your organization, what ideas are shared the most? What words get repeated around here that shape the direction and future of the ministry?

What words still echo in the walls of this church from previous seasons of leadership?

- Hall of fame: If you were fighting for which stories belong in your church's hall of fame, which ones would make the top three? If your ministry had a shoebox of memorabilia, which objects would be in it? What were the two biggest defining moments in the ministry's history? What happened, and how did the event shape the character of the organization?

In this section, we have discussed the nature of clarity, its benefits, and its prerequisites, including the need to be in tune with God and the opportunity to learn from other visionaries. Up to this point, Part Two has been preparatory. Next, we explore how you can discover your Church Unique.

9

DISCOVER YOUR KINGDOM CONCEPT

HOW TO ASCERTAIN VISION

Most artists look for something fresh to paint; frankly I find that quite boring. For me it is much more exciting to find fresh meaning in something familiar.

—Andrew Wyeth

MY FAVORITE PLAYGROUND GROWING UP was the meandering Brandywine River in Southeastern Pennsylvania. Full of refreshment and surprise, rarely would a summer day pass without inner tube and fishing tackle in hand. Little did I know that my personal stomping grounds in that picturesque countryside were becoming world-famous through the work of a local artist, Andrew Wyeth. He is considered one of America's most significant artists, an unparalleled genius of realism. This celebrated painter can capture the eternal moment of a moonlit landscape with exquisite detail, or the fleeting moment of a rushing stream with mysterious beauty.

What's particularly interesting about Wyeth is that in more than fifty years of painting he never tried to capture a landscape outside of the immediate surroundings of his home in Chadds Ford, Pennsylvania, and his family's summerhouse in Maine. Ponder this startling fact for a moment. This man has touched the world with an ability he never exercised outside of his own backyard! Wyeth has a love for locale. His creative mind and brilliant skill, turned loose for ten hours a day and for years on end, can be forever satisfied by radically full attention to the familiar.

Wyeth's local focus reinvigorated my interest to learn more about his life and work. It seemed to me that he was doing something inherently visionary, and critically important for ministry leaders to do as well. His ability to observe his immediate surroundings enables him to discover and express meaning in life that others miss. It is as if he can enter more deeply into what he has already possessed. Then he masterfully recreates and patiently reimages the scene until it becomes more powerful than reality itself.

These skills are also required for those leading a Church Unique. How do you observe the all-too-familiar in order to discover new meaning and discern the activity of God that others miss? What do you look for? The purpose of this chapter is to outline specific practices to this end—what I call ascertaining vision.

The work of ascertaining deals with the present. That is, how do we simultaneously explore, inspect, discover, and define what God is up to and where he wants us to go? This stands in contrast to the prior chapter, about learning from visionary legacies from the past. As we have said, uncovering the visionary work of others does not give us ours directly, but it sets the stage for our own journey.

Your Kingdom Concept

The first step in ascertaining a unique vision is to discover your Kingdom Concept. The Kingdom Concept is the simple, clear, "big idea" that defines how your church will glorify God and make disciples. Please note the important point of the last sentence: your Kingdom Concept is not to "glorify God" or to "make disciples" in and of itself. These ideas reflect the biblical mandate for every church.* Rather, your Kingdom Concept is what differentiates you from every other church in *how* you develop followers of Christ for God's ultimate honor. The Kingdom Concept answers important questions such as "What is our greatest opportunity to have an impact on the kingdom?" and "What can we do better than ten thousand other churches?" Think of it as your organizational sweet spot. It is the place where your church's unique experiences flow as a body of Christ. With a clear understanding of a Kingdom Concept, your leadership can capture and release amazing energy toward a better future.

---

*My purpose is not to develop this assertion, because much has been written on this topic in the last two decades. If a church does not see glorifying God as its ultimate purpose and making disciples as its earthly mission, then it is not a church by biblical definition.

Figure 9.1. Your Kingdom Concept

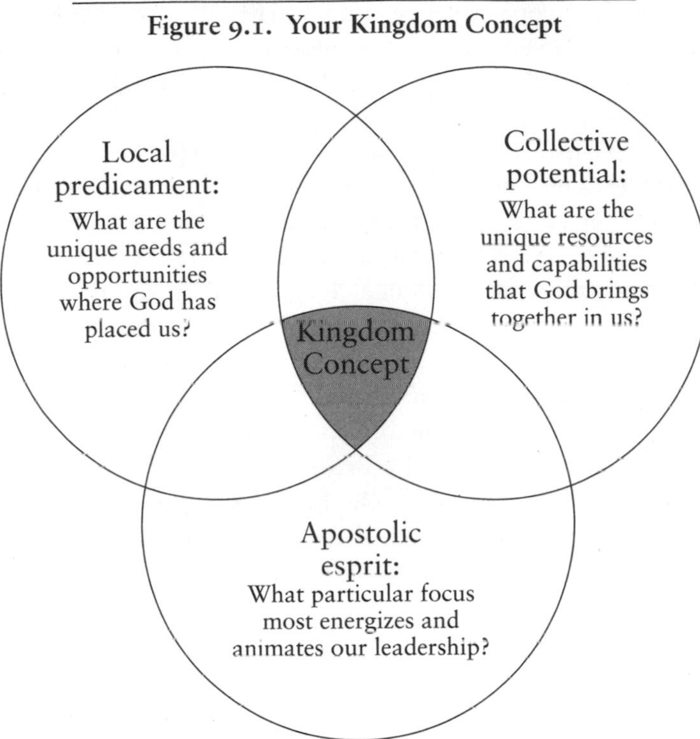

In the second half of the twentieth century, there has been a movement toward refocusing on the Great Commission. Within this context, think of your Kingdom Concept as your "Great Permission"; *being free to live as God has created and called you to do in your unique setting.* (Of course, your Great Permission is always subordinate to God's mandate in the Great Commission.) The book of Acts reminds us that David found his permission and specific calling: "For when David had served God's purpose in his own generation, he fell asleep; he was buried with his fathers and his body decayed" (Acts 13:36).

The best way to find your Kingdom Concept is to look at the intersection of three circles that represent aspects of your church's God-given uniqueness (see Figure 9.1).

Circle One: Local Predicament

Your community has all kinds of specific challenges. Do you know what they are? Defining your local predicament answers the question, What are the unique needs and opportunities where God has placed us? Understanding your local predicament is about having an intimate grasp of the soil where God has called you to minister. It is about walking firsthand your contours of locality.

Can your vision be separated from where God has sovereignly embedded you? One church is across the street from a high school, and one is across the street from a medical center. Another church is in a booming suburb, and in contrast to one that is in a transitioning urban area. I worked with one church in a city that is 65 percent Catholic and then flew across the country to church that is across the street from the world training center for Christian Science. These locations speak volumes about their Kingdom Concept.

John Hus was a priest and martyr in the early fifteenth century and a key player in the lead-up to the Protestant Reformation. Where he preached in the city of Prague, the Bethlehem Chapel, there is a strange feature in the southeastern corner of the sanctuary: a huge well. Legend has it that the prostitutes and swindlers in the town had spoiled the local water source. Besides their bully presence around the well itself, some were known to have thrown their unwanted babies down the well. The horrific scene created two burdens: the tragedy of lost life and the loss of usable water. Compelled to provide a viable water source, the chapel dug the well just yards from the pulpit. A new door was placed in the side of the church so that people could draw from the protected water source inside the church, even during the services. They also demonstrated their care and compassion for the innocent babies that were murdered in the artwork on the walls of the chapel. In a nutshell, the people of the Bethlehem Chapel responded to their local predicament.

What about your square footage on planet earth? Here are some questions that can help you and your leadership team explore your local predicament:

- What are the unique needs where God has placed us? in our city? in our neighborhood?
- How are these needs reflected socially, economically, ethnically, environmentally, politically, and religiously?
- What arena of our community is the furthest from the utopia that God wants to restore?
- What special opportunities are found within our immediate sphere of influence (within a half-mile)?

- What burning issues are alive in the public's eye and brought to attention by the media?
- What needs and opportunities do the industries specific to our area create?
- What is the most significant change in our community in the last decade, and what need does this create?
- What are the largest community events, and what needs or opportunities do they create?
- Because of our specific location, what solution could we provide that no other church does?
- How would we describe the "atmosphere of lostness" in our community?
- What is the creation story of our particular community, and what insight does this afford?
- Does the history of our community bring to light any spiritual strongholds?
- What one positive change in our community would have the most dramatic effect in people's lives?

Answering these questions obviously requires much prayer, reflection, dialogue, and research. It may take some digging around and a financial investment to get good demographic and psychographic data. If you are serious, the best approach is to do your own primary research; you will uncover a treasure chest of information.

KEEPING THE PULSE OF LOCALITY IN THE EARLY CHURCH. The leaders of the early church were so well versed in culture it is (somewhat ironically) easy to miss. We are so culturally removed from the context of the writers themselves that in our inclination to get practical teaching it's all too easy to miss the their habitual attention to locality. We see this most clearly in the life of Paul in his evangelistic and church-planting work. Two snapshots show how Paul kept the local pulse.

When Paul comes to Athens (Acts 17), he demonstrates exquisite skill in adapting his communication of the gospel. Invited to speak at the Areopagus (v. 19), he uses their "statue to an unknown God" as a religious loophole by which he commends their spiritual fervor. He argues not from Scripture first but from culture, quoting two philosophers in verse 28, probably from Epimenides of Crete and from Aratus' poem, "Phainomena." How did Paul so quickly adapt his communication to this new context? In verse 22 Paul says that he "perceived" their ways, and in verse 16 we see him "provoked" in his spirit by what he saw. These two words offer insight into Paul's ability to read the culture. Eyes that perceive and a heart that's provoked defined his two-step stride as a cultural exegete.

Paul's ability to adapt to culture is also seen during his church-planting work on the Island of Crete. He opens his letter to Titus, his point man for the project, with a description of God as the "God who never lies" (1:2). That's funny; Paul never used such language in the opening of other letters. Was this reference a random thought of the day from his quiet time? Hardly. Almost every sentence in this short letter contains nuances to the local culture on the Island of Crete. He references the truth-telling character of God precisely because the tendency to lie is a local predicament (1:12–13). When he writes to Timothy about establishing a leadership community on the island, he adapts his qualification for elders according to the sin patterns of that particular cultural context. His emphasis is on sound doctrine and not only the ability to teach it but the character to "hold firm" and the skill to refute liars who will contradict it (1:9). These are two small examples of the contextual nuances that run through Scripture.

KEEPING THE PULSE OF LOCALITY TODAY. How have some churches successfully defined their local predicament?

- Bandera Road Community Church in San Antonio has identified teenage pregnancy as a social issue to tackle in response to the fact that San Antonio has one of the highest teen birth rates in the country.
- Life Church in Portland, Oregon, has identified its local predicament generally as a culture of "self-reliance" and specifically as underresourced education facilities.
- First Presbyterian of Midland, Texas, insightfully realized that as an "oil town" everything of value in the community lies literally beneath the surface. They see their local predicament as exposing the same dynamic from a spiritual-kingdom perspective: the need to explore and enter the deeper realities of Christ.
- Hope Baptist Church in Las Vegas has identified multiple issues, but one they are currently giving their attention to is homeless children, whose numbers continue to grow in the area.

- A church in Aspen, Colorado, recognized the opportunity to touch the world from their backyard, because a significant constituency of their fluctuating community is eighteen to twenty-four years old, young people who come from the upper crust around the globe. When I checked in at my hotel, the twenty-one-year-old woman from Norway had never heard the gospel.

Circle Two: Collective Potential

The second circle looks at the collection of individuals in your church and answers the question, What are the unique resources and capabilities that God brings together in us? The resources reflecting cooperative potential are multifaceted: spiritual gifts, training and education, shared experiences, financial capabilities, motivated abilities, common possessions, a particular anointing of Holy Spirit, and so on. Most churches don't look for common patterns of collective capabilities, but you might be surprised what you find when you look for it.

One immediate difficulty in identifying cooperative potential is our tendency as Westerners to focus on the individual and not on the community. When we read verses such as 1 Cor. 6:19 ("Or do you not know that your body is a temple of the Holy Spirit within you?"), we jump to the conclusion that the term *you* is singular when it is in fact plural. Paul is telling the church that their *corporate* body is the temple, not their individual bodies. This verse is commonly misinterpreted by referring it to the believer's physical body with regard to the abuses of sexuality, drinking, smoking, and even tattoos.

Chuck Colson writes, "Modern Christians, especially evangelicals, see the Christian faith primarily if not exclusively as the gospel of 'Jesus and me.' Christianity is simply a personal relationship with Jesus. Accept Christ into your personal life and you will be saved. This is true as far as it goes, but it falls woefully short. Although we are justified through our faith, Christianity is much more than a private transaction with Jesus. . . . According to Scripture, Christianity is corporate."[1]

JESUS AND WE VS. JESUS AND ME. Spiritual leaders often tend to emphasize the potential of the individual to the neglect of the whole when spiritual gifts are identified and released. In the positive emphasis on "every member ministry," a church can subconsciously create a one-to-one relationship between a spiritual gift and a ministry initiative. So when

Sally discovers her gift, a mix of faith and mercy, we bless her in starting a hospital visitation ministry. Now please hear me clearly: I am not suggesting that we minimize Sally's gifts. I am advocating the importance of viewing Sally's gifts in light of the whole, or in view of the Kingdom Concept. If we don't, the church can become a chaotic mess of everyone wanting to do her own thing. Would you rather rally a hundred people into one effective initiative, or have a hundred people going in a hundred directions? Inadvertently, most churches tend toward the latter. When they do, they often sacrifice their cooperative potential for the well-intended whims of the individual.

An important verse in Romans 1:11 again reinforces the capabilities of the group compared to the single unit. Paul expresses his desire to visit the Roman church so that "I may impart to you [plural] some spiritual gift." Again this "you" is not singular but plural, indicating the possibility that Paul is talking about a "collective gifting" or "corporate grace." The idea is so foreign to the common way we think of spiritual gifts that it is hard to imagine what Paul meant. Can an entire congregation be defined by a singular strength, motivation, or spiritual gift? I believe so.

GROUP GRACE. Scriptures teach that grace empowers us to serve the Lord not only as individuals but also as groups. David Cannistraci cites several passages as biblical examples of what he calls "group grace": Acts 4:33 and 11:23; 1 Corinthians 1:4; 2 Corinthians 8:1, 6, 7, and 9:14; Ephesians 3:2; Philippians 1:7; and 1 Peter 3:7.[2] In each of these verses, grace *(charis)* is corporate—shared by two or more people. Examples in biblical history of group grace:

- The seventy elders under Moses (Num. 11:17, 25)
- The armies of Israel (as in Exod. 17:11–12)
- Priests at the Temple of Dedication (2 Chron. 5:11–14)
- Saul and the prophets (1 Sam. 10:4–6, 10)
- The disciples at Pentecost (Acts 2:1–4, 38)
- Apostles as witnesses (Acts 4:33)
- Cornelius's household (Acts 10:44)

Another biblical example of corporate identity is the twelve tribes of Israel. Before Jacob's death, he speaks a blessing to each of his sons, who become the representative tribes or communities of Israel. In Genesis 49:28, it says the he "blessed each with a blessing suitable to him." In other words, each son had uniqueness, and that uniqueness would come to reflect the cooperative strength or personality of the tribe. For example, Jacob likens several tribes to animals:

- Judah is a lion.
- Issachar is a strong donkey.
- Naphtali is a doe.
- Benjamin is a ravenous wolf.

Through Israel's history we see tribal decisions and tribal heroes reflecting their tribes' group grace. For example, references to the tribe of Dan reflect their ability to judge and fight. Samson, a Danite, was a more familiar judge of Israel, and well known for his aggressiveness and superstrength.

The same collective abilities are seen in the church. Specifically in Revelation chapter 2, we see dialogue between Jesus and seven churches. Several times he commends them on their corporate character:

- Ephesus: patience and discernment
- Smyrna: faithfulness amid persecution
- Thyatira: increasing productivity of service and love

In fact, most of the New Testament is written to the church as a community and not to individuals. Therefore Paul's commendations and warning in all of his epistles except those to Timothy and Titus reflect the successes and failures of the community's collective potential.

What about your church? I find that this is usually harder to discern than the local predicament. Most churches are like an animal at the zoo that only looks in the mirror. They have a hard time seeing their unique potential because there is little experience comparing and contrasting with other animals. This is why an outsider can be particularly helpful, especially one who has seen many churches. Outsiders can bring the perspective of the zookeeper who appreciates the beauty and uniqueness of each creation. Here are some questions for you to consider to help you discover your collective potential (these will also help you discern the perception of outsiders):

- If a guest visited our church several times and answered the question, "What did you like best about this church?" what would the guest say?

- If you were bringing a friend to our church for the first time, what singular promise (that is, what she will receive or experience from coming) would you be most willing to make?
- If we were to stop nonmembers who drive by the church regularly and ask them how they feel about the church, what would they say?
- If our church was immediately uprooted from the community, what would people in the community feel is missing?
- How would a local group of pastors or denominational fellowship describe the strength of our church?
- What is the biggest impact our church has made in the community? in the world?
- What is the most significant thing our church could do in the community? in the world?
- Who comes to our church? How does ethnicity, age, gender, life stage, and the spiritual maturity of our people define our congregation's make-up?
- What capabilities tend to cluster in our church? What are common aspects of training, education, or occupational history?
- What spiritual gifts seem to be prominent in our church?
- What shared motivations, spiritual growth markers, or views of sanctification characterize people in our church?
- What is the most significant ministry inside our church? outside?
- If we had to only do one ministry outside our church walls, which would we choose?
- What atmosphere do we tend to create when our people get together?
- How do new members talk about what attracted them to the church?
- If our church were a hotel or department store, which one would it be?

Answering these questions can be an arduous, albeit rewarding, task. It requires hours of dialogue with many kinds of people. (Remember the reference to the "tunnel of chaos"?) Keep in mind that your core leadership, as well as the first impressions of newcomers, can offer equal insight into answering these questions. I recommend beginning this assessment in a retreat setting where prayer, reflection, and observations of outsiders can be included.

I also recommend listening tools such as surveys (three kinds: leadership, congregation, and community), focus groups, and exit interviews. A particularly good focus group is a collection of diverse people who started attending the church in the prior six months. Use the questions given here as a starting point for developing these tools.

STUNNING IMPACT. When churches understand their collective potential, amazing things happen. The work of John Hus, cited earlier, eventually led to unification of believers who followed his teaching in Bulgaria and Moravia. In the early eighteenth century, a local community of believers gathered as Moravian refugees in the town of Herrenhut, Germany. After a revival that occurred in 1727, the Moravian community, which started with three hundred people, birthed a worldwide missionary movement that in eight years was the most ambitious program the Protestant world had ever known. A local church unleashed a collective capacity that touched the farthest corners of the earth, including unreached black communities in the West Indies and Eskimos in Greenland.[3]

A more current example of collective capacity is the 2006 film release of *Facing the Giants,* a feature film written and produced by Sherwood Baptist Church in Albany, Georgia. The cast and crew was made up of more than five hundred members of the church. The film, which was shot for a mere $100,000, was shown in more than a thousand theaters and grossed more than $10 million. The movie was filmed as an ambitious goal of one local church community that wanted to produce a family-friendly and Christ-honoring alternative for the box office.[4]

The marks of collective potential are always beautiful, but they may not always receive recognition. I was working with a church outside of Ft. Lauderdale years ago that discovered a cooperative capacity centered on a shared salvation history. As it turned out, a large majority of their church had all come to Christ through a season of brokenness after age forty. The group then began to shape the vision around being a church "where life begins," for adults experiencing difficulty in midlife. Another church in Dallas identified a common background of having been set free from legalism. They identified a vision around the idea of "life beyond boundaries" and focused on reaching those in desperate need of "radical grace" inside and outside the church.

In both cases, these churches were unaware of the common threads and cohesive forces that defined the culture and collective potential.

The epiphany came only after an intentional season of dialogue and listening with an outside facilitator present. What possibilities of cooperative potential are lying beneath the surface of your Church Unique?

Circle Three: Apostolic Esprit

A church's "apostolic esprit" is the area of focus that arouses an energetic style in its leaders. By apostolic I mean that this source of liveliness and animation is anchored in a missional mind-set—the self-understanding of "being sent." Esprit is more than your passion. Esprit captures both the empowering and direction of the Holy Spirit and the human side of fervor and vitality that springs from team morale. Think of esprit as "the hot place in a man's consciousness, the group of ideas to which and from which he works, the habitual center of his personal energy."[5]

Although the local predicament finds its locus outside of the church and collective potential finds its meaning within the congregation, apostolic esprit lives in and through the leadership community. The very existence of the gift of leadership (Rom. 12:8) infers that directional leadership is stewardship of the leadership community. The record of Scripture demonstrates that vision is communicated through the personality of leaders. For example, when God wanted to speak to a nation he chose Moses; when he wanted to speak to the Gentiles, he chose Paul.

There are several launching pads for expressing your church's apostolic esprit. Different models may try to present the right way to think about passion and gifting. I prefer to see the various models as interrelated and dynamic, and I encourage leaders to devour any and every one to hone their self-understanding and self-discovery. Perspectives that all contribute to apostolic esprit:

- Spiritual gifts (Rom. 12: 3–8, 1 Cor. 12:1–11, 1 Pet. 4:10–11)
- Natural talents as inborn predispositions (Ps. 139:13–16)
- Strengths or motivated abilities that combine talents with knowledge, skills, experience, and context*

*The Clifton Strengthsfinder defines strengths as "the ability to provide consistent, near perfect performance in a given activity." *Living Your Strengths,* p. 3.

- ❍ Personality as relating behavioral preferences*
- ❍ Leadership orientation (APEPT, from Eph. 4:12–16)**
- ❍ Special calling from God (Jeremiah in Jer. 1:4–5, or Paul in Acts 9:6)
- ❍ Maturely developed fruits of the Spirit
- ❍ Focused compassion on a social concern, target area, or people group
- ❍ Impressions of the Holy Spirit in daily relationship with God

Again, the key is not a magic formula for defining your esprit but freedom to be specific through many possible routes as God leads you.

Have you ever watched someone's disposition change when she discusses a certain topic? You sense a deeper conviction, you see a spark in her eye, and you hear the certainty of victory in her words. That's the apostolic esprit at work. Noel Tichy calls it "E^3"—a leader's emotional energy and edge.[6] Bill Hybels refers to it as a "holy discontent."

A leader's apostolic esprit can find its shape through emphasis on *ideas* or *actions*. Here are some examples of leaders with whom I have worked.

ESPRIT AS IDEA

Nonstop spiritual growth: When David Loveless at Discovery Church in Orlando, Florida, talks about the history of his church, it parallels aggressive pursuit of sanctification in his own life. The passion translates to the whole church. His esprit is felt most when he articulates with clarity, "We believe that there is always more to discover in Christ; each year, each month, each week, each day." Hence the church's name.

Gentleness: The fruit of the spirit, gentleness, marks Jim Nite and the leadership community at Center Point Community Church in Naples, Florida. With a strong commitment to preaching the

---

*Jungian psychology is the basis for many of the most respected personality assessment profiles (Insights Discovery Personal Profile, Myers-Briggs Type Inventory, DiSC). According to Jung, personal development emanates from self-understanding of our attitudes and behavioral preferences as well as understanding of how we relate to others.

**I agree with Frost and Hirsch (The Shaping of Things to Come) that every believer in the body has an orientation around the fivefold framework of Eph. 4:13: apostle, prophet, evangelist, pastor, and teacher, commonly referred to as APEPT.

Word, the atmosphere of gentleness is identified, modeled, and celebrated as they "connected one person at a time, to a family of committed followers of Jesus Christ."

Storytelling: As Oak Hills Church, led by Max Lucado, explored its Kingdom Concept, the idea of accomplishing the Great Commission as "storytelling disciples" came to the surface, guided by the missional idea of "living to bring God's story to life."

"Grace-life": Through a long history of strong preachers and aligned theology, Castle Hills First Baptist Church in San Antonio, Texas, finds esprit through the grace emphasis of "Keswick" sanctification or "exchanged life" teaching. This was carried by Jack Taylor, George Harris, and Si Wood and is currently shouldered by James Shupp, who came in passionately supporting the existing mission: "To invite each individual from every background to really live in Christ."

ESPRIT AS ACTION

Reaching seekers: When Bruce Wesley planted Clear Creek Community Church in the suburbs south of Houston, the guiding esprit was to create a place where unchurched friends could experience a safe haven for exploring the person of Christ. The church's leadership fifteen years later keeps a white-hot focus on reaching seekers, having led thousands of people across the line of faith.

Building servants: Park Place Methodist, also in Houston, had a very different esprit from reaching seekers; they want to reach servants. They see their Kingdom Concept through the lens of "hard core" service that embraces an ethnically diverse neighborhood. Their missional mandate is to "build a fellowship of servants whose diversity enriches growth in Christ."

Transforming cities: Vance Pitman, who started Hope Baptist in Las Vegas, has an unmistakable esprit for city transformation. The goal is to make sure what happens in Las Vegas spreads all over the world: the transformation of a city that only God could get the credit for!

Discipling families: Bannockburn Baptist in Austin, Texas, led by Ryan Rush, decided to measure the Great Commission not one person at a time but one family at a time. Their esprit is a radical focus on family discipleship, captured by the idea of "guiding generations to passionately follow Christ, one home at a time."

I hope this sampling gives you a good idea for thinking through your own apostolic esprit. To help you, here are some questions to ask and answer:

- Review the list of perspectives that contribute to your apostolic esprit. Write down the best of your self-understanding for each bullet (or that of other leaders on your team).
- What one thing bothers you most about the world?
- If you knew you couldn't fail, what one thing would you pursue for God?
- What do you tend to pray for the most?
- What gives you energy?
- What have you secretly believed you would be really good at if only you were given a chance?
- What do others say that you are good at? that you are not good at? (Have you asked lately?)
- What projects or accomplishments, though probably unnoticed by others, created a deep sense of satisfaction on your life's journey? what projects or accomplishments from grade school years, high school, college, and early career?
- What would you want people saying about you at your funeral? State three words that reflect "who you were." State three words that reflect "what you accomplished."
- Who are your heroes? Why do you admire them? Who have you wanted to emulate or spend time with but have not been able to?

Use these questions for you and for your leadership team to answer the primary question, What particular focus most energizes and animates our leadership? Once this is accomplished—and it may take a long time, even several months—you can begin to understand the overlap of the three circles that identify your Kingdom Concept.

The three circles are simple yet profound. The real secret to discovering them is found in our opening illustration of Andrew Wyeth. He did not look constantly for fresh things to paint; rather, he was excited to find fresh meaning in things that were familiar. Your job in finding your Kingdom Concept is nothing less than the work of scrutinizing the obvious. As the three circles come into focus, you may feel that one or two may have more influence over your Kingdom Concept than the others. That's OK; just keep looking for the points and patterns of overlap.

In the next chapter, we provide further illustration to help you navigate the discovery of your own Kingdom Concept. As we do so, I urge you to consider this exercise, which I hope you'll take a moment to complete now, and revisit after the next chapter. You will want the final expression of your Kingdom Concept to be the most specific phrase possible that fills in the blank. After you nail down this phrase as your Kingdom Concept, you will have successfully answered the question, "What can our church do better than ten thousand others?"

○○○

Our church glorifies God and makes disciples by:

____.

10

TAKE A CLOSER LOOK

NAVIGATING YOUR DISCOVERY PROCESS

Social sector leaders pride themselves on "doing good" for the world, but to be of maximum service requires a ferocious focus on doing good only if it fits your Hedgehog Concept. To do the most good requires saying "no" to the pressures to stray and the discipline to stop doing what does not fit.

—Jim Collins

FOR THE LAST DECADE, I have worked with church leaders with the firm conviction that every prevailing church is an original. When I look in the eyes of a Vision Pathway team, I can see their doubt. I imagine their questions: "Does this guy really know what he's talking about?" or "He hasn't spent much time around here" or "We're already clear on our five purposes." From whatever bias, the idea of a Kingdom Concept seems either too good to be true or utterly unnecessary. But somewhere on the journey, something clicks. Team members, one by one, are converted. They become excited about what God *is* doing and *could be* doing uniquely through them.

In a way, knowing that I cannot be personally present as your vision navigator breaks my heart, because I know God wants to do something fantastically special in your church. I wish I could be there to see yet another one-of-a-kind vision emerge—a new picture of God's better intermediate future.

Since I can't, I am writing this chapter to get into the nitty-gritty with you. First, I want to let you peek into an ongoing process, and see how the overlapping circles of the Kingdom Concept can emerge real time.

Second, I want explore how some popular ways of thinking about leadership inhibit your Kingdom Concept from emerging.

Kingdom Concept in Real Time

Take a walk with me as I discover the local predicament, the collective potential, and the apostolic esprit of a local church.

Snapshot One: Weekend Visit to the Church, October

The church is well established and runs about twenty-five hundred in attendance. It is a downtown church in one of America's midsized cities; the church building is a wonderful monument to the Christian era of yesterday. For five years, the ministry has experienced a plateau. Leaders are frustrated and want to go to the next level but don't know how. The church employees are the finest professional staff money can buy.

It is evident that most of the attenders drive by many other churches (average drive is eight miles) to come to this church—much more than the typical situation. I wonder why, and I plan to ask as many people as possible both inside and outside the church.

I attend worship and immerse myself in the church culture through all the weekend programs. Our team spends all day Saturday, talking to people in the area about church in general and this church in particular. There are several things that strike me about the church from my "secret worshipper" experience:

- The church has one of the nicest student facilities I have ever seen.
- The pastor was most animated on Sunday morning when he interacted with an eleven-year-old boy on the stage (and he was amazing at it).
- A local high school football team sat in the front area of the sanctuary. They received special appreciation during the service.
- The children's facility was quite underdeveloped, in contrast to the student facility.

On Sunday night, I have the opportunity to sit in on a small-group experience. When the group finishes early and the leader identifies my role as "vision consultant," an awkward silence ensues. I realize the unplanned opportunity and decide to add a few questions and bake up an instant focus group. My questions reveal two common threads. First, what people like best about their church pertains to such inward-facing aspects of church life as fellowship, caring, and personal knowledge development (that is, they don't tend to be missional). Second, there is no self-awareness of what makes their church different. Any questions signaling strengths or corporate grace come back random and scattered.

Snapshot Two: Meeting with the Church Staff, November

Immediately I am impressed with the tenure of the staff. They seem to have a bond of brotherhood that is a strength on the staff level at the very least. During the meeting, I learn that one of the staff knows a lot about the local community. He is the church's primary contact with the city. I keep fishing from his deep well of facts as we process them as a group. Several observations struck me that day:

- The church has an unusually good relationship with the city; in fact, city officials often come to the church to use the student facility, a state-of-the-art meeting place.
- The trends are seeing more life coming back to the city and into proximity of the church.
- In this city 40 percent of kids in the ninth grade will not graduate from high school.

Snapshot Three: Hallway Conversations, October-November

By the end of the second visit, I have drilled the question home to many: "So why do you people drive by other churches to come to this church?" Almost all answers fell into one of two categories: the strength of the preaching ministry, and the strength of the student ministry.

One evening I get together with a local Christian leader who does not attend the church. Because of his keen awareness of many churches in the city, I ask him the same question. He responds instantly, "That church is built around a strong student ministry; that's why people go."

Snapshot Four: Meeting with the Staff, January

The two most important things that happen occur outside of our planned meeting. First, there are conversations with three staff people:

- In getting to know the executive pastor, I learn that the ministry prior to his current role was leading a specialized ministry for mentoring student pastors. I note that he still has a passion for mentoring but does not have the same outlet for doing so.

- While spending time with the communication pastor, I get a tour of an in-house radio station fully operated by volunteers in the church. The station provides the area's only Christian alternative targeting student and college-age listeners. It strikes me as an impressive operation.
- I discovered that the senior pastor's ministry prior to his current role was teaching at seminary. He demonstrates a youthful spirit as a passionate teacher who gels with students of all ages.

Between visits to this church, I also gain insight into two ministries that were launched from this church. One is a national sports ministry for children and students. The other is a writing and speaking ministry for teenage camps across the country.

Snapshot Five: The Flight Home, January

The Kingdom Concept is coming into focus with amazing clarity. I am astonished at the overlap of the circles. In my mind's eyes, I jotted out some bullets in our Kingdom Concept circles (see Figure 10.1).

I write down a phrase as a tentative idea: This church exists to glorify God and make disciples by *reaching and discipling students in a way that transforms the local education system.*

Troubleshooting the Kingdom Concept

Expect immediate objections upon introducing the Kingdom Concept. Reasons will vary; some are well intended and others frankly stem from selfishness. Let's deal with some of the pushback and consider how to address it.

What If the Kingdom Concept Does Not Emphasize "My Ministry Area"?

At first blush, this is a legitimate concern. When I introduced the idea of a student ministry focus to the staff of the church cited here, I was most concerned about the children's pastor. Would he think I was trying to pull the rug out from under him? Well, he did a little, as did the worship pastor.

The Kingdom Concept challenges the "egoless clarity" of the team, forcing them to decide if they are present for the sake of the mission or for their own advancement. One mentor of mine had a quote on his wall: "Imagine how much more we would get done for the kingdom if

Figure 10.1. Kingdom Concept in a Local Church

Local predicament

- The education system is a huge failure; gaping community need is evidenced by high percentage of high school dropouts
- There is a huge concentration of public schools and colleges around the church
- The city is looking to outside organizations and facilities to host important events
- Community interests are heading back downtown, including development of restaurants and bars

Collective potential

- The church has very strong student ministry leadership and facilities (and has prioritized this in the past)
- The church has a unique, self-run radio station ministry for students
- The people of the church are primarily white-collar and well educated
- The senior pastor and church at large are known for quality teaching; the senior pastor has taught seminary
- The church has the best meeting facility in the city

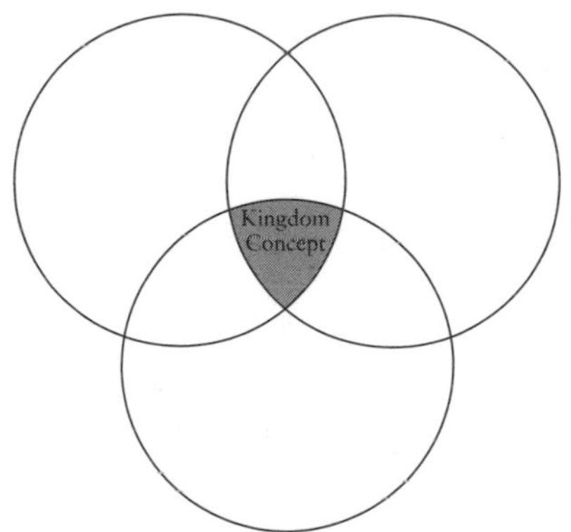

Apostolic esprit

- The church has a history of raising up people and ministries with passion for students
- The church's top staff in nonstudent-related positions have a passion and demonstrated performance in student ministry
- The senior pastor models exuberance best when talking with and on behalf of students
- The worship planning actively pursues opportunities to honor students

no one cared who got the credit." The first question should not be "What about my ministry area?" but "What area is God wanting us to address?" If God is truly demonstrating a strategic area on which to focus, many will be magnetically attracted; if some refuse to acknowledge the church's uniqueness, a stronger but loving urge to repent may be in order.

Aren't We Just Doing Less Ministry by Focusing in One Area?

No, not at all, because *focus expands.* In fact, the focus that the Kingdom Concept brings will most likely enhance surrounding ministries that horizontally align with the area of focus. For example, a church that focuses on reaching thirty-somethings and does so really well may have a better chance at reaching their fifty-to-sixty-year-old parents than a church that tries to be all things to all people. Or, using our example of the children's pastor, imagine if he saw his ministry as an important ramp-up to the student ministry. Or what if he collaborated with the student pastor to use the children's area as a primary service opportunity for students? The key is to let the defining strength of the church enhance every other ministry, not overshadow or eclipse them. The worship pastor of the church soon saw the student choir trips as a major point of overlap and horizontal alignment. Is it possible that the worship pastor would do more for the kingdom in his lifetime by combining his talents and love for worship with the church's strength in student ministry rather than trying to compete with it?

The principle that focus expands is true in the business world. When I go to California, I can't wait to eat at an In and Out Burger. The place is always ten times busier than the McDonald's across the street. Yet it has only two things on the menu: burgers and fries. The fries are fresh cut and there is more time and energy put into serving them than into having employees scurry to offer a variety of food options such as fish and chicken and salad. Fewer options but tons more business. Or consider Southwest Airlines: they only offer a ride on one plane model—the 737. The focused approach behind the scenes, including focused pilot training, focused maintenance process, and focused parts delivery, has led to mind-blowing breakthroughs in staying on mission. They have the longest record of profitability in the industry. The company reports, "In May 1988, we were the first airline to win the coveted Triple Crown for a month—Best On-time Record, Best Baggage Handling, and Fewest Customer Complaints. Since then we've won it more than thirty times, as well as five annual Triple Crowns for 1992, 1993, 1994, 1995, and 1996."[1] Southwest accomplished more with its focused approach than any other airline in history.

These business stories are but a glimpse of what many have learned. This is why researcher Jim Collins reports, "Maximum service requires a ferocious focus on doing good only if it fits your Hedgehog Concept [his version of our three circles]."[2] Thom Ranier chimes in after his recent research on the same dynamic in churches. His reminds us that "focus is the ability to eliminate everything that falls outside of the simple ministry process . . . it is the most difficult element to implement."[3] Why are these men so adamant? They both have piles of research that screams the good news that focus expands.

What About All of the "Five Purposes" of the Church?

When it comes to discovering your Kingdom Concept, we run into a predicament with the "purpose driven" emphasis. When Rick Warren penned his landmark book in 1995, *The Purpose Driven Church*, he single-handedly helped thousands of pastors.* His book legitimized a new perspective on being the church, which cultivated new levels of intentionality. He reflected deeply on the people God called him to reach. He designed processes with clarifying genius to help people understand new levels of commitment in their walk with God. He even created a visual icon—a baseball diamond—for communicating his strategy in a simple and relevant fashion. In a nutshell, he challenged the process of "doing ministry as usual" at a time when the church was at a record breaking low in its impact on culture.

But in Warren's reorientation to the purposes of God generally, we lose something very important specifically. There is uniqueness within the call to "love God and love others" that goes unmentioned. There is nuance underneath the Great Commandment and the Great Commission that remains unexplored. For Warren, the primary level of specificity is allegiance to a fivefold framework: worship, fellowship, discipleship, ministry, and mission. Many churches have intentionally sought to be purpose-driven or have been unconsciously influenced by Warren's work. These churches gravitate to and are defined by the fivefold framework. But it is there, in the name of being purpose-driven, that they get stuck. Thinking they have arrived at being clear and visionary, they fail to push through to a more specific reality: their unique Kingdom Concept.

Take Alex Kennedy, for example. When he took the senior pastor role at Kingsland Baptist Church in Katy, Texas, he immediately articulated a

---

*The Saddleback Website (http://saddleback.com) indicates that more than two hundred thousand church leaders have been through some type of purpose-driven training.

vision using Warren's vocabulary. Yet three years later something unique—a very specific call to the spiritual formation of the family—was bubbling to the surface. In his case, the purpose-driven language was blocking something more organic from being expressed. Or take Vance Pitman, the senior pastor of Hope Baptist Church in Las Vegas. As a recent church plant, Vance relied heavily on purpose-driven language. But in his heart, he knew that more specific words were needed. Their desire for city transformation in a modern-day Nineveh needed a fresh expression that the five purposes couldn't touch. In a nutshell, although the purpose-driven model has helped many churches jump-start a new ministry paradigm, it left many churches ill equipped to define something *purposefully specific.*

Is the Kingdom Concept Taking Us Away from the New and Innovative?

The practical application of this chapter represents a paradigm shift for leaders. To many pastors who are looking for the next new thing, the practices of defining their Kingdom Concept may seem irrelevant. Yet the resolve to discover your Kingdom Concept is the most relevant thing you can do. It takes you to the heart of God's divine design of your church. It equips you with a "community intelligence" to meet the real needs around you. On the surface, the leader's ability to scrutinize the obvious may seem a little dull and uninteresting. In response, I go back to the words of Andrew Wyeth: "Most artists look for something new to paint. Frankly, I find that boring. I prefer to find fresh meaning with something that is already familiar." It is time for leaders to look for the extraordinary in the ordinary. It is time to find exponential impact

Figure 10.2. The Church Unique Process: The Vision Pathway

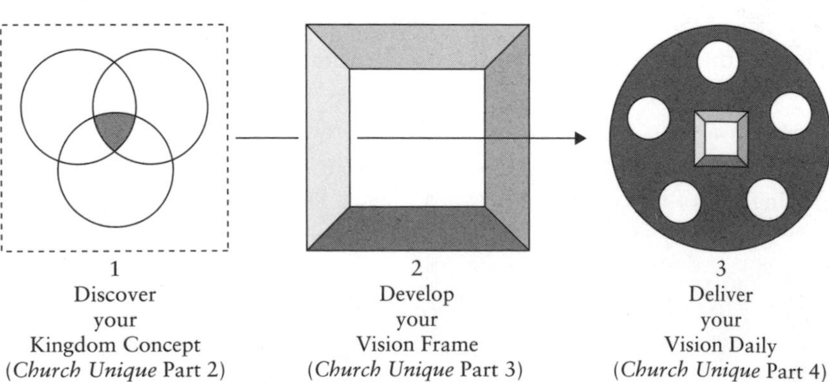

through a simple and local focus. This wisdom flies in the face of our ministry instinct to find new meaning in the next new program or ministry model. So, rather than running off to the next conference, let's learn how to find something fresh while driving to work.

Having reviewed the story of one church and some common objections, you can no doubt generate much team discussion about your Kingdom Concept. As you do, know that your long, drawn-out discussion will bear fruit. Remember: you *have to* navigate the tunnel of chaos if dialogue is to be successful. As you do, I will be anxious to see your story. Either send an e-mail directly to me (will@churchunique.com) or post your Kingdom Concept at churchunique.com.

Now that you have reviewed step one of the Vision Pathway (Figure 10.2) it is time to move to step two, Developing Your Vision Frame.

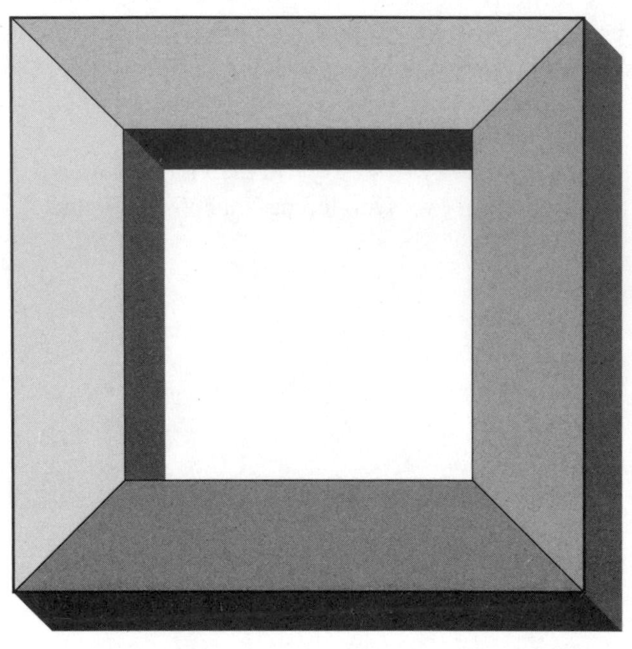

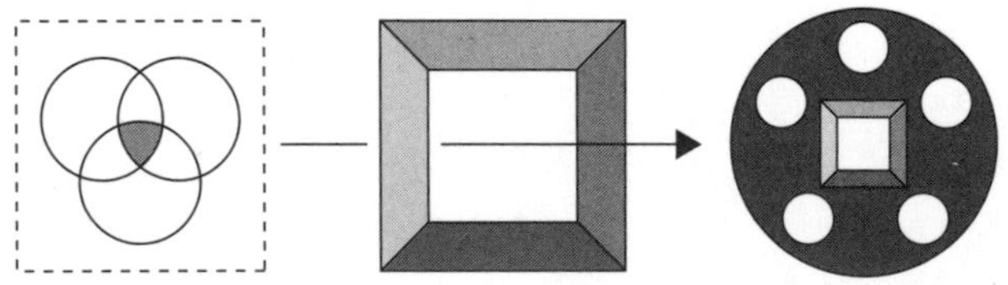

PART THREE

ARTICULATING VISION

REMEMBER THE LAST TIME YOU SAT down to do a jigsaw puzzle? The work proceeds in two basic steps. First, you put the edges together. Finding all of the little pieces with straight edges is the easiest way to begin. As you piece together the top and bottom and sides, the puzzle is framed up within a relatively short period of time.

The second part of the process is now ready to begin, because you have defined the basic shape and outline of the puzzle. Before building the frame, it would have been exceedingly difficult to put many of the middle pieces together. But now, all of those elusive jigsaw shapes and unclear image fragments have perspective and boundaries.

Even though the frame makes the puzzle building project easier, more work remains. You pick up awkward shape after awkward shape, twisting and turning them and turning again, until you get just the right fit and—snap—the image develops, one piece at a time. After a long journey that may take days or even months, the final image emerges.

In Part Three, we show you how to articulate your vision the same way you would build a puzzle: in two basic steps. As we introduce the Vision Frame, we guide you to first articulate the four outer edges—the components of your church's identity and direction that frame everything else you do. These edges anchor the second part of the process, which involves living and articulating the dynamic vision of your Church Unique through the daily work of turning and twisting the pieces of the organization. The edges of the frame are definitive, but the middle of the puzzle is dynamic. The fixed nature of step one, building the frame, anchors the fluid nature of step two, where your vision picture slowly develops into *the better intermediate future* God has entrusted to you.

11

SEE WITH NEW EYES

DEFINING YOUR VISION FRAME

Words create worlds.

—Anonymous

THE FOCUS OF THE LAST TWO CHAPTERS has been on content, not word choice. Think of your Kingdom Concept as the operating system of your church that is running in the background largely unnoticed. The Kingdom Concept is the basis for understanding your Church Unique but not the words you use to cast vision. The purpose of this next chapter is to move from operating system to operating language, from hidden hard drive, to colorful screen. The previous chapters dealt with the work we do in the kitchen. Now we address the sizzling steak that we serve to our dinner guests.

As we turn our attention to articulation of your vision, we want nothing less than an ultimate expression of clarity. The framework we use will allow every aspect of your missional vision and your Church Unique to shine through. Remember, we said earlier that we must state our framework before we frame our statement. In this chapter, we introduce the framework that keeps a leader from merely stabbing at the future with a few nifty vision phrases.

Your Church, in Ten Words or Less

The "signal versus noise" blog, by the company 37signals.com, presented an exercise in clarity: "Explain podcasting in ten words or less." Here are ten definitions that respondents submitted:

- Internet radio broadcasting for the common man via iPods + MP3
- Podcasting is to radio what Tivo is to TV

- ○ Ham radio for the Internet
- ○ Digital audio newsstand
- ○ Portable. Audio. Blog. People. Connections. Open. Communication. Music. Thought. Fun.
- ○ Podcasting is the hypesatisfactic marketage for distribulation of auditory snips
- ○ A fad that I don't care to understand
- ○ Audible Websites to go
- ○ Subscription radio by and for everyone
- ○ On-demand radio distributed over the Internet into mobile devices[1]

According to your personal background and your level of experience with an iPod and iTunes, you will find these definitions either more or less helpful. With that reality in mind, how would you describe your church in ten words or less? The way you answer this question will likewise be more or less helpful to the myriad people who call your church home. Keep in mind that these people have widely differing backgrounds: unchurched, dechurched, overchurched, and the antichurch. Will your words communicate well? Will they capture attention? Will your words serve up crystal clear understanding of what God is doing in the world in and through the church?

Notice how this little exercise shows us some common mistakes we make when we try to foster clarity as church leaders. The first two definitions reference other technology to define podcasting (Tivo, MP3, and iPods). Many in need of clarity will not understand these more technical words. Pastors often do the same thing in using "technical" religious language.

The third and fourth definitions use dated or local concepts. Will young people know what a ham radio is, and is a newsstand a common feature in everyone's experience? Similarly, church leaders sometimes use special language based on traditions that not everyone shares.

The fifth definition loses meaning by trying to be too creative. In the sixth definition, the novelty of making up words hints toward the full-blown frustration of the seventh, which screams, "I don't care." (In church meetings, I have seen the full range of these responses.) The final three definitions are most helpful.

Should we resist the forced limitation of ten words? Hardly. This is not an unfair restraint, but the best-kept clarity secret: say more by saying less. Fewer words that are well focused have further reach.

A Framework for Missional Clarity: The Vision Frame

The central thrust of Church Unique is introduction of a framework called the Vision Frame. The Vision Frame contains five components that define your church's DNA and creates the platform for all vision casting. No leader should lead, no team should meet, and no initiative should start without a clear understanding of the Vision Frame (Figure 11.1).

Each component is critical to answering one of the five irreducible questions of leadership:

- Mission as missional mandate ([m]*Mandate*): *What are we doing?* The missional mandate is a clear and concise statement that describes what the church is ultimately supposed to be doing.
- Values as missional motives ([m]*Motives*): *Why are we doing it?* The missional motives are shared convictions that guide the actions and reveal the strengths of the church.
- Strategy as missional map ([m]*Map*): *How are we doing it?* The missional map is the process or picture that demonstrates how the church will accomplish its mandate on the broadest level.
- Measures as missional life marks ([m]*Marks*): *When are we successful?* The missional life marks are a set of attributes in an individual's life that define or reflect accomplishment of the church's mandate.
- Vision Proper as missional mountaintop + milestones ([m]*Mountaintop + Milestones*): *Where is God taking us?* Vision Proper is the living language that anticipates and illustrates God's better intermediate future.

In my work with churches, it is extremely rare to find a local church that has all of these vision components developed and the questions answered. On close examination of these churches, we see that many of

Figure 11.1. The Vision Frame

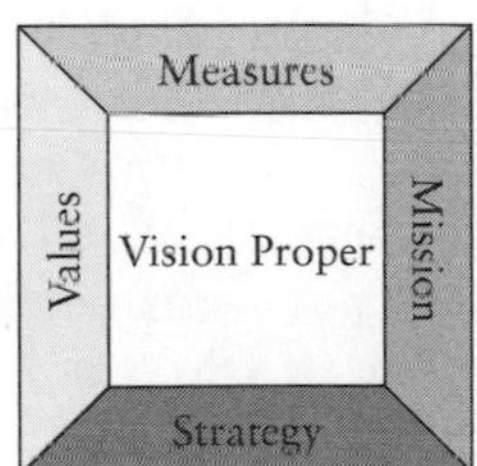

their challenges can be traced back to the problem of not having clarity first. Developing your Vision Frame may be the most significant *strategic* step you take in your ministry career.

Why the Vision Frame Works

The Vision Frame is an amazing leadership tool. By using it, I regularly see existing ministry teams feel like a team for the very first time. I see the light bulbs going off for leaders (even gifted visionaries) who exclaim that they have never understood visionary leadership more clearly. Why does this framework work so well? There are three aspects to highlight.

IT CARRIES THE KINGDOM CONCEPT. Your Kingdom Concept influences your Vision Frame anywhere and everywhere. Therefore it "lives" as it is translated and forged in the Vision Frame itself and not as a separate statement. Because there are several facets to the Vision Frame, the nuance of your Kingdom Concept finds many possibilities for expression. For example, it may be most prominently expressed in the strategy, or perhaps in the values.

IT IS COMPLETE YET CONCISE. A mission statement by itself or a values statement by itself still allows competing pictures of how the church should function or what the future looks like. This is why so many leaders grow disenfranchised with standard approaches to visioning. The Vision Frame, however, does not leave the irreducible questions of leadership unanswered; it closes the gaps, so to speak. It is comprehensive and addresses the function and future of the church in a real and tangible way. The genius of its completeness, though, is how it is packaged so concisely, enabling the DNA of the church to be "carryable" in the life of the church. Given my passion for brevity, you may be surprised to see five components at first, but I will show how they all work together with the ten-words-or-less approach.

IT COMMUNICATES A MISSIONAL REORIENTATION. You will notice that the Vision Frame components use words that are connected to traditional approaches to planning: values, strategy, and measures. I employ these terms because they are both useful and familiar. However, I define them a little differently, according to a missional reorientation. As a result, you will discover how to translate this traditional jargon into something priceless. The Vision Frame is a powerful tool to capture culture—drawing *on* the best of who God made you to be, drawing *out* your best as people to live and serve in the community. As we progress, you may choose to use either the classic terms or missional language. I continue to use both as we develop and illustrate the Vision Frame in the next chapter.

Putting the Pieces Together

We used an illustration of a jigsaw puzzle at the onset of Part Three as an aid to understanding how to develop the Vision Frame. The frame represents how your church views the future. It gives your team a shared reference point for all decision making, planning, and future talk. As the future develops, the work of leaders is like putting a jigsaw puzzle together.

These framing statements can and should be hammered out by responsible pastor-leaders in a given period of time. The order of development is dynamic, based on the history of the church and the presence of what we call existing vision equity—aspects of the Vision Frame that are currently alive and well articulated. Generally speaking, the development of the frame moves from Missional Mandate (^m*Mandate*) to Missional Motives (^m*Motives*) to Missional Map (^m*Map*) to Missional Marked Life (^m*Marks*).

The primary usefulness of the jigsaw puzzle picture is how Vision Proper inside the frame is differentiated from the frame itself. In our turn away from vision as statement toward vision as lifestyle, I am depositing Vision Proper in the realm of a living vocabulary that moves and turns and evolves over time, just like puzzle pieces in the hands of the puzzle builder. There are no simple answers with Vision Proper. The work is never completed; you cannot write a phrase that has a fifty-thousand-foot-altitude perspective and be done. Nor can you write a few eloquent paragraphs to frame, file away, and send to prospective staff.

Consequently, there is an ongoing dynamic tension among the four-sided frame and the Vision Proper inside the frame. To furnish perspective on what the process of frame building should feel like, there are two primary ways to falter. The first is by taking too long to put together the four outer edges. If significant progress cannot be made in multiple day sessions (over six months, for example) with leaders sitting around a table, something is wrong. But for Vision Proper inside the frame, the opposite dynamic is true; indeed, there is something wrong if you do this too fast. The goal is not to put a one-page vision on paper and be done but to keep the work of visioning in the daily flow of leadership. The four edges of the Vision Frame should be finished within six months, but Vision Proper takes a lifetime.

Keeping Vision Viral

Obviously the value of the Vision Frame is directly related to how well your words are crafted. When collaborating as a team on the Vision Frame, you will want to keep some rules for good articulation in mind. In my work with church leaders, I insist that we adhere to the "five C's" as our measure of success. The Vision Frame components must be *clear, concise, compelling, catalytic,* and *contextual*:

- Clear is measured by the Junior High Rule: Is our language clear enough that a twelve-year-old boy who has not been to church would understand it?
- Concise is measured by the One Breath Rule: Can any part of the Vision Frame be stated in one breath?
- Compelling is measured by the Resonance Rule: When the Vision Frame components are stated, does this make people want to say them again because they are delightful to hear?
- Catalytic is measured by the Actionability Rule: Does our terminology inherently remind the listener to act rather than define success as what professional ministers do?
- Contextual is measured by the Bouquet Rule: Do the words communicate biblical truth for the listener's time and place, thus going to the garden of the Word and arranging the perfect bouquet for our people?

If these five attributes are fused within the Vision Frame, amazing energy is released. People understand the vision because you have broken it down into meaningful bite-sized chunks. Credibility is enhanced by virtue of the fact that it is comprehensive without being overwhelming. Ownership is increased because it is portable; people can remember it, use it, and share it. It all funnels into an important reality: *the vision is contagious.*

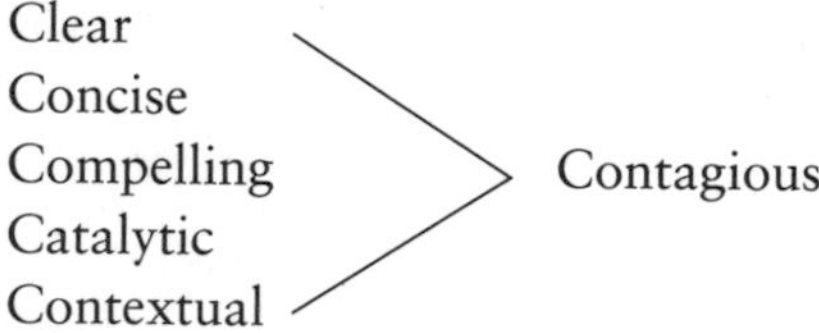

Missional leaders have agreed: we need a new language for evoking our imagination and forging a new identity for the church at large and for our individual Church Unique. The Vision Frame is the framework for missional clarity that equips you to create this new language.

Developing your Vision Frame is like finding that perfect set of cordless power tools at Home Depot with which you can build your ministry. Christ is our foundation. The Holy Spirit is our power source. The Word contains our blueprints. Our people are the living stones. How do these four come together each day as Christ builds his church? Through the visionary pastor-leader who shows up with a Vision Frame in hand. Guided by a stunningly unique, movement-oriented vision, saints collide with the Savior, the Spirit, and the Sacred Text. Jesus had a movement-oriented vision; with compelling and beautiful simplicity it can be captured in what I refer to as "red-letter vision." I use this to show how Jesus' words from the book of Mark could be easily fit into the Vision Frame.

RED-LETTER VISION FRAME: HOW JESUS ARTICULATED HIS VISION IN THE BOOK OF MARK

Missional Mandate

"For even the Son of Man came not to be served but to serve, and to give his life as a ransom for many." (Mark 10:45)

Missional Motives

- Submission ("Abba, Father, all things are possible for you. Remove this cup from me. Yet not what I will, but what you will." Mark 14:36)
- Focus ("Those who are well have no need of a physician; I came not to call the righteous, but sinners." Mark 2:17)
- Team ("Follow me and I will make you become fishers of men." Mark 1:17)
- Compassion ("Go home to your friends and tell them how much the Lord has done for you." Mark 5:19)

Missional Map

"And he called the twelve and began to send them out two by two. . . . 'Whenever you enter a house, stay there until you depart from there. And if any place will not receive you and will not listen to you, when you leave, shake off the dust that is on your feet as a testimony against them.' So they went out and proclaimed that people should repent. And they cast out many demons and anointed with oil many who were sick and healed them." (Mark 6:7–13) (See Figure 11.2.)

Measures as Life Marks

- Radical generosity ("With the measure you use, it will be measured to you, and still more will be added to you." Mark 4:24)

- Downward mobility ("If any would be first, he must be last and servant of all." (Mark 9:35)
- Personal purity ("If your eye causes you to sin, tear it out. It is better for you to enter the kingdom of God with one eye, than with two to be thrown into hell." Mark 9:47)
- Gospel intentionality ("Go into all the world and proclaim the gospel to all creation." Mark 16:15)

Vision Proper

"For whoever would save his life will lose it, but whoever loses his life for my sake and the gospel's will save it. For what does it profit a man to gain the whole world and forfeit his life?" (Mark 8:35–36)

"Truly I say to you, there is no one who has left house, or brothers, or sisters or mother or father or children or lands for my sake and for the gospel, who will not receive hundredfold now in this time." (Mark 10:29–30)

"But in those days, after the tribulation, the sun will be darkened and the moon will not give its light, and the stars will be falling from heaven, and the powers in the heavens will be shaken. And then they will see the Son of man coming in clouds with great power and glory. And then he will send out his angels and gather his elect from the four winds, from the ends of the earth to the ends of the heaven." (Mark 13:24–27)

Figure 11.2. Red-Letter Strategy

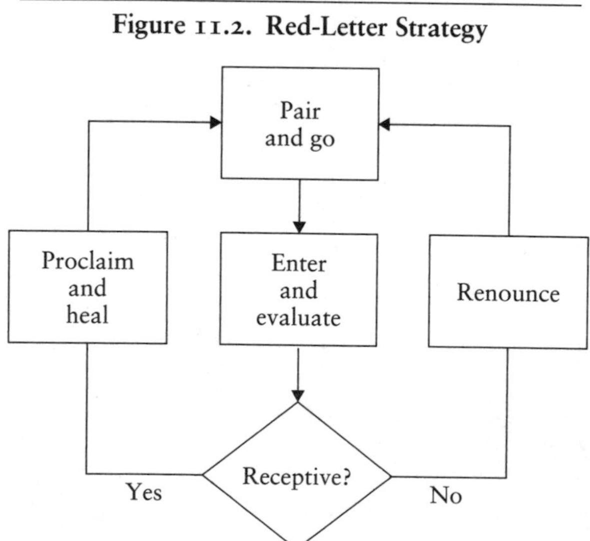

12

CARRY THE HOLY ORDERS

MISSION AS MISSIONAL MANDATE

My uncle once told me that during World War II if an unidentified soldier appeared suddenly in the dark and could not state his mission, he was automatically shot without question. I wonder what would happen if we reinstituted that policy today.

—Laurie Beth Jones

IS IT A STRETCH TO THINK THAT knowing our mission is a matter of life or death? I don't think so.

Being confronted with the need to know one's mission would force millions of us to reexamine who we are, and what we're really about. It would save immeasurable amounts of money, tears, and heartache. Casual church attendance would drop. Volunteerism would soar. Leaders of large churches, small churches, house churches, organic movements, church starts, and small groups would be forced to exchange rhetoric for real and meaningful action. People who linger in the shadows, leading unfulfilled lives, would burst into the sunlight of kingdom possibilities and Spirit's power. Those who have never known what it's like to feel a passionate commitment to a cause would be catapulted from their couches onto the playing field, tasting the dirt, feeling the sweat and the sting of tears, and having the wind knocked out of them . . . and in the process become fully alive.[1]

Leaders in today's church carry holy orders from Jesus. As his body, we must champion the cause of the kingdom, ruthlessly avoiding what

Reggie McNeal has described as "mission amnesia." The clarity and vitality of the saints that God has entrusted to your care depend on it.

Mission as Missional Mandate

The first side to our Vision Frame is the missional mandate (ᵐ*Mandate*; see Figure 12.1), defined as *a clear and concise statement that defines what the church is ultimately supposed to be doing*. The ᵐ*Mandate* answers "question zero"—the question before all other questions. Why do we exist? What is our raison d'être? The ᵐ*Mandate* is your church's compass and guiding North Star. As such, it provides direction and points everyone in that direction. The mission as ᵐ*Mandate* is like the heartbeat of the organization. It should touch members on an emotional level and act like a cohesive force and binding agent.

From a biblical perspective, the church's ᵐ*Mandate* is anchored in the "sentness" of Jesus Christ, reflected in the Great Commission as the church's sentness into the world. Our mission lives within the boundaries of making disciples, teaching personal obedience to Jesus as Lord, and taking the message of the gospel to the Nations (Matt. 28:19–20). This makes our Bouquet Rule (Chapter Eleven) critical. From the garden of God's timeless Word, we arrange a bouquet of truth—in this case the all-encompassing mission of Jesus—for our time and place. We don't invent from scratch but articulate from Scripture. How do you remind people in your particular church culture that they are sent from God as missionaries everywhere, and every day? What words do you use to enlarge their imagination and ignite their heart for a redemptive focus?

One amazing snapshot of the radical call to live as sent ones is found in John 20:19–22. In this postresurrection appearance, the disciples are gathered in fear ("On the evening of that first day of the week, when the disciples were together, with the doors locked for fear of the Jews"; v. 19). Sensing their trouble, Jesus tells them not just once but twice: "Peace

Figure 12.1. The Vision Frame: Mission as ᵐ*Mandate*

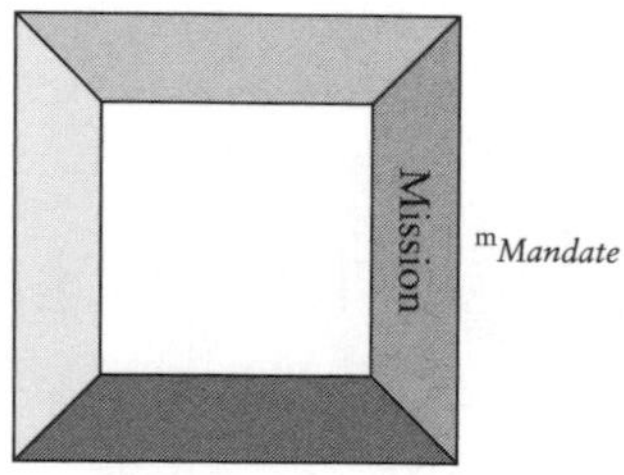

be with you" (vv. 19, 21). Then Jesus gets outrageous. Immediately after pronouncing peace, he declares, "As the Father has sent me, I am sending you." Can you imagine the disciples huddled up, doors triple-locked, windows barred, scared that any minute the bad guys will come crashing in? And Jesus comes in and basically says, "Guys, let's go out there and get 'em!" Note that his words of peace were not for comfort's sake; they were for *mission's* sake. This is one of the precious few times (John says there was only three appearances) the Lord spent with the disciples after his resurrection. We have few words in red ink. In these fleeting moments, we see the deepest desire of our Savior: that his redeemed flock would unlock their doors and latch their hearts to a lost and dying world. In this gospel cameo, we see *missio Dei* transmitted in pristine form. So again I ask what words you use to remind people that your church is sent. What is your ^{m}*Mandate?*

By describing the idea of mission as ^{m}*Mandate,* I am not encouraging a wholesale swap of terminology. Rather, I want to infuse clearer meaning in the often used language of mission. Therefore I use them interchangeably. What are the benefits? First, it allows the "missional" adjective to inform the church's understanding. Using the word *mission* itself may crack the door to be confused with "missions."^{m}*Mandate* more clearly subsumes everything that the church does as part of Christ's mission, not just our two-week service projects in the third world. Second, it is a personal word that connotes transfer of authority. The Latin literally means to give into one's hand. The image is of one passing the baton or of Jesus handing you holy orders. It is not just a piece of paper you carry but the authority of Christ himself, the King of Kings and the Lord of Lords (as he reminds us before pronouncing the Great Commission; Matt. 28:18). Third, the word *mandate* directly implies obedience or disobedience to our Lord's command. Sometimes when we describe "mission drift," the edge is taken off the reality of defiance. We can't slip into seeing our commission as a "Great Suggestion" (like the bumper sticker that says, "Jesus is coming; look busy"). Finally, the word mandate can be broken into the words "man" and "date." This breakdown, though totally arbitrary, is useful in that it reminds us that our time is limited and that God has set a date specifically for our lives ("teach us to number our days"; Psalm 90:12), and for mankind ("It is not for you to know the times and date the Father has set for his own authority"; Acts 1:7) So our ^{m}*Mandate* reminds us that mankind-on-earth is dated. As a leader you do have someone holding a gun to your head; the enemy is time. We don't have forever to make disciples as we take the gospel to every nook and cranny of the planet.

Stoking Redemptive Passion: Your Primary Growth Challenge

Jesus modeled an amazing redemptive passion in his earthly ministry. In Luke 9:51–55, we witness a pivotal moment. Luke the physician records that Jesus "set his face to go toward Jerusalem." This idiom, repeated twice, conveys the unwavering focus of a man on a mission, in this case a Savior with a destination. The emphasis is on Jesus' redemptive resolve to reach the cross. Nothing could stop him. In fact, the surrounding passage shows us that this redemptive passion offended the worship preferences of some (v. 53) and that his own disciples, his core group, were still suffering from mission drift (v. 54).

In discussing barriers to growth, most churches lose sight of the taproot issue: the redemptive passion of their people's hearts. Someone once said that a thousand people hack at the branches of evil for every one that hacks at the root. Turning the statement around for church growth, I would say there are a thousand who fertilize the branches for every one who fertilizes the root. When it comes to growth challenges, leaders jump too quickly to the branches: parking lots, seating capacity, finances, staff, and so on. But when God's people are deeply stirred with redemptive passion, the church becomes an unstoppable force, hurdling other barriers with ease. The question then becomes, What is keeping your people from strengthening their redemptive heartbeat?

I can't answer that question for your church. But the probability is that you don't have a mission, your ᵐ*Mandate*, designed to stoke redemptive passion. If your clear and concise mission does not wave an unmistakable evangelistic banner, nothing else will. Remember, it's question zero. It's the primary cue for your church's culture. As such, it will either guide a missional movement or validate a missions department.

To be an effective tool, the ᵐ*Mandate* must counteract the "gravity inward" of Christian fellowship. Dietrich Bonhoeffer said that the church is only the church when it exists for others. What keeps your church focused externally? Who do you think the most important person is to the Coca Cola company? The consumer? Which one? The coke drinker? Nope—it's actually the Pepsi drinker. Missional leaders need to polarize this same reality for their people. It should be clear that the most important people are those *outside* the church. Neil Cole sums it up well when he reminds believers, "If you want to reach people for Jesus, you're going to have to sit in the smoking section."[2]

Have you ever seen a warped plank? To straighten a board, you can't just put it in a frame to hold it straight. You have to put it in a frame that holds the wood bowed in the opposite direction. Likewise the ᵐ*Mandate* should keep the church mind-set bowed in the redemptive, outward direction, applying opposite force to inward tendencies and temptations. In a similar way, Bill Hybels encourages leaders to apply a disproportionately greater emphasis on evangelism at the beginning of the day in order to have a balanced church at the end.

The Golden Thread of Redemption

Think of the ^{m}*Mandate* as the golden thread of redemption that weaves its way through every activity in the organization. For example, Morgan Hill Bible Church's mission is "connecting the disconnected into a vital relationship with Jesus Christ." The golden thread means that whether you are leading a bible study, changing a baby's diaper, rehearsing for worship, standing in the grocery store checkout line, typing in your cubicle, or watching your son's soccer game, you are at that moment connecting the disconnected into a vital relationship with Jesus Christ. Mission is everywhere! When someone gets it for the first time, it is like throwing a giant electric switch whereby *everyone can be energized* by mission and *everything can organized* for mission. It is this electricity that enables the brick maker to do tedious work with tireless energy. The big picture of the beautiful cathedral stays alive in the mind's eye.

THE MISSION STATEMENTS OF YESTERDAY. The easiest way to embarrass a pastor is to ask him to tell you his mission statement. Most don't know it. Why? The average mission statement has these characteristics:

- Too long (twenty words or more)
- Too generic (all things to all people)
- Too technical (focuses on theological content and accuracy)

These attributes render most statements useless and irretrievable from the leader's conscious.

Let's use an older mission statement from one of my clients as an example. Here is their previous mission, which contains *seventy-seven words:*

> We exist for the purpose of fulfilling the Great Commission and the Great Commandment: Seeking to love God with all of our being and others as ourselves, we will strive to worship God together in peace and unity, share the Good News of salvation through Christ with our community and throughout the world, encourage individual Christian

> growth and service, and provide for the needs of individuals through social ministry as the Holy Spirit leads and gives power.

This mouthful kills memorableness and short-circuits cultural electricity. Statements like this end up framed and forgotten, for two primary reasons. First, the team that developed it didn't understand the "weight load" of a mission statement. A mission statement by its nature is a relatively small container. It's more like a serving tray than a three-quarter-ton pick-up. It is intended neither to carry a theological treatise nor to communicate strategy. It is a synthesis; therefore it communicates your big idea with a few small words. The greater the mission, the more simply it can be stated. The second reason this type of mission statement fades into obscurity is that too many people are involved in crafting it. Too many opinions lead to too many words and too many complex sentences. One time, the pastor of a large church shared proudly that eight hundred people worked through their visioning process. (I call a group this size a "conjunction factory.") After asking permission to put him on the spot, I asked him to tell me the resulting mission statement; two minutes later he was still stuttering.

Let's take a look at the same church's mission after a makeover—fifteen words. This statement surely has more clarity, more simplicity, and more impact:

> We exist to lead people into a life-changing, ever-growing relationship with Jesus Christ.

If your church has a current mission statement, does it resemble the one before or after the makeover?

THE MISSIONAL MANDATE OF TODAY. Every church needs a compass to set its bearing. As the missional church reorients identity to "be the church," certain characteristics are necessary. The ᵐ*Mandate* should:

- Remind the church that it exists primarily for those outside
- Eliminate an us-versus-them mentality with outsiders
- Emphasize the reality of "being the church" twenty-four, seven
- Reinforce the lifestyle of engaging in relationships and conversation with others
- Connote process for both evangelism and discipleship
- Highlight features of the Kingdom Concept

As your team carefully considers the words it uses to define the ᵐ*Mandate*, evaluate each term. Hold it up as a gem to the light, turning it to look for just the right nuance. Explore how the language reinforces or detracts from the bullet points given here. Remember, you are shooting for the five C's: clear, concise, compelling, catalytic, and contextual. This may sound like a tall order, but I have seen some remarkable articulations of a church's ᵐ*Mandate* capturing these ideas. Here are some good examples:

> Colonial Heights Baptist: "*Inviting everyday people to experience Christ in every way.*"
>
> Life Church, Portland: "*Guiding self-reliant people toward a Christ-centered lifestyle.*"
>
> Faithbridge United Methodist: "*To make more and stronger disciples of Christ by being a bridge of faith to people every day.*"
>
> First Presbyterian, San Antonio: "*Renewing minds and redeeming lives with the steadfast love of Jesus Christ.*"
>
> Bannockburn Baptist: "*Guiding generations to passionately follow Christ, one home at a time.*"
>
> Trinity Lutheran: "*Encouraging more life in Christ, one life at a time.*"
>
> Bandera Road Community Church: "*To lead people who are far from God to be fully devoted followers of Christ.*"
>
> Grace Point Church: "*To lead unsaved people into a relationship of full devotion to Jesus Christ.*"
>
> Westlake Hills Presbyterian: "*To invite people into God's larger story as we follow Christ together.*"
>
> Crozet Baptist Church: "*To encourage people in our ever-expanding community to follow Christ with ever-increasing passion.*"
>
> The MET: "*Connecting people each day to the real Jesus in a real way.*"

Capturing God's Mission to Be Captured by It

One irony of trying to capture God's mission in a meaningful ᵐ*Mandate* is that the mission ought to be continuously capturing us. This fact, by the way, should motivate you to spend adequate time in distilling just the right words. We want to state a mission that can perpetually nourish a sense of God's calling to us. This emphasizes our attribute of "compelling" (the Resonance Rule). Did you sense this dynamic when you read the statements just above? Milfred Minatrea highlights the largeness of the ^{m}*Mandate* when he writes:

> As author John Steinbeck was preparing to embark on a journey across the United States, he described the nature of the trip with these words: "We find after years of struggle that we do not take a trip; the trip takes us." Missional churches understand this statement. They have not chosen God's mission; God has chosen them for a missional purpose. The initiative for mission lies in God. Jesus said, "You did not choose me, but I chose you, and appointed you, that you should go and bear fruit" (John 15:16). The impetus for mission resides in Christ, who invites the church to become His missional body.[3]

Having raised the bar on articulating your mission as ^{m}*Mandate*, let's turn to some practical tips for developing your own.

BOIL DOWN YOUR CURRENT STATEMENT. Most churches have some form of mission statement. Don't read this chapter and just decide to chuck it. Better to look at what you have first and make it as clear and concise as possible by removing unnecessary elements. One you have boiled it down to purest form, run it through the five C's. Do this as a leadership team, and decide together whether you need to start from scratch, tweak the existing statement, or use the boiled-down statement as is.

START WITH THE A TO B STRUCTURE. To best capture the five C's in the shortest synthesis, I recommend trying the A to B structure. "State A" represents the people or the context to which the church is sent. "State B" represents what we are becoming as followers of Christ. The advantage of this framework is that it can communicate movement, incarnation, process, and completion with efficient use of words. Here are a few of the church missions that I listed previously broken into this format:

A	B
Everyday people	Christ in every way
Self-reliant	Christ-centered lifestyle
Far from God	Fully devoted follower
Ever-expanding community	Ever-increasing passion
Unsaved	Relationship of full devotion

The best way to experiment with this format is to brainstorm a list of ideas for state A and state B separately. After you are finished, compare the lists and look for any ideas that contrast meaningfully. Sometimes it is difficult to articulate state A explicitly; it can be left implicit. For example, the implied state A of "inviting people into God's larger story as we follow Christ together" is "small living." The tension between small living and God's larger story drives the identity and missional heartbeat of the church.

KEEP REVIEWING THE FIVE C'S. As the team collaborates, it is imperative that you have the five C's on a white board in front of you. As potential ideas arise, evaluate each statement with every C on a scale of one to five. Resist the temptation to evaluate a mission without referring to one of the C's. For example, one statement might be more clear and less compelling; another might have a catalytic punch to it even though it is not concise. Talk through the give-and-take of each C until you make your final decision (remember the 100–80 rule from Chapter Seven?).

Teaching for Practice, Not Knowledge

When I give my final exhortation to groups defining their ^{m}*Mandate*, I remind them that Jesus taught people to act; the emphasis was *practice* over *knowledge*. He did not discuss the ins and outs of forgiveness; he simply told them to forgive "up to seventy times seven." He didn't teach them a course on life-changing bible study; he commanded them to "feed my sheep." As Mark Twain said, "It is not what I don't know about the Bible that bothers me; it is what I know."

We will all stand before Jesus someday. As a leader, you will be held accountable for your words of guidance. I fear for pastors who lead as if Jesus will be giving out an IQ test that day. Taking our cue from the Savior, I believe it is clear that he will be measuring not how much we know but how well we loved. The test is not IQ but EKG; he will note the strength of redemptive passion in the people we led. We desperately need words that will move them into God's grand mission. The ^{m}*Mandate* that you articulate and lead from is your primary missional tool.

13

FEEL THE COMMON HEARTBEAT

VALUES AS MISSIONAL MOTIVES

You won't do ministry that really matters until you define what matters.

—Aubrey Malphurs

IN 1963, PRESIDENT JOHN F. KENNEDY articulated his vision for space exploration on behalf of freedom, peace, and democracy—and he challenged the nation to land a man on the moon within the decade. This amazing vision and subsequent accomplishment is a compelling picture of the need for values and the difference between having a clear mandate (the subject of our last chapter) and knowing the motives behind the mandate (the subject of this chapter). Kennedy's mandate was to put a man on the moon, to get a human being from point A (earth) to point B (moon). It couldn't be clearer. But within his overall Vision Frame, if you will, were important values. Which one was the clearest? Preservation of human life. Kennedy unmistakably embeds this value into the mission. The big idea was to get a man on the moon and return him safely.

If you remember the movie *Apollo 13*, you will recall the great edge-of-your-seat moments were about getting home safely. The NASA engineers who were working under fierce time restraints and with brilliant ingenuity pieced together off-the-cuff solutions to preserve human life. Imagine how much money the entire race for space could have saved if after that giant step for mankind we just turned off our monitors, celebrated, and wished our astronaut heroes farewell. That would be ludicrous. The nation's ownership in the mission was inextricably tied to its ownership in the value of life. The values, our ᵐ*Motives*, on the deepest level are those mission nonnegotiables, or as one pastor put it, the "die-fors"—things that we are ready and willing to die for. They represent what we are not willing to sacrifice in accomplishment of the mission.

We define these missional motives (ᵐ*Motives*) as *the shared convictions that guide the actions and reveal the strengths of the church*. They are the values that represent the conscious and collective soul of your church because they express your most deeply held ideals. They define your ministry's ethos. ᵐ*Motives* are filters for decision making and springboards for daily action. They are the constant reminder of what is most important to church.

Doing More of What You Do Best

A church without ᵐ*Motives* is like a river without banks—just a large puddle. It is missing an opportunity for white-water movement. As with any organization, your church has a set of shared motives, or values, underneath the surface of everyday activity. The problem is that they stay weak because they are unidentified and unharnessed in guiding the future. The role of the leader is to identify the most important values and pull them above the waterline of people's perception. Once they are in clear view, the leader can nurture their development, enabling the church to do more of what it does best. Once your people know and own the ᵐ*Motives*, it's like creating the banks of a river to channel energy and momentum.

Values as missional motives can be the most difficult aspect of the Vision Frame to grasp (see Figure 13.1). They differentiate any two churches that share many similarities such as size of staff, budget, facility, and denominational heritage. Given these likenesses, two churches would still have very different assumptions and commitments driving their ministry. Think of ᵐ*Motives* not as what we do but rather as what characterizes everything we do.

Figure 13.1. The Vision Frame: Values as ᵐ*Motives*

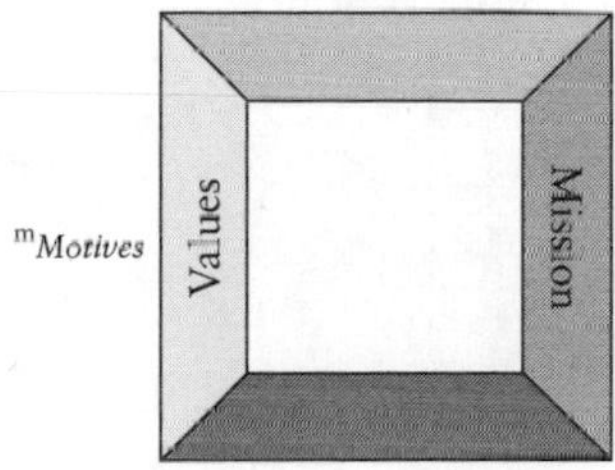

When your mMotives are clearly defined and adequately aligned, the benefits are numerous. You will:

- Define good decision making that releases leaders on the front line of ministry
- Demonstrate a God-honoring unity
- Attract more staff, leaders, and members who share your values
- Free the church to not do a lot of things that other churches may do
- Increase commitment because people know clearly what we stand for
- Enhance leadership credibility because everyone knows what's most important to the church as a whole
- Navigate change more easily because people are emotionally connected to the values that never change

Discovering Your Missional Motives

In uncovering the m*Motives* of the church, I bring together six inputs (Figure 13.2).

The first is a survey of the leaders. I do this early in the process in an attempt to catch input unfiltered and unbiased. The second is an exercise

Figure 13.2. Values Discovery

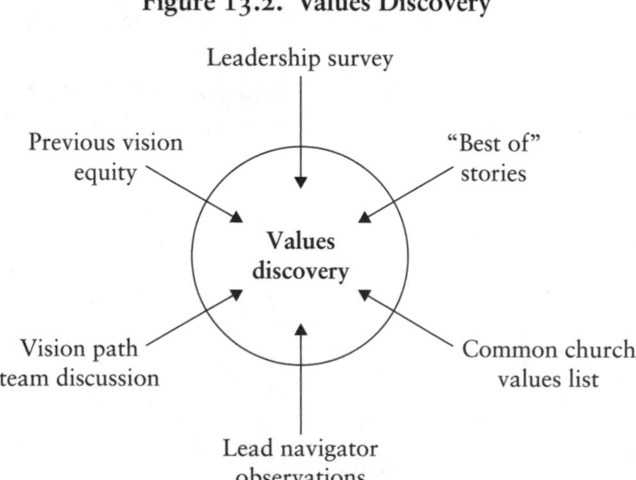

that looks at the hall of fame stories (discussed in Chapter Nine). The third is a list of the most common values from other churches. I use this to stimulate thoughts in the group after I have solicited their initial input. A fourth component is my perspective as an objective outsider; I can usually pick up on one or two defining values after a few meetings with a church. The fifth is the dynamic collaboration of the Vision Pathway team. I anticipate that through training, prayer, and vibrant discussion new things will come to the surface. Finally, I look at previous vision equity—what kinds of statements the church leaders have used in the past.

THE VALUES STATEMENT OF YESTERDAY. Through conferences and leadership training events, most pastors have been exposed to the idea of having values but don't experience the value of values. There are five reasons:

- Most values statements have too many values listed (more than six is too many—they can't be remembered).
- Values tend to be reactionary (saying what we are not rather than what we are).
- Values often present meaningless redundancy because they repeat doctrinal beliefs or rehash general purpose ideas, such as worship, evangelism, and fellowship (the latter fails to differentiate your church).
- Values aren't words crafted to be catalytic (they fail the Actionability Rule).
- The values don't represent reality and lose credibility.

It distresses me when I hear people say that they don't get the values. But when you look at how church values are articulated most of the time, it's easy to understand where the confusion comes in. Let's take a look at how to move values toward being ᵐ*Motives*.

THE MISSIONAL MOTIVES OF TODAY. You can take your values to a place of unprecedented freedom in expressing your Church Unique. ᵐ*Motives* are the most fluid component of the Vision Frame for your Kingdom Concept to be reflected. At the risk of sounding too harsh, I would say differentiate or don't exist. Your people deserve to know why your church is special, what God is doing uniquely through your leadership, and why they should sacrificially contribute. Your ᵐ*Motives* can push through to this exciting reality.

Be proactive, not reactive. The most common reactive values are "excellence" and "relevance." In effect, they say, "We are not like the all the dead and dying churches around." So what? Don't tell me that you are excellent or relevant; tell me *what makes you* excellent or relevant.

Guard your doctrine and free your values. Your doctrinal heritage is very important, but it doesn't necessarily need to be repeated as [m]*Motives*. Keep these statements separate so that your [m]*Motives* can express more nuance and ideas about why you do ministry in addition to the doctrine you believe.

Let your strengths shine through. The church is engaged in the battle for souls. If you were at war, wouldn't you want to know why you have a chance at victory? If you're on a team, don't you want to know the secret to a winning game? Of course you do, and so do people who attend your church. Let your [m]*Motives* reveal your strengths and instill a God-honoring confidence in your people. Tell them why your Church Unique is going to win the day. Inspire the attitudes and actions that harmonize with the collective potential.

Have some personality. Some churches are embarrassed by their uniqueness. Like an awkward adolescent, they gaze into the mirror wishing they had the features of everybody else. To adapt a phrase I heard from Max Lucado, your church can't be anything it wants to be, but it can be everything God wants it to be. Don't shy away from who you are; embrace and exploit it on behalf of your mission. One church expressed the value of "laughter: we promote an atmosphere of enjoyment and fun as a part of experiencing the life God offers."

In the end, identifying your deeply held values is like defining your team colors. A good friend of mine drives only maroon cars, as a Texas A&M grad. I met with a pastor yesterday who was proudly wearing his North Carolina blue. Imagine gearing up for the big game for a team that had no colors—nothing but white on white. That's what going to a church with no articulated [m]*Motives* feels like.

Shaping Culture with Missional Motives

As you clarify your deeply held values, they become tools for shaping culture only to the extent that they are captured and carried. Here are a few guidelines for multiplying and transmitting your [m]*Motives* while you lead.

Say More by Saying Less

Keep your ᵐ*Motives* set to a list of no more than six. Four is ideal. Any more, and people cannot remember them. If they can't remember them, the motives can't shape their action. If they can't remember them, they can't share them. Sure, your church values ten or eighteen or forty things you *could* list. But would you rather have a list of eighteen with a 2 percent retention rate, or a list of five with a 60 percent retention rate? Keep the top list the top list. What *most deeply* motivates you?

Live Before You Label, But Don't Forget to Label!

You can teach what you know, but you only reproduce what you are. ᵐ*Motives* cannot multiply without modeling. As a pastor, the best thing you can do is to create a culture of shared accountability where those at the top of the organization *live* the ᵐ*Motives*. For example, when I was on staff at Clear Creek Community Church the pastoral staff would discuss and pray weekly for the "people far from God" whom we were getting to know. I was expected to share weekly how I was intentionally investing in people's lives. Consequently, the racquetball court became my mission field. As a young pastor, my value for lost people was forged through the modeling of the senior pastor and through loving accountability.

But modeling must be enhanced with labeling. In other words, our deepest values must be interpreted so that they can be caught more readily by others. Labeling is being quick to define the values in action, whether in casual conversation or in a planned moment, worship programming, a formal evaluation, or moment of celebration. Leaders label best when the values not only saturate all forms of internal media but also initiate enough conversation that values become "copy room talk" with their people.

Demonstrate, and Demonstrate Again

The Actionability Rule is critical in communicating ᵐ*Motives*. Each is useful only to the extent that it stimulates new thoughts, priorities, attitudes, and behaviors in people. If the motive or value communicates an idea and not an actionable idea, it is a piece of deadwood. The best way to do this is to articulate a "demonstrated by" statement for each value. The statement answers the questions "What does the value really mean?" and "How does this value really make a difference?" and many times can be a long bullet list. It's a way to give your ᵐ*Motives* teeth. For example,

Gateway Community Church in Houston has this demonstrated-by statement in its value for lost people: "demonstrated by . . . intentionally focusing our time and resources toward the needs and interests of people outside of the church."

Sugar Creek Baptist developed a statement for their value of Mutual Respect as "demonstrated by going out of our way to listen, communicate, support, and celebrate one another, so that each person and their contribution in ministry is held in high regard."

Life Church in Portland has Acceptance as a value, with the imperative "We accept others because Christ has accepted us even when we didn't deserve it." The value is further explained with the statement "demonstrated by reordering our lives to build healthy, loving, and grace-filled relationships in every area of our lives including family, church, neighborhood, and work."

As a final example, at Auxano we use bullet points to show our demonstrated-by statement. Our first core value is Egoless Clarity, which is demonstrated by:

- Pursuing self-knowledge through intentional dialogue and ruthless self-evaluation
- Living from our strengths
- Embracing our limitations without excusing them
- Speaking the truth in love to our clients even if it risks our business relationship
- Believing that team process will produce better results when it would be easier to work alone
- Describing our clarity as a model and inspiration to others

Anchor in Reality But Create the Future

Some values are "realized"—that is, they are held deeply and widely in the organization's culture. Other values are "aspirational"; they define the reality we hope to create, not the one we have. The ratio of aspirational to realized values ought to be no more than one to three; there should be no more than two aspirational values in a set of six, or one in a set of four. When you have an aspirational value, be sure that you state it as such. You do not want your people second-guessing your ability to size up the situation, or perceiving that you are leading with rose-colored glasses. When you identify a value as aspirational, you are signaling to your people the kind of culture you want to nurture together.

By the way, it is easy for the leader to know which values are aspirational and which ones are realized. Just ask! Most of the time a group's consensus can shed significant light on the strength of a church's [m]*Motives*.

14

SHOW ME THE WAY

STRATEGY AS MISSIONAL MAP

Churches with a simple process for reaching and maturing people are expanding the kingdom. . . . Conversely, churches without a process or with a complicated process for making disciples are floundering. As a whole, cluttered and complex churches are not alive.

—Thom Rainer

IN 1999, THE U.S. MINT LAUNCHED AN INITIATIVE to develop the strategic thinking of its employees. The important meeting was limited to twenty-five people, who were invited to apply from any level within the organization. More than 150 employees applied. The twenty-five slots were filled not just with executives but also with production managers, accountants, and even a custodian. One of their assignments was to design a graphic that would show all of the steps going into making a coin, a complex process that only a few people understood from start to finish. Development of this simple little graphic led to dramatic results. As *Fast Company* magazine reports, "After the U.S. Mint retreat, the depiction of the coin-minting process was turned into posters that now hang in every Mint location. Just sharing that information allowed each Mint employee to see how his or her job related to the big picture—and how changes that they might make in their jobs could ripple through the rest of the process. The changes that employees themselves suggested over the next year helped the Mint increase production from twenty billion coins in 1999 to twenty-eight billion in 2000—without increasing the resources required to produce them."[1]

Strategy = Quantum Leap Clarity

The results at the U.S. Mint testify to the importance of having a clear map that shows how things get done. If you have a map, the effectiveness of your mission will go through the roof. For the mint it was a 40 percent increase of efficiency. Would you like to improve your assimilation process by that much in one year? Strategic clarity can birth a quantum leap in your ministry.

In 1999, Ken Werlein started Faithbridge United Methodist Church in Northwest Houston with a white-hot vision and clear strategy. Five years and a thousand people later, it came time to reclarify and refocus for the future. Was the secret to their future finding something new? No. The key was going back through the original Vision Pathway. The team spent seven months refining their Vision Frame together. They discussed at length how success had caused them to drift from their initial strategy. Like a busy household full of kids, they realized that more people, more staff, and lots of energetic ministry quickly led to cluttered ministry mind-set.

At a size when many churches begin to plateau, Faithbridge's attendance doubled over the next eighteen months. To what does Ken attribute the quantum leap in growth? He would tell you two primary things. The first factor was moving into a larger permanent building that seemed to legitimize their presence in the community. The second was regaining fundamental clarity on their strategy.

Defining Strategy as Missional Map

As we move to explore strategy as Missional Map (^{m}*Map*), keep in mind that 98 percent of churches in North America are not functioning with this piece of the Vision Frame. Many have some kind of expression for mission and values, but not for strategy. The absence of strategy, as I am defining it, is the number one cause of ineffectiveness in a *healthy* church. Note my qualification. By healthy, I mean that there is some foundation of spiritual unity in the church and trust among the leaders. Unfortunately, many churches think that being more effective is simply a matter of trying harder, being more obedient, or praying more. The battle belongs to the Lord, but the Lord also asks us to prepare the horse for battle. In other words, kingdom effectiveness and missional movement require more than spiritual unity; they require strategic clarity (see Figure 14.1).

The ^{m}*Map* is the piece of the Vision Frame that brings this crucial dimension (Figure 14.2). It is defined as *the process or picture that demonstrates how the church will accomplish its mandate on the broadest*

Figure 14.1. Missional Movement

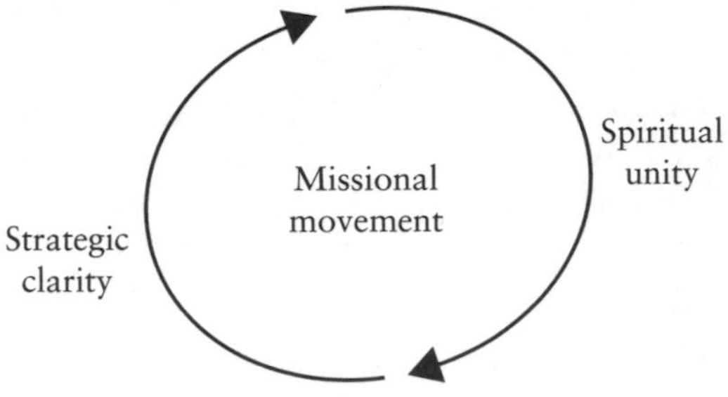

Figure 14.2. The Vision Frame: Strategy as ᵐ*Map*

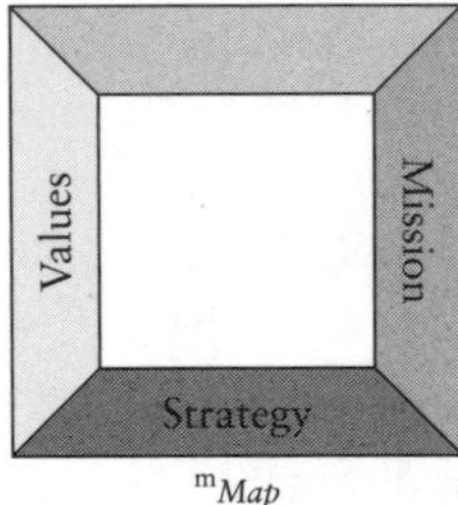

level. This map, or strategy picture, is like a container that holds all church activities in one meaningful whole. Without this orientation, individuals within the organization will forget how each major component or ministry activity fits into the mission.

The ᵐ*Map* can be described as:

- The church's organization logic for achieving the mission
- The pattern of how ministry fits together for fulfilling the mission
- The rhythm of church life as the body of Christ on mission

The word *map* implies that the strategy serves as both a locator and a guide. Think of the "you are here" map at the mall. It orients you in the middle of a three-level, one-hundred-store complex. Then it helps you find your way. The ᵐ*Map* does the same; it orients you in the complexity of a church environment and guides your next step. Keep in mind that about 50 percent of the people in our churches have never taken a step beyond the worship service itself.

Figure 14.3. Typical Church Brochure

No strategy = Meaningless ministries = Confusion about next steps

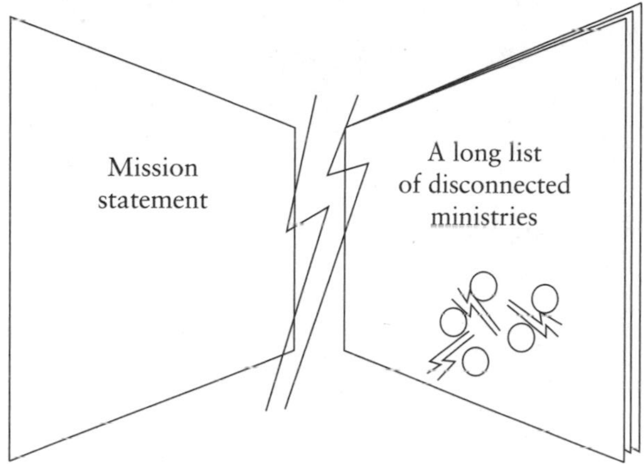

To clarify why churches need a strategy, imagine this scenario. You walk into a church you have never attended and pick up a guest brochure at a welcome center. On the inside flap you see a nice mission statement. Then on the next page (and the rest of the brochure) you see umpteen ministries, listed from A to double Z. As you stare at the brochure, a paralytic effect ensues. "What in the world do I do next?" you momentarily wonder. Then you choose to do nothing at all (Figure 14.3).

This guest scenario reveals a threefold problem for most churches that have no strategy or [m]*Map*. First, they have too many ministry or program options. Second, the ministry options have no relationship with one another. Finally, the ministries themselves have no connection to the mission—in fact, never the two shall meet. Another way to say it is that ministries have no *vertical* alignment with the mission and no *horizontal* alignment with each other. This creates complexity and confusion for people, which is hard for most pastors and ministry staff to appreciate. Individuals stay lost with regard to where they are and what to do next. For the average attender, ministries exist in a disconnected soup of meaningless activity.

With the [m]*Map*, your church has a much needed strategy bridge between the mission and all of the activities. The strategy becomes a powerful connector not only to the mission but for the individual ministries as well. In this connection, the ministries find their meaning and programs find their purpose. The relationship between ministries yields clarity for everyone, from staff to core leadership to members and to guests.

Figure 14.4. Church Brochure with [m]*Map*

Strategy = Meaningful ministries = Clarity about next steps

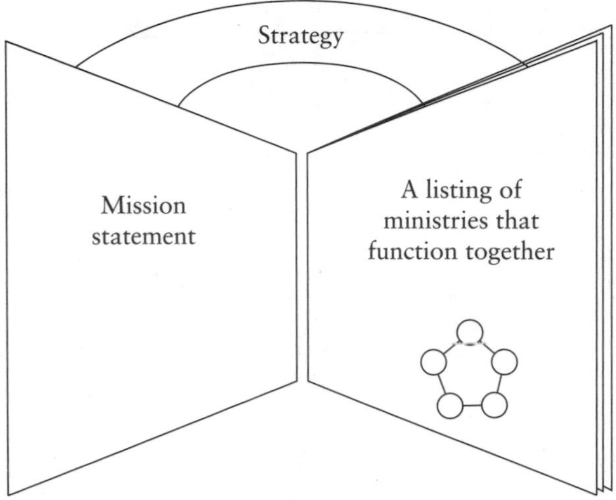

In the church culture, people are attuned and structure is aligned. Members know not only "why we exist" but "how we get there together." To go back to our guest scenario, the [m]*Map* brochure would show the newcomer a simple and obvious pathway of involvement (Figure 14.4).

The Good Samaritan and the "Bad" Martha

When I suggest that churches might have too many ministries, some grow concerned. When sharing the perspective of less is more, I picture one disagreeable saint who practically belched out, "Isn't it possible that doing less is actually just . . . doing less?" Yes, I suppose it is, but that misses the point.

Consider an interesting juxtaposition of stories in the gospel of Luke. In chapter 10, the familiar passage of the good Samaritan constitutes the quintessential snapshot of service—being a neighbor to the needy within one's sphere of influence. Right after this important teaching event, Jesus enters the home of Mary and Martha with his disciples. The two sisters respond to Jesus' presence differently. Mary sits and listens at Jesus' feet. But Martha is "distracted by all of the preparations that had to be made" (Luke 10:40). To make matters worse, Martha blurts out a complaint about Mary's passivity. But Jesus mildly rebukes her: "You are worried and upset about many things, but only one thing is needed. Mary has chosen the better. . . ."

So on the heels of the famous parable we see Jesus giving a corrective on pursuing service for service's sake. He ultimately defines *us*, not our "service to him." Is it possible that Luke brilliantly places these two stories side-by-side as if to say, "You had better spend your life ready and willing to serve" on the one hand and "you had better be careful not to be distracted in too much service" on the other? There are a lot of Martha churches out there, and defining your ᵐ*Map* will help you reduce the distractions of many things, even those "good things" that are enemy to the best.

Illustrating the Missional Map

Let's take a peek at Faithbridge's ᵐ*Map* to gain the benefit of an illustration before moving on. At Faithbridge the ᵐ*Map* has four components: three weekly time commitments held together by the lifestyle of "being a bridge of faith to people every day." The three time commitments are represented by three venues offered each week: (1) worship services, (2) grow groups, and (3) serve teams. These are the three standing invitations for church involvement and the church's simple process for making disciples. At Faithbridge, the people call this the strategy of "worship + 2." The ᵐ*Map* is represented by the icon in Figure 14.5.

This picture represents how the church accomplishes its mission on the broadest level—its operational logic and pattern for ministry. No program exists without some relationship to this strategy, and no guest or member encounters a random menu of programs without first seeing this ᵐ*Map*.

Figure 14.5. Faithbridge UMC ᵐ*Map* Icon

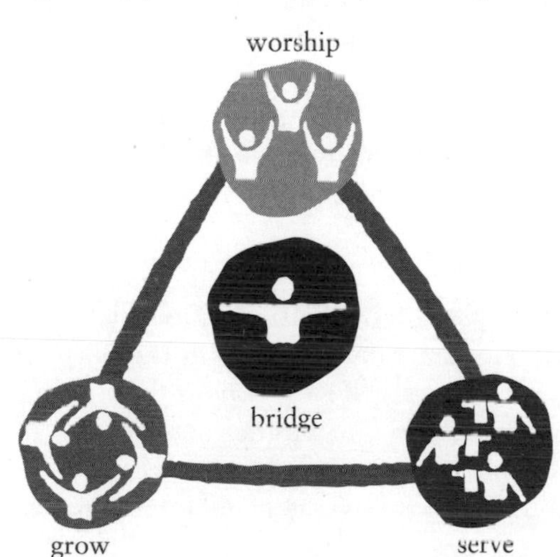

Simple Design Equals Vibrant Growth

Let's consider more fully the advantages of this critical piece in your Vision Frame. The ᵐ*Map* brings profound benefits to both the personal side and the organization side of your church's ministry. Think of it like two sides of the same coin. Each side has a corresponding benefit, "for me" and "for us." Using Faithbridge as an example, let's explore the benefits.

FEWER CHOICES FOR ME, SIMPLER STRUCTURE FOR US. Because the how of the mission is organized around a few highly developed ministries, the first benefit for people is that there are fewer choices. People no longer want endless options. A marketing test conducted recently gave people the option to purchase jellies from two sample platters in a grocery store. One sample platter had twenty-four samples and the other had six. The result? The tray with only six samples sold ten times more![2] One time I was developing the ᵐ*Map* for a church that had an executive chef in the Vision Pathway process. He was enthused about the process and understood the less-is-more philosophy. He told me, "In the restaurant business we have learned that the fewer specials you have, the more specials you sell." That is exactly what a strategy or ᵐ*Map* enables your Church Unique to do: serve up a few great ministry specials.

At Faithbridge, they serve three specials, and three specials only! The average church, however, offers five to twelve separate ministry opportunity invitations each week. One could easily burnout on a weekly diet of Sunday morning worship, Sunday afternoon life enrichment seminars, Tuesday night Bible study, Wednesday night rehearsal after the Wednesday night service, and Friday morning men's prayer breakfast.

The opportunity of fewer choices for the individual allows a correspondingly simpler organizational structure in the church. The work of organizing, staffing, and budgeting ministry becomes easier with fewer balls to juggle and less clutter in the closet.

CLEARER PATHWAY FOR ME, REAL SYNERGY FOR US. Fewer options is not about doing less in and of itself; it's about helping people develop relationally and with spiritual maturity in the body of Christ. But it doesn't happen automatically. Fewer options become meaningful when they exist in relationship to one another and show a clear pathway. In Faithbridge's example, you see a triangular pathway with multiple entry points. Worship is at the top of the triangle, representing the primary entry point.

The corresponding benefits to the staff are numerous, but all are rooted in the opportunity for real synergy. Ministry is no longer measured by "butts in seats in my ministry area" but by how people progress through the ᵐ*Map*. Because the pathway is clear, leadership teams share a common goal: they know what it means to score a touchdown together. For example, the Faithbridge small-groups pastor can celebrate when someone stops double dipping by attending two small groups and gets involved in a serve team instead. Another benefit to the leadership team is the ability to readily decide what fits and what doesn't. With a clear pathway, it is more obvious when programs or initiatives create a counterflow or distraction to the defined process. Likewise, the staff can continually experiment to create initiatives and events that enhance assimilation through the pathway. On this note, I salute the mantra initiated by Andy Stanley: "Think steps, not programs!"[3]

BETTER QUALITY FOR ME, FOCUSED ENERGY FOR US. The ᵐ*Map* allows the church to channel more resources in the form of time, money, creativity, prayer, and planning into the best ministry initiatives. The result is a better experience for all aspects of "life together." It is important not to read consumerism into the idea of quality. It is a quality of spiritual substance as much as it is clean restrooms and tight harmony. Is your teaching better with three sermons to prepare each week, or one? Do the worship team members experience meaningful community before they lead or not? Are you constantly worn out as a spiritual leader, or are you attending to your people with energy and passion? By *quality* I mean the quality of life Jesus referenced when he talked about "life to the full" (John 10:10).

With your ᵐ*Map*, the collective potential of your leadership is as effective as sunlight shining through a magnifying glass. What was mild and "effect-less" becomes concentrated and potent—even burning hot. At Faithbridge, leaders log many hours, not talking about philosophy of ministry issues and evaluating all kinds of new programs but in working toward improving their worship +2 strategy. They focus on doing more of what they do best.

MORE LIFE FOR ME, LESS ACTIVITY FOR US. For the individual, the ᵐ*Map* means more life—that is, more life change, and more life outside of church to be the church. In the end, the greatest argument for the ᵐ*Map* is that it frees people from overprogrammed environments to embody the life of Jesus in the world. When I left church staff to start consulting years ago, I stopped going to a Wednesday night service. Permanently. I am now a better dad and neighbor because I quit that habit.

The corresponding benefit for the staff and other church leaders is nothing short of sanity. Not all activity is progress; the blood, sweat, and tears of many pastors are the fuel of a church machine with little life-change output. Developing the ᵐ*Map* for your church is critical not just to leading but to living a life worth giving away to those who follow us.

ᵐMap, *Take Two (and Three, and Four)*

Here are a few more examples to inspire your own journey toward a unique ᵐ*Map*.

CALVARY BAPTIST, CLEARWATER, FLORIDA. Calvary's mission is "building relationships that bring people to dynamic life in Christ." In the Vision Pathway process, the team developed the ᵐ*Map* to show five components that describe the journey in accomplishing the mission. It is represented by the tagline "For life's journey." Each step has its own icon, and the overall ᵐ*Map* is referred to as "signs for life's journey" (see Figure 14.6).

Figure 14.6. Calvary Baptist ᵐ*Map* Icon

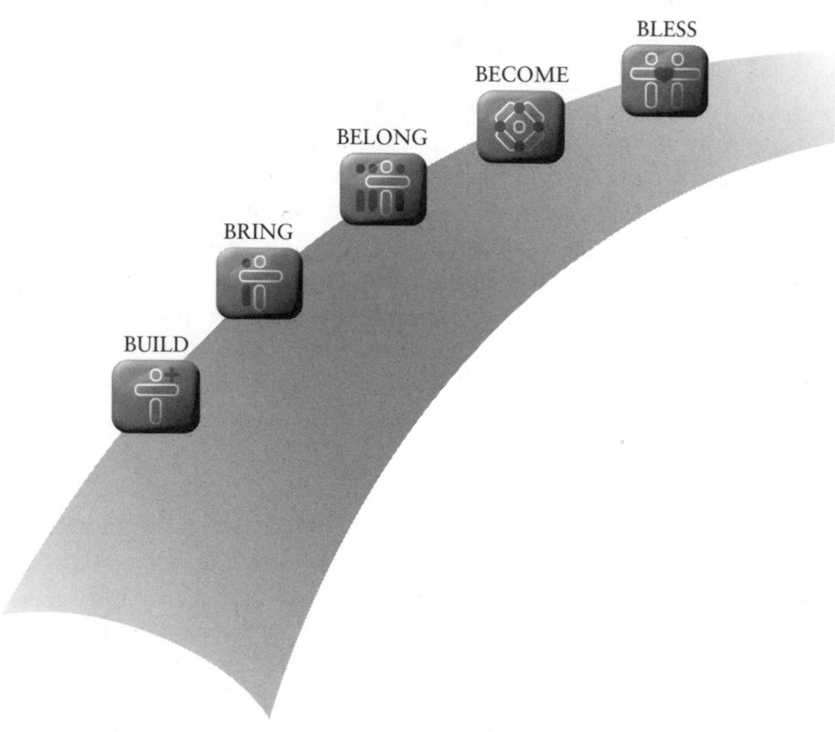

Here is the meaning of each step:

- *Build* means to build relationships. The icon represents always being willing to add someone to your life while being intentional for Christ.
- *Bring* represents bringing yourself and others to worship on weekends.
- *Belong* represents the life-groups component of the strategy (Calvary does on- and off-campus small groups).
- *Become* is the sequence of equipping seminars offered seasonally at the church; here we use the baseball diamond to represent a curriculum pathway.
- Finally, *bless* is the lifestyle of service both inside and outside the church.

Again, as with Faithbridge, everything at Calvary is connected to this clear ᵐ*Map*. Even the internal language is rooted in the strategy vocabulary. A grand opening was promoted as the "Big Bring." When the church launched off-campus small groups, they called it "Belong 2.0." One special initiative to serve the community was coined "Blessfest." By aligning their communication, the church helps keep everyone focused on the vision.

DISCOVERY CHURCH, ORLANDO, FLORIDA. When Discovery Church developed its ᵐ*Map*, the inspiration came from the metaphor of a home (developed before North Point's became popular) where new rooms represented new "discoveries" about Jesus. Their ᵐ*Mandate* is "to lead people to discover their home in Christ." As a media-savvy and innovative church, Discovery needed colorful and multiple graphic images to create a multifaceted communication approach that would help people understand their strategy (see Figure 14.7). The strategy unfolds as follows:

- The front door represents their weekend services.
- The family room is their small-group community.
- The kitchen represents ministry and volunteer teams.
- The study reminds people to encounter Jesus personally each day through prayer and bible study.
- The neighborhood icon reminds people to live intentionally for Christ where they live.

Figure 14.7. Discovery Church ᵐ*Map* Icon

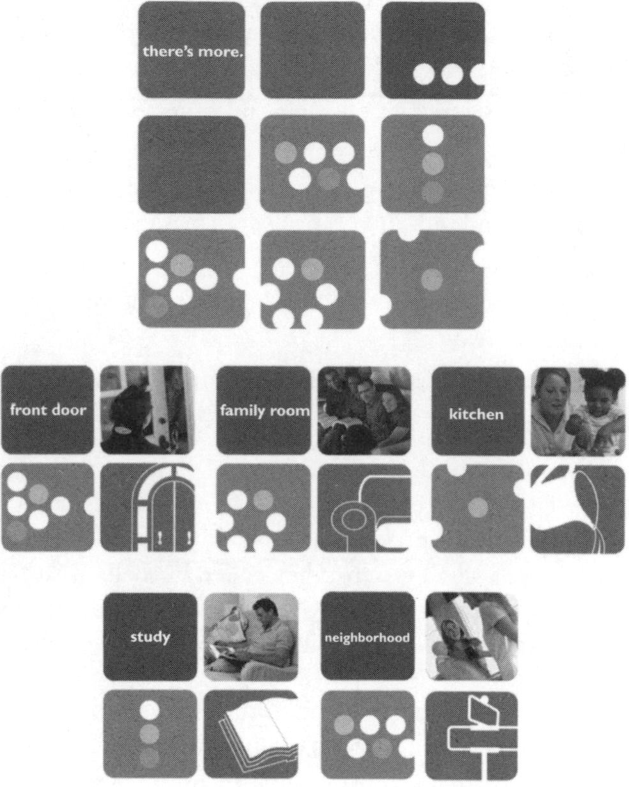

The first component is the use of dots to show connection to the logo (the mark of the upper right hand corner of the master icon). The three dots in the logo show an ellipsis; there is always something more to be discovered in Christ. The use of these dots for strategy components creates a playful, media-driven graphic that conceptualizes aspects of each component. The second component is a house graphic as an illustration to show visual connection to the specific part of the home. The third aspect of the interactive icon is the photographic style, which can also be used to show connection to the home.

FIRST PRESBYTERIAN CHURCH, HOUSTON. When First Presbyterian developed its ᵐ*Map*, missional emphasis was carried through the idea of a lifestyle of inviting (represented by the "*i*"), that is, inviting people to know Christ and experience the life he offers (Figure 14.8). This key

Figure 14.8. First Presbyterian Houston ᵐ*Map* Icon

step in the cycle of the ᵐ*Map* is the beginning and ending of everything the church does, indicating by a swoosh that begins and ends at the *i*. (The two parts of the swoosh come from their mission, which includes "engaging minds and guiding hearts.") The *w* represents worship, and the *g* represents "grow" in Sunday school, where components of teaching and fellowship come together in a traditional on-campus format. The *s* represents areas of service. Again, everything at First Presbyterian is connected to these four ᵐ*Map* components.

Every Church Needs a Strategy

Please note that having an ᵐ*Map* does not represent a certain way of being the church. Rather, it is simply being clear about how your Church Unique works. To illustrate, consider the differences in the four examples of this chapter (Table 14.1).

Strategy Development in Recent History

The history of churches that have a strategy is pretty short. Here are the five most notable checkpoints in development of the ᵐ*Map* or strategy as I have defined it.

Table 14.1. Four Unique ᵐ*Map* Structures

Church	Heritage	ᵐ*Map* Structure	Graphic Presentation
Faithbridge	Methodist	Mosaic	Organic, relational, literal icons
Calvary	Baptist	Linear	Clean, progressive, stylized icons
Discovery	Nondenominational	Interactive	Bold, innovative, conceptual icons
First Presbyterian	Presbyterian	Cyclical	Traditional, elegant, typographic icons

Rick Warren's Baseball Diamond

Popularized through the release of the 1995 book *The Purpose Driven Church*, many churches have "stepped up to the plate" and use the diamond. The diamond is ingeniously clear and offers a simple progression. With the missional orientation, however, two problems emerge: (1) the metaphor suggests running by yourself, which punts the value of community, and (2) when you cross home plate the implication is that you have scored—you're done. So much for discipleship as a process! The most unfortunate reality with the baseball diamond, however, is that nine of ten churches misuse it as a strategy by watering it down to be a curriculum pathway only. This is not how the diamond was intended to be used.

Bill Hybel's Seven-Step Strategy

The Willow Creek Community Church strategy was made popular through the increasing attendance at Willow's conferences, starting in the 1990s and continuing today. The first three steps of the strategy were "build a relationship with the unchurched," "share a verbal witness," and "invite to a seeker service." At their August 2007 Leadership Summit, they announced results of a significant study in a book titled *Reveal*, which exposed the need to revisit their strategy. The pivotal discovery is articulated as, "Involvement in church activities does not predict or drive long-term spiritual growth."[4] I appreciate the way Willow Creek has been transparent in sharing what they are learning. As they rethink their strategy, they admit freely that their vision for a new strategy is still developing. One observation that guides their current thinking is the desire to "move people from dependence on the church to a growing interdependent partnership with the church."[5]

Andy Stanley's Three Environments of the Home

North Point's strategy is popularized by its Catalyst and Drive conferences, which have gained momentum in the previous decade. The home metaphor is wonderfully relational and intuitive, following a three-step progression from foyer to living room to kitchen, to represent the kinds of ministry that people must encounter to be in a growing relationship with Christ.

Auxano's Consulting and Creative Team

In 2001, members of our team coined the term "strategy icon" and pioneered a process for development of the ᵐ*Map* for hundreds of churches across the country. Driven to help churches discover their own DNA, we embedded the ᵐ*Map* in our unique brand development process.

Thom Ranier's Simple Church

Published in 2006, this is the first book dedicated to the idea of having a clear, simple process for disciple making. Thom used his research base to confirm that "there is a highly significant relationship between a simple church design, and the growth and vitality of the local church."[6] I am delighted that Thom heralds a message so many need to hear.

Summing It Up: Wal-Mart, or Starbucks?

Both Wal-Mart and Starbucks are supersuccess retailers in North America. Wal-Mart attracts people because of how many low-priced products it can cram on the shelf. Starbucks attracts people because it does one thing well: serving coffee in the people business. In fact, quality is so important to Starbucks that their stores don't have microwaves even though they serve hot beverage.

Is your church a Wal-Mart or a Starbucks? Does your church exist to put as many programs on the shelves as possible, in hopes that more people will come? Or is your church a Starbucks, providing a stunningly clear, quality process for missional living that makes disciples? Before leaving this chapter, remember this defining principle: *programs don't attract people; people attract people.*

Table 14.2. Benefits of the ᵐ*Map*

Church Without a Strategy (More Is More; Wal-Mart Approach)	Church with Strategy (Less Is More; Starbucks Approach)
Churches are stuck thinking that more programs means more ministry	The ᵐ*Map* shows how to accomplish the mission with a few right ministries
Churches are deceived by the myth that people want more choices	The ᵐ*Map* clarifies a simple pathway of involvement
Churches inadvertently think that time at church equals spiritual maturity	The ᵐ*Map* limits and stewards time "at church" to release people to "be the church"
Churches can't say no to their people's ideas even when the ideas are ineffective	The ᵐ*Map* filters which ideas fit best and which ones don't fit
Churches allow an immature knowledge-centered spirituality to dictate program offerings	The ᵐ*Map* presents and guides people through a balanced process of discipleship
Churches make religious consumers	Churches make Christ followers

There is real beauty in clarifying, focusing, and strengthening the ministries as defined by your ᵐ*Map*; the people who are growing in the process will take other people along with them (Table 14.2). Growing people grow people. Consuming people consume programs. We cannot miss the way of Jesus in this regard. At the end of the Christian era, we cannot expect a Wal-Mart approach to have sustained viability. With a strategy or ᵐ*Map*, your church can develop its unique approach to growing disciples.

15

TALK THE WALK

MEASURES AS MISSIONAL LIFE MARKS

The true measures of a church are not "how many" but "how loving," not "how relevant" but "how real."

—Robert Lewis

MATT EMMONS WAS ONE TRIGGER PULL away from winning his second gold medal at the 2004 Olympics. In the lead position of the fifty-meter, three-position rifle competition, Emmons was so far ahead that his last bullet needed only to hit the target—anywhere. With unwavering calm and unbelievable precision, he fired his bullet and watched it pierce yet another bull's-eye. But a few seconds passed, and no score lights appeared on the board. When three red-jacketed officials approached, Emmons was sure that the scoreboard was just broken. But it wasn't. He was in shock, when the officials informed him that he had hit the wrong target. While standing in lane two, he had fired at the target in lane three. That day, the officials awarded him a zero, and Emmons didn't even place in the competition.

Cross-Firing Ministries

Though extremely rare in elite competition, there is a technical term for hitting the wrong target: "cross firing." Unfortunately, cross firing in a different way is all too common in our churches today. Why do I say this? Imagine that you are sitting in front of five or six people at your church. They may be elders, council members, volunteer leaders, or members of your small group. For the sake of our illustration, imagine that these people are paid staff at the church. Then you ask them the simple question, "What ministry bull's-eye are you all aiming at together?" Every week I see blank stares when I ask this question. Or if the staff does attempt an answer, the bull's-eye descriptions are never the same. In other words, it is almost impossible for me to walk into a church where the top leaders have a shared articulation of what results they are looking for. What happened to Emmons is happening right now in tens of thousands of churches in North America: well meaning leaders are shooting across lanes at other targets. I wish I could report it differently. Lord help us!

Measures as Missional Life Marks

Thus far, we have discussed three components of the Vision Frame: mission, values, and strategy. The question I now want to pose is, How do you know when all of these components are working as they should? In other words, when do you hit the bull's-eye? The answer introduces the fourth piece: Measures as the Missional Life Marks, or ᵐ*Marks* for short (Figures 15.1 and 15.2).

We define ᵐ*Marks* as *a set of attributes in an individual's life that define or reflect the accomplishment of the church's mission*. The ᵐ*Marks* are the church's portrait of a disciple and definition of spiritual maturity. ᵐ*Marks* supply the standard by which the mission can be measured with respect to an individual's development through the ministry of the church.

The old maxim goes, "Your mission is what you measure." As discussed earlier, every church feels the gravitation pull to measure only the ABC's (attendance, buildings, and cash). The problem is that you can be very successful with the ABC's but be a circus. So what measures are appropriate for kingdom-minded leaders in the missional church? By defining ᵐ*Marks* as your measures, you can focus your church on the

Figure 15.1. The Vision Frame: Measures as ᵐ*Marks*

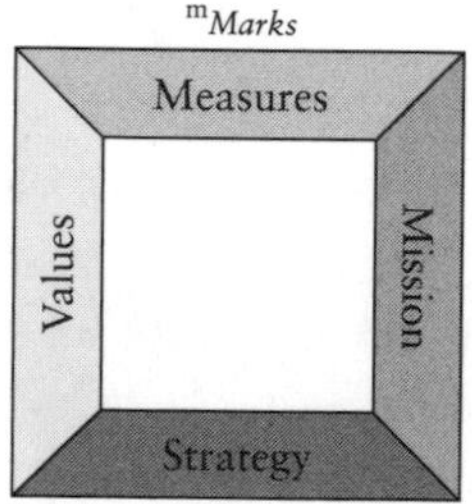

Figure 15.2. Hitting the Bull's-Eye

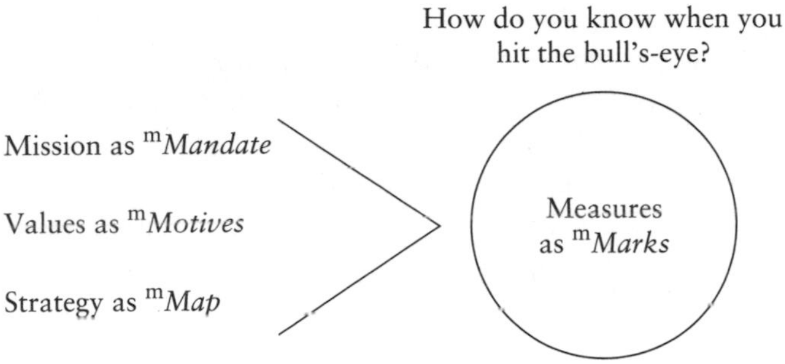

How do you know when you hit the bull's-eye?

Mission as ᵐ*Mandate*

Values as ᵐ*Motives*

Strategy as ᵐ*Map*

Measures as ᵐ*Marks*

Spirit's work of soul formation, and Jesus' agenda for multiplication. When a young leader in Austin was exposed to the ᵐ*Marks* in our visioning process, he was relieved beyond belief. He shared that his primary hesitancy to enter the ministry was from the broken metrics of his past church experiences. He was visibly thrilled that the leadership team was behind the ᵐ*Marks* that we crafted.

What Kind of Christian Is Your Church Designed to Produce?

Several leading pastors offer a glimpse into the value of ᵐ*Marks*. One is Randy Pope of Perimeter Church in Atlanta. As Randy chronicles his journey, he shares the problem of having a mission (ᵐ*Mandate*) and a process (ᵐ*Map*) but no "clear ideal." As you read his words, keep in mind that his vision uses the metaphor of a safe home; therefore, he refers to his congregation as "residents." Randy writes:

> They [leaders in the church] asked a revealing question: So if you are faithful to all of the guidelines of a church "safe home," what kind of residents do you expect to develop as a result? The variety of answers we gave only proved one thing—we had a lot of ideas, but no clear ideal. We had never clearly identified what the residents of our safe home should in time ideally look like. We were throwing around terms such as *trained disciples, mature believers,* and *equipped Christians*, but had no agreed-upon description for such persons. What kind of Christian was Perimeter designed to produce? I can think of few healthier exercises in our church's life than when we wrestled with the issue and developed a working definition.[1]

Randy Frazee addresses the subject as well, saying, "We must adopt from the ancient church and redefine for the postmodern church what a follower of Christ looks like. . . . Whatever the model of spiritual formation, it should be promoted by the spiritual authority of the church, it should be taught at all levels, it should form a common language by which the people of the community speak to one another, and it should be the benchmark against which we examine our lives as an individual and a community."[2]

For Perimeter Church, their ᵐ*Marks* are the "clear ideal" and the working definition of a disciple. For Pantego Bible Church, their ᵐ*Marks* are the "common language of the people" that serve as benchmarks for examination. These two very different churches share the conviction that the local church must clarify its bull's-eye—the attributes of an individual that reflect accomplishment of the mission.

Simple Concept, Missing Practice

Although the ᵐ*Marks* is a straightforward and simple definition for pastors, it's strangely missing in our churches. On a typical leadership team, most people could scratch out a basic definition of a disciple within five minutes. Yet years and years go by without ministry staff ever having a shared definition to work from. I see four reasons for this. First, planning and vision models have not emphasized it. Second, because we traffic in teaching so much we miss the need for it. Third, once a team sees the need for a shared set of ᵐ*Marks*, it can be extremely difficult to forge. Fourth, some pastors resist accountability. Let's examine each of these reasons further.

VISION AND PLANNING MODELS HAVE NOT EMPHASIZED IT. The best corporate vision gurus build models that are helpful, but not complete for the church. The desired outcome of life change is more elusive than "six-sigma" on the Motorola assembly line, on-time delivery for FedEx, and the customer-service-smile of a Southwest Airlines flight attendant. These are important measures no doubt, but how do we get our leadership minds around something more mysterious, like the Holy Spirit giving Bob a deepening hunger for Scripture, or convincing Betty that her overeating is idolatrous? Many vision models stop after identifying mission, values, and vision. Jim Collins's popular concept BHAG (big, hairy, audacious goals) is a helpful mind-stretching idea for leaders, but it is hardly useful to capture the outcomes of spiritual formation. Many writers in the ministry category have missed it as well. I have dozens of ministry books on vision that won't take you there. A few are beginning to do so. Aubrey Malphurs has recently added a "maturity matrix" to his work on strategy that brings in a concept like the ᵐ*Marks*. In *The Present Future,* Reggie McNeal touches on it with emphasis on "results" as an addition to his list, which includes mission, vision, and values. He writes: "I am convinced that the reason for so much burnout, lack of commitment, and low performance in our churches among staff and members is directly related to the failure to declare the results we are after. We don't know when we are winning."[3]

WE ARE SO BUSY TEACHING WE DON'T REALIZE IT'S MISSING. The classic syndrome of missing the forest for the trees is a massive problem. In fact, it is significant enough to have drawn the attention of George Barna, who articulates the problem lucidly. Listen to his description of the top three reasons that churches are unsuccessful at making disciples today:

- Few churches or Christians have a clear and measurable definition of spiritual success.
- We have defined discipleship as "head knowledge" rather than complete transformation.
- We have chosen to teach people in random, rather than systematic, ways.[4]

I have reflected on his third observation for years and have been stunned by its piercing accuracy. Our failure to offer a basic framework of spiritual formation has left people awash in fragments of spiritual truth, missing an integrated vision for following Christ. A personal story illustrates the point. I was walking out of McDonald's with my five-year-old daughter, Abby. She had one of those kiddy-size orange drinks in her hand. As we walked out the door, her concerned little eyes glanced up as she asked an important question: "Dad, can I put my cup in the drink spot when we get to your car?" Just as Abby needed a drink spot, people in our churches need a holder for truth in their mind, so they can integrate it into their lives. People need the "truth spots" that the ᵐ*Marks* create. Barna continues his description with a penetrating explanation of why churches need a tool like ᵐ*Marks*:

> As we survey the practices of churches across the country, we find that most churches are content to provide their people with biblical substance. The problem is not that the content itself is bad, but that the content is not presented in a purposeful and systematic manner. The result is that believers are exposed to good information without context and thus lose that information because they have no way of making sense of it within the bigger picture of faith and life. Consequently

> we rate sermons on their value to what we're experiencing at the moment, or assess the usefulness of books and lessons in terms of how entertaining or erudite they are. Ultimately, believers become well versed in knowing characters, stories, ideas, and verses from the Bible, but remain clueless to the importance of each.
>
> Think of the way we teach people about Christianity as a massive game of "Connect the Dots." The problem is, in our version of the game, we do not put numbers next to the dots. . . . We push everyone through the same generic journey, expecting everyone to "get it" at the same time and in the same way, simultaneously developing into mature believers. It doesn't work that away. Until we assume a more strategic approach to delivering insights and outcomes within a viable mental and experiential framework we will continue to be frustrated by the results of our well-intentioned but poorly conceptualized efforts to grow disciples.[5]

The ^{m}*Marks* become the mental framework for people to catch and digest truth. Think of this as a net, matrix, or grid inside the head that prevents teaching from going in one ear and out the other. Your mission measurements as ^{m}*Marks* are an antidote to the three challenges noted by Barna and listed above; first, they create the definition of a disciple, second, they correct a knowledge-centered spirituality, and third, they constitute the foundation for systematic teaching.

IT'S DIFFICULT TO FORGE A SHARED DEFINITION. In the last decade, I have worked with hundreds of teams through this process. Remember that we are looking for a simplicity on the other side of complexity that requires walking through the tunnel of chaos. Remember that Randy Pope, as I mentioned earlier, referred to it as wrestling. A shared definition of a follower of Christ takes blood, sweat, and tears to develop. It also takes a lot of egoless clarity. One exhortation I often give leaders is that they don't have the right to invent their own language with every initiative or every ministry department. There is too much at stake. Even a small church has so much communication complexity that people won't catch the measures if the language is not clear and aligned. In fact, it takes consistent use of the same language over three years for the culture to be affected. If various team members change the language, they are always resetting the three-year counter back to zero.

SOME LEADERS DON'T WANT THE ACCOUNTABILITY. With all of the benefits of having ^{m}*Marks*, some leaders would prefer not to have a bull's-eye.

It may be too painful if they miss, or just be too scary to know that someone is watching. These leaders' unspoken metrics are how many criticisms they can avoid, or how many days they can get home early without disrupting the status quo. How do leaders get to this point? My guess is that it stems from one of four sources: their own insecurity, strong wiring as a peacemaker and harmonizer, inherent doubt about the methods or tools they are using, or just low emotional energy.

Widely Used ^{m}*Marks*

In your Christian journey, you have probably run into numerous "portraits of a disciple." There are a few that I have found to be prominent. The first is the Navigator's Wheel. As a parachurch ministry with a military background, the Navigator's ministry has been marked by emphasis on one-on-one discipleship and personal discipline. To transmit their understanding of the Christian life, they use a wheel diagram (Figure 15.3). The strength of the diagram is its simplicity, with an engaging teaching point that "when the wheel is in motion, you don't see the spokes; you see Christ at the center."

But for church leaders, the wheel leaves a few things to be desired. What about worship, service, or stewardship—vital elements to a local gathering of believers? So church leaders have made appropriate modifications. Leading the way is Willow Creek's five G's statement. (I have seen this statement modified or adopted more than any other even though Willow Creek technically stopped using it even before the study was published in *Reveal*.) The five

Figure 15.3. The Navigator's Wheel

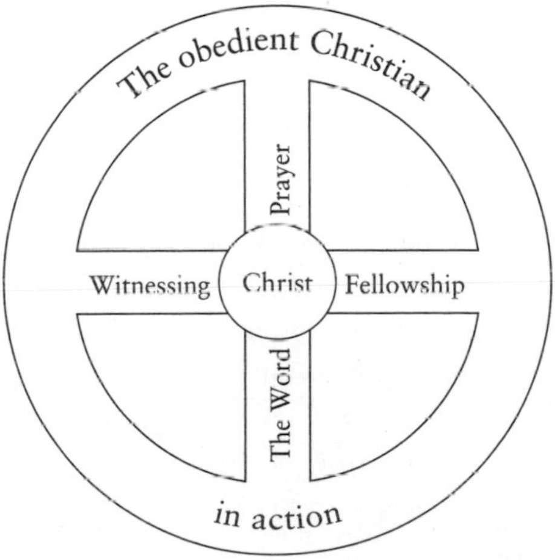

G's answer the question, "What does a fully devoted follower look like?" Here are the G's (my summary, not theirs):

- Grace: Refers to both receiving grace and being a person of grace
- Growth: Speaks to the disciplines of personal spiritual growth
- Groups: Refers to the practice of gathering in larger and smaller group settings
- Gifts: Means using your spiritual gift for the edification of the body
- Good stewardship: Highlights the giving of your time, talent, and treasures

Another example of [m]*Marks* is the set used by Fellowship Bible Church in Little Rock, Arkansas. They have developed the characteristics of a life of "irresistible influence":

- Passionately committed to Jesus Christ (a heart for God)
- Biblically measured (everything by the Book)
- Morally pure (in a morally compromised age)
- Family-centered (healthy homes are a priority)
- Evangelistically bold (willing and confident in sharing one's faith)
- Socially responsible (the community around us is our business)

A final perspective, developed by Pantego Bible Church, is more comprehensive. The church uses "30 core competencies" that are found in their "Christian Life Profile." The competencies are listed in Table 15.1 as three sets of ten core beliefs, core practices, and core virtues.

Table 15.1. Thirty Core Competencies

10 Core Beliefs	10 Core Practices	10 Core Virtues
Trinity	Worship	Joy
Salvation by grace	Prayer	Peace
Authority of the Bible	Bible study	Self-control
Personal God	Single-mindedness	Humility
Identity in Christ	Spiritual gifts	Love
Church	Biblical community	Patience
Humanity	Give away my time	Faithfulness
Compassion	Give away my money	Kindness and goodness
Eternity	Give away my faith	Gentleness
Stewardship	Give away my life	Hope

These examples from four strong, but differing, ministries are helpful reference points as you think about your own spiritual journey. Refer back to them as you walk the path of developing your own.

Developing ᵐ*Marks*

As with all of the components of the Vision Frame, I hope you are getting the feeling that you wouldn't want to lead another day in the church without nailing this down. When I share the Vision Frame and build the ᵐ*Marks* with mission, values, and strategy, the lights start coming on for many. In particular, strategy and measures as life marks are welcome discoveries that most leaders are missing. Of course, it does take some time to see how all the parts of the frame work together.

Leading with your own Missional Life Marks requires you to take some important steps to *articulate* and *saturate* before you can actually *enculturate*. Let's walk through the first step, articulate.

Articulating Your ᵐMarks

Articulating your ᵐ*Marks* requires four basic steps. First you will want to make sure you understand the difference between your ᵐ*Marks* and your ᵐ*Map* (between measures and strategy). Second, you build the content of your ᵐ*Marks* as a top-level outline with participation from leaders. Third, you refine the articulation to be based on your unique vision. Fourth you'll want to build out the subpoints of your ᵐ*Marks*.

KNOW THE DIFFERENCE BETWEEN ᴹ*MARKS* AND ᴹ*MAP*. Now that we are into the fourth part of the Vision Frame, it is important to distinguish the components and know how they work together. To use a simple analogy, think of a paint company. Years ago, I had a job in a company that produced paint. When we made the paint, we would use three large 2,000-gallon kettles for cooking and mixing. Then we had a quality control lab check the paint on a six-point checklist: the paint's viscosity, color, gloss, dry time, and so on. How we made the paint (three kettles) and how we validated good paint (QC lab) represent the difference between strategy (ᵐ*Map)* and measure (ᵐ*Marks*). When clarifying the difference with leaders, I also use a fictitious member named Joe Grow. We would say that the ᵐ*Map* is where Joe *goes* and the ᵐ*Marks* are what Joe *becomes*. Using churchspeak, we would say that the ᵐ*Map* is about assimilation into the organization and the ᵐ*Marks* are about spiritual formation for the individual.

Table 15.2. Differences Between ᵐ*Map* and ᵐ*Marks*

ᵐ*Map*	ᵐ*Marks*
Strategy	Measure
Three kettles	QC lab
Organization	Individual
Venues	Virtues
Assimilation	Spiritual formation
Where Joe Grow goes	What Joe Grow becomes

Table 15.2 summarizes the differences between the ᵐ*Map* and the ᵐ*Marks*.

We have not broached the subject yet that the obvious test of the ᵐ*Map* is if it is producing the ᵐ*Marks* for the people in the process. At the paint factory, we could not tell the customer that the paint was good just because it went into the three kettles; it had to be validated! Think about your leadership for a moment. Will it be enough to stand before Jesus and say, "We accomplished your mission" just by pointing to attendance at worship and small groups? Or will you have something more to validate the fruit of your mission? With the distinction of the ᵐ*Marks* clear, let's go to the next step.

DETERMINE THE TOP-LEVEL OUTLINE OF YOUR ᴹ*MARKS*. I recommend that teams create four to six categories as the outline of their ᵐ*Marks*. More than six will be difficult for people to remember. To stimulate creative juices, I use several exercises, available in a tool called the Vision Deck (visiondeck.com). Here is a sample of ideas to get you started:

- *Mission man:* Have small groups of leaders draw a stick figure on a large white pad. Using parts of the body as a creative spark, develop a list of the attributes of a disciple that corresponds to the body part.
- *Red-letter maturity:* Have groups scan the red letters of the gospel—the words that Jesus spoke directly. Organize them into no more than six categories that describe a mature follower of Christ.
- *Missional interviews:* Bring in three to five people who represent the most missionally minded people in your church. Talk to them about their story and life practices of following Christ. Ask them to list the six most important characteristics of their walk with

Jesus. See how their individual lists compare and from them develop your own.

Obviously, these exercises are meant to stimulate the expression of biblical foundations already present on the leadership team. For a more thorough treatment, find books and Bible studies to work through together. Of course you can always study the mMarks of other churches like those in this chapter. But don't get too preoccupied with the expressions of others. Do the hard work of your own process! At this stage of the process your focus should be on content—what are the most important four to six ideas you want to use to describe the missional life. With the next step, we will focus on how you *say* it.

REFINE THE ARTICULATION ON THE BASIS OF YOUR UNIQUENESS. Now make sure that you capture your culture and allow your Kingdom Concept to drip through. How can the m*Marks* be best communicated to your people? What aspects of your Kingdom Concept can be nuanced into it? They may be stated as alliteration, questions, poetry, or simple one-word bullet points. Here are a trio of examples:

Story metaphor One church used the idea of roles in the story of redemption to drive its m*Marks*. Living into God's larger story means living the four key roles as Christ-followers: the Beloved, knowing and embracing your identity in Christ; the Companion, walking in accountability with others on the pilgrimage of faith; the Servant, adopting the mind-set of concern and practice of care for others; and the Ambassador, representing Jesus to the world through words and actions.

Poetic expression A simple acronym wouldn't fly for the culture of First Presbyterian Houston. Through the process, they coined memorable phrases that can be used independently or woven together:

Worship beyond Sunday
Study and pray each day
Connect for accountability
Serve and give generously
Invest and invite to show the way

The expression answers the question, "What does a life-changing relationship with God look like?"

Kingdom Concept–focused Hope Baptist church is focused on reaching the Nations and leveraging the work of God in Las

Vegas to that end. In their ᵐ*Marks*, they chose to emphasize this Kingdom Concept with an explicit reference to the Nations. Their ᵐ*Marks* answer the question, "What does it look like to live the life of a Jesus follower?"

The life of a Jesus follower is all about relationships.

- A relationship with the Father that is personal and daily.
- A relationship with one another that is connected and caring.
- A relationship with the world that engages neighbors and nations.

Notice how each of these Missional Life Marks hits the five C's; they are all clear, concise, compelling, catalytic, and contextual. Can you imagine walking into a church environment where these are owned with passion and clarity?

BUILD OUT THE SUBPOINT OF YOUR ᴹ*MARKS*. Once you have arrived at your final expression, you can drill down and flesh out the subcategories of each ᵐ*Marks* component. This part of your ᵐ*Marks* is not for memorization, but for saturation into the church's culture by way of systematic reference through teaching. The earlier example of thirty competencies demonstrates this level of detail. When you have this tool, it can become a "neo-lectionary" or scope and sequence for your church's overall teaching diet. The beauty of this articulation is that it can expand like an accordion at any time. It can represent a measure of the church's mission in five short phrases, or it can unfold and yield a twenty-point list, if for example you choose to develop four subpoints for each one.

Guiding Decisions on the Front Line of Ministry

While onsite at a church that uses its own ᵐ*Marks* (the acronym GUIDE), I was discussing the selection of small-group curriculum with a young leader named Mike. He is a twenty-eight-year-old who sells gas turbine engines for a living. Amazingly, he grabbed a pen and napkin to aid him with his response. What did he write down? His church's ᵐ*Marks*, of course! He started by listing the letters *G, U, I*, etc. on the napkin. As a volunteer leader, Mike leads with awareness of his church's primary measure. As he diagnosed the need for small-group curriculum, his decisions were based not on a whim but an intentional, systematic framework that saturates the culture of the church.

That day Mike told me about his group, about Teresa and Bill, and Tim and Holley. He felt that it was time for them to study something under the category of "exercising stewardship." What Mike was doing that day was profound. He was helping connect the dots for people and upholding the clear ideal for people in his little flock. What Mike did that day, most full-time pastors in North America never do: he made a simple ministry decision with the benefit of a clear bull's-eye in front of him. He hit the mark of missional leadership because his church had clearly articulated the target it was aiming for.

16

FRAME THE FUTURE

PREPARING FOR A VISION LIFESTYLE

Missional leadership will require skills in evoking a language about the church that reshapes its understanding on its purpose and practices.

—Darrell Guder

IN THE LAST FOUR CHAPTERS, we have covered the four sides of the Vision Frame. My intention is to clarify how vision can be articulated with incredible brevity and clarity, yet without comprising completeness. This chapter turns the corner to work not on the frame but on what it holds. Using our puzzle analogy, we have completed the straight edges that frame our puzzle; now we can start putting the individual jigsaw pieces together inside—inside the frame we define as Vision Proper (Figure 16.1).

Figure 16.1. The Vision Pathway: Vision Proper as ᵐ*Mountaintop + Milestones*

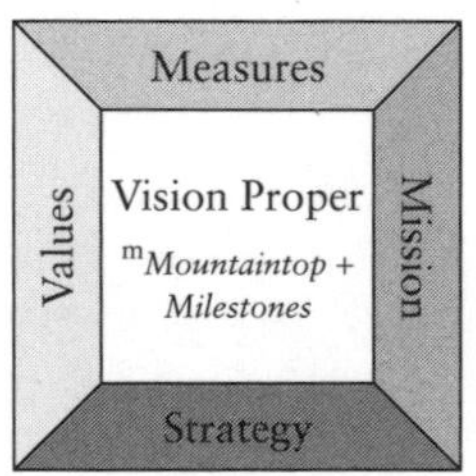

Visionary Jazz

Vision Proper is very different from the sides of the frame we have just developed. The difference between building the sides of the frame and the inside is similar to the difference between an architect and a jazz musician. The architect uses creativity within the bounds of science and completes her work before the actual task of building is done. The jazz musician continually creates by blending the science and art of music—his work is never done. In every moment, the visionary musician creates with nuanced spontaneity. The skill of the musician remains flexible as the patterns of sounds evolve, bouncing heart to heart, artist to audience and back to the artist. Likewise, the work of vision is fundamentally living and not static; there is constant nuance, surprise, and art as leader and followers "play into the future" together. In this chapter, we develop an understanding of Vision Proper that follows the likeness of jazz. As Warren Bennis wrote, "Leaders must encourage their organizations to dance to forms of music yet to be heard."[1]

Part One discussed the "fall" of strategic planning. We suggested that planning cannot assume fixed points of reference in the future. We also suggested that the leader will need the tools for navigation in a more fluid environment, as in navigating the ocean. This chapter explains that the Vision Frame is such a tool. It is not a strategic plan per se but exactly what we need to navigate the times: a strategic framework for thinking and acting. As we develop Vision Proper—thinking specifically about what the future will look like—we do so with the advantage of the Vision Frame.

A Stroll on the Pathway

The journey of working the frame to arrive at what we now call Vision Proper makes the process of seeing and describing the future more accessible. Many models describe the definitions and benefits of vision but do not make available an adequate *pathway.* The goal is to create a walkable pathway to enhance passion and effectiveness for the visionary. Let's do a short review of our progress (Figure 16.2).

We began by anchoring the Vision Pathway not in the future first but in the past. What has God always been up to? What is God specifically doing in your local context? I urged you to discover your Kingdom Concept as *the way* your church glorifies God and makes disciples. That discovery requires serious reflection on the overlap of your local church's three realities or circles: your local predicament, your collective potential, and your apostolic esprit.

Figure 16.2. The Vision Pathway: Review

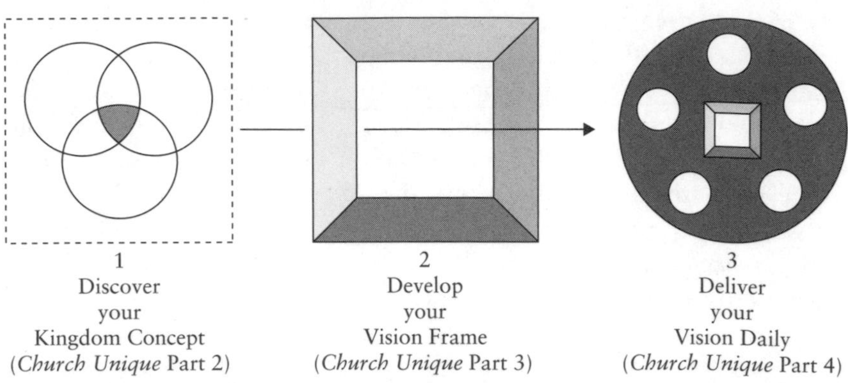

From the Kingdom Concept we moved to the Vision Frame as the best model for expressing your church's identity and DNA. We started with mission as missional mandate (^{m}*Mandate*). The mission answers "question zero," the question before all questions: What does God want us to do? We don't have to dream up an answer; rather, we articulate for our time and place the timeless ^{m}*Mandate* given by Jesus. Then we moved to the second part of the frame: values as missional motives (^{m}*Motives*). Values answer "question hero": What deepest motives and convictions would characterize a hero in our organization? We stressed the importance of being yourself as a church and leveraging your strengths.

Having acknowledged that most church visions stop with just mission and values, we added two more critical components, because without the next two sides of the frame almost any ministry initiative can live justifiably under the mission and create competing pictures of where the church is headed. So the third component of the frame is strategy as missional map (^{m}*Map*). The strategy answers "question how": What is the basic process of how we do what we do? This ^{m}*Map* brings amazing clarity to both the leadership team and individuals, allowing us to break silos and work together as never before. The last component of the frame is our measures as missional life marks (^{m}*Marks*). Your life marks answer "question now": What defines success today? ^{m}*Marks* create the shared bull's-eye that we either hit or don't hit each day. The life marks focus our attention on the missional outcomes of life change, not just on attendance, building, and cash.

Once you have developed your Vision Frame by defining mission, values, strategy, and measures, you are poised for the first time to look at Vision Proper. Vision Proper answers "question wow": What is the breathtaking

Table 16.1. Vision Frame Summary

Frame Component	Missional Reorientation	Answers	Irreducible Question of Leadership
Mission	mMandate	Question *zero*	What are we doing?
Values	mMotives	Question *hero*	Why are we doing it?
Strategy	mMap	Question *how*	How are we doing it?
Measures	mMarks	Question *now*	When are we successful?
Vision Proper	mMountaintop + Milestones	Question *wow*	Where is God taking us?

snapshot of the future God has in store for us? We break Vision Proper into two parts, Missional Mountaintop + Milestones, with explanations to come. To summarize the Vision Frame once again, refer to Table 16.1.

Defining Vision Differently

As we move toward a definition of Vision Proper, I am interested in nothing less than a radical reorientation to the concept. Vision is still the most talked about and least understood term in the leadership lexicon. Why, after so many books and conferences on the subject, is it true that "less than one out of ten senior pastors can articulate what he believes is God's vision for church he is leading"?[2] How can it still be said that "the most important problem in the church today is a fundamental lack of clear, heart-grabbing vision. The church in America has no vision. It has programs and institutions and property and ministers and politically correct hymnals, but no vision"?[3] How do we account for this gap between prolific writing about vision and the floundering practice of vision? Is there something wrong with how we think about vision? The answer is both yes and no.

Eloquent Impotence: The Vision Statements of Yesterday

Various definitions, books, and consultants have been the product, over the past several decades, of a focus on equipping leaders. They have been helpful, but limiting. The definitions themselves are good; we have been taught correctly that the vision is a "mental image of a preferred future" or a "memorable picture of what tomorrow will look like." Many books have walked through the features and benefits of having a vision. I don't think there is a pastor alive who doesn't want to be more visionary. But the results of our definitions have been limiting. Specifically, the vision statement has found its expression trapped in one of two ruts. Let's examine these two types of vision statement, each of which has its own weaknesses. Keep in mind that almost any ministry that does have a vision statement fits into one of these two kinds: the "compelling page dump" or the "lofty one-liner."

THE COMPELLING PAGE DUMP. This is roughly a one-page statement that describes the future of the church with vivid and compelling language. Some attributes of the page dump:

- One person wrote it.
- The document remains static over time.
- No one other than the originator uses the document.
- The vision is used only in formal vision casting settings.
- The vision is primarily read, not heard, by the vision receiver.

The compelling page dump was made popular when Rick Warren published his "I have a dream" vision statement in *The Purpose Driven Church*. Several books on ministry vision have underscored this type of expression, notably Aubrey Malphurs's *Advanced Strategic Planning*. Where do you find the compelling page dump most frequently? It is usually on a Web site somewhere, framed on the wall, or filed away for photocopying for the new member class or a prospective staff member.

Although the effort to produce the page dump vision is worthwhile and noble, the usefulness of such a document is bounded. The primary limitations are that the statement is static rather than dynamic, it is reserved for formal communication and not daily use, and it tends to be used by the primary vision caster and not the leadership team.

As a staff pastor, I can remember reading a compelling page dump prior to signing on with my first church after seminary. Two years later, I remember pulling out that same vision statement and reading it with discouragement. It had not changed, but our church had changed. It glamorized what we were doing a bit. It was never revisited in any staff meeting or planning retreat. I was not taught how to use it. In a nutshell it felt, to borrow a term from Eugene Peterson, like ecclesiastical pornography: it presented something scintillating without the possibility of real relationship.

THE LOFTY ONE-LINER. This second kind of vision statement hopes to express a picture of the future as a noble, future-oriented ideal and boil it down into a short phrase or sentence. Some attributes of the one-liner:

- It is usually developed as a group.
- It is intended to be motivational.
- It looks to the future by presenting an unreachable, transcendent concept.
- It never changes.
- Most leaders in the organization wouldn't repeat it day to day.
- The vision is primarily read and not heard by the vision receiver.

Many models and strategic planning consultants promote this kind of vision phrase. It could sound something like, "Making disciples globally by mobilizing every generation locally" or "Quenching the thirst of every man, woman, and child with the good news of Jesus" or "Growing a diverse community of passionate worshippers who will love people toward Jesus."

These statements may contain some important vision elements for the church, but by themselves they are incomplete. First, they don't paint a vivid description of a future reality or any of the intermediate steps to get there. In fact, the intent of the statements is to present something unattainable, like a North Star that guides you but that you literally can never reach. The problem with this idea is twofold: first, who wants a vision you can't reach? Second, to the extent that it provides directional value, it becomes redundant to mission. Most of the confusion between a mission statement and a vision statement has arisen because of this misapplication. People create a vision statement that competes for attention with the mission as a loftier or more eloquent generic restatement of it. The second limitation is that you can't use it practically on a daily basis. It is so lofty that it would not roll off the tongue; one feels forced to say it because it sounds so formal. Additionally, it is too generic to be useful in real ministry decisions.

I recently worked with a large parachurch ministry. I noticed they not only had a lofty one-liner but used it everywhere. During our first meeting, we reviewed all of their vision equity. I asked each of them to write anonymously the most meaningless or empty part of their vision language. Half of the team wrote down the lofty one-liner. It was so removed from their vernacular and so unnecessary to the leadership that they had actually begun to resent it. Once I showed them it was redundant to the mission, it was happily discarded.

Primitive Sophistication: Missional Vision Today

What is the solution for missional leaders today? We need a way to think about vision articulation that is at the same more primitive and more sophisticated. By primitive, I mean it must be hearty and raw—connected to reality. It is powerful because it is first authentic. By sophisticated, I mean it must take into account the complexity of teams, the messiness of change, and the sensitivity of spiritual guidance without compromising boldness. Sophistication allows true collaboration toward God-sized dreams. The definition of vision can be nuanced to accomplish this: Vision Proper is *the living language that anticipates and illustrates God's better intermediate future.*

LIVING LANGUAGE. The importance of living language is that the vision is always a developing Polaroid picture. Never static, vision is always evolving. Like a sequence of smaller mountains that give view to larger mountains on reaching the summit, today's new accomplishments give view to tomorrow's possibilities. Our definition moves us away from *vision as statement* to *vision as dynamic vocabulary.* Picture a treasure chest of phrases, ideas, metaphors, and stories that is the container of vision vocabulary. The beauty of a treasure chest like this is that the whole team can put words and dreams into it, and the entire leadership can pick ideas and stories out of it. It empowers a shared vision in a unique way that the compelling page dump and lofty one-liner do not.

Living language also reminds us of the importance of verbal communication and eyeball-to-eyeball exchange of dialogue. Because communication is primarily nonverbal, personal presence in vision casting is everything. In other words, the posture, tone, voice inflections, and facial expressions of the person communicating convey more meaning than the words themselves. A vision should never be designed to be read. What would have happened to Martin Luther King Jr.'s "I Have a Dream" speech if he made it a PowerPoint presentation or decided to just send out flyers? People do not follow your compelling page dumps; they follow you! The vision cannot be separated from the vision caster, and the vision caster cannot separate his message from his life as a model. What Charlie Parker, the legendary jazz saxophonist, said of music is true of vision: "Music is your own experience, your thoughts, your wisdom. If you don't live it, it won't come out of your horn."

ANTICIPATING GOD'S FUTURE. The use of vision has so emphasized a static snapshot that communication risks becoming information, not inspiration. Therefore the idea of anticipating becomes larger than just describing or painting the picture. It pulls in conviction, passion, and emotional commitment. It's not what the leader thinks *can be* or even *should be*, but what *must be*. Vision that does not engage the heart and touch the emotions is nothing more than flowery words on paper. Simply put, a shared anticipation fuels participation in a shared vision. Because the visionary embodies the anticipation of the future, he or she brings more to the table than just a picture; he or she brings a contagious longing for what God wants to do.

GOD'S BETTER INTERMEDIATE FUTURE. The foundation for this language was formed earlier in the book. It is the reminder that our vision is one of many in the course of redemptive history. It reminds us that God is the Chief Visionary who is bringing us into a final Utopia, our final rescue to the joy of His undiluted presence. Until that day we push forward, not with arrogance but with confidence, because we know we are a part of a divine chain reaction. The inherent accountability in this definition is that the leader must know the vision is from God.

In 2004 the founder of Big Idea Productions, the company that brought the world Veggie Tales, explored why the company was brought to bankruptcy. In his story, he explains that after reading a book on vision he felt he needed to have his own, big hairy audacious goal. This is how he describes what came to him: "I had always felt that God wanted me to tell the stories and teach the lessons He laid on my heart, but He hadn't given me any particular big, hairy audacious goal. But the book said I needed one to inspire and focus my employees. Okay . . . deep breath . . . 'We will build a top-four family media brand within twenty years!' Huh? Where did that come from? *I had no idea.*"[4] (Italics mine.) It is critical to know that your vision finds its source in God. If after writing down a vision you have no idea where it came from, it is probably not God's vision. Again the musician's point of view is instructive. Chick Corea, jazz pianist and composer, said, "Only play what you hear. If you don't hear anything, don't play anything."

Vision Proper Within the Vision Frame

Now that you have this new definition of vision, you can benefit from seeing how the Vision Proper fits within the Vision Frame. Specifically, there are three important principles to capture.

Principle One: Vision Proper Within the Frame Provides Dynamic Tension

The missional visioneer must embrace an important dynamic tension (Figure 16.3). Going back to our earlier thought, this is illustrated by the difference between an architect and a jazz musician. The architect produces a fixed product, while the musician is constantly creating. In our model, think of the outer frame as the preset part, and so that we look into a flowing future through a fixed frame. Think of the outer frame as the objective connection to Scripture. It expresses the basic direction of the Great Commission (ᵐ*Map*) and what our definition of a disciple should look like (ᵐ*Marks*). This allows us to work from revealed Word with revealing Spirit. In other words, we bring the objectivity of God's Word to the vision as we look to the subjective leadership of the Holy Spirit.

Before a team explores and discerns Vision Proper, the leadership team has already answered four of our irreducible questions of leadership. Therefore, it is easier to extrapolate the future, and do so with clear biblical boundaries. Once mission, values, strategy, and measures are known, it is easier to imagine what our tomorrow will look like. Think of it as a more grounded vision, a more rooted future, or a more actionable dream (Figure 16.3). The missional leader understands that the journey is changing and unpredictable. Therefore, the leader needs adaptability, humility, reflection, openness, and dependence within a boundaryless perspective. But these attributes by themselves may leave the vision ungrounded.

Figure 16.3. The Dynamic Tension of the Vision Frame

Fixed frame: objective		**Fluid future: subjective**
visionary architect grounded rooted actionable		visionary jazz vision future dream
Four outside parts	← →	Vision Proper inside
Based on the revealed Word		Based on the direction of the Holy Spirit

So the missional leader also understands authenticity; he or she is not going to throw around any spiritually decorated rhetoric. Therefore, the leader needs an approach that is anchored, responsible, confident, directed, assertive, constant, active, bold, and defined. The Vision Proper allows this dynamic tension to coexist as it lives within the Vision Frame.

GROUNDED VISION WITHIN THE VISION FRAME

Anchored adaptability

Responsible extravagance

Confident humility

Directed release

Constant emergence

Active reflection

Assertive openness

Bold dependence

Defined unboundedness

Principle Two: Vision Proper with the Frame Permits Distributed Application

Dynamic tension yields an amazing benefit to the leader when it comes to team leadership. Because of the sophistication of the frame, the vision speaks adequately to the diverse roles within the leadership community. For example, someone with strengths in process thinking may grow frustrated with the pastor who is always jumping from one thing to the next. I meet many pastors who are distractible and always trying new things. This can drive their staff crazy. But with a team-endorsed Vision Frame in place, everyone has what they need to lead, and it is defined at the top of the organization. Process people have strategy defined for them. The results-oriented person has measures defined, and so on. Or consider an introverted pastor whose primary gift is teaching. Many may wish to have a more emotive, energetic point leader. With the Vision Frame in place, however, other members of the team can speak from the treasure chest of vision vocabulary and bring a passion and visionary presence that complements the role of the senior pastor.

APEPT AND THE VISION FRAME. The team-based, apostolic approach of a missional reorientation has brought greater attention to the leadership roles of Ephesians 4:11: apostle, prophet, evangelist, pastor, and teacher (APEPT for short). Frost and Hirsch present the idea that every single person in the church (and therefore the leadership team) has one of these divinely provided motivated abilities.[5] In support of their view of Ephesians 4, I see the Vision Frame as a critical tool to engage all five functions of APEPT. For example, the forward drive of the apostle (one who is sent) as an entrepreneur, pioneer, and strategist tends to drive the mission forward. This person deeply resonates and thrives on the missional mandate of the church. The prophet (one who knows) may look at the measures and how well the mission is being accomplished. As the catalytic questioner, he looks at the organization and is not afraid to call the mission into account. The pastor (one who cares) makes sure that people are appropriately nurtured. He grabs hold of the values to ensure that the movement of the church does not happen to the neglect of relational integrity of the community. Table 16.2 shows how these functions of leadership attend to and thrive on the several aspects of the Vision Frame.

The purpose of the table is to peek into the diverse functional make-up of leaders in the church. Leaders who want to engage these roles will benefit from the concise yet complete nature of the Vision Frame. The key is that we transform the compelling page dump and the lofty one-liner from something that only one leader could use into a vision expression that the entire leadership team can produce and promote.

Table 16.2. APEPT Leadership and the Vision Frame

APEPT Function	Definition as One Who . . .	Role	Orientation Toward Vision	Vision Frame Attention
Apostle	Is sent	Initiates	Charges the vision forward	Mission and Vision Proper
Prophet	Knows	Inspects	Challenges the vision upward	Mission and measures
Evangelist	Recruits	Invites	Champions the vision outward	Mission and strategy
Pastor	Cares	Instills	Chaperones the vision within	Values and measures
Teacher	Explains	Integrates	Channels the vision into	All equally

Note: *I am grateful to Frost and Hirsch's work on APEPT generally. Specifically, I use their terminology in the definition column.*

Principle Three: Vision Proper with the Frame Promotes Daily Usefulness

One of my deepest frustrations on behalf of leaders is the inability to use vision daily. Your vision vocabulary should inform much more than just a formal vision statement or a "vision night" by being injected into the flow or rhythm of daily leadership. Think of vision-casting moments on the scale of informality (Figure 16.4).

From this figure, you get a taste of vision as a lifestyle. For the skilled leader, every day brings "insertion points" for vision. They might be when a church member talks to a neighbor—a vision-casting moment. It might be a teaching, transitioning toward application—another vision-casting moment. It might be the children's director inviting someone to be on the team . . . or the lead pastor trying to recruit a stellar leader from the business world . . . or a small group of pastors praying together for the same vision—all vision-casting moments. What makes this daily use possible? As soon as we define it as living language, we can rearrange the expectations of what vision is about. As soon as vision is unshackled from the vision statement, we put it back into people's hands and it becomes part of daily life. Missional leaders crystallize their reality to see life as a sequence of vision-casting opportunities. Pushing the future forward is the natural inclination of the apostolic bent.

Figure 16.4. Vision-Casting Opportunities

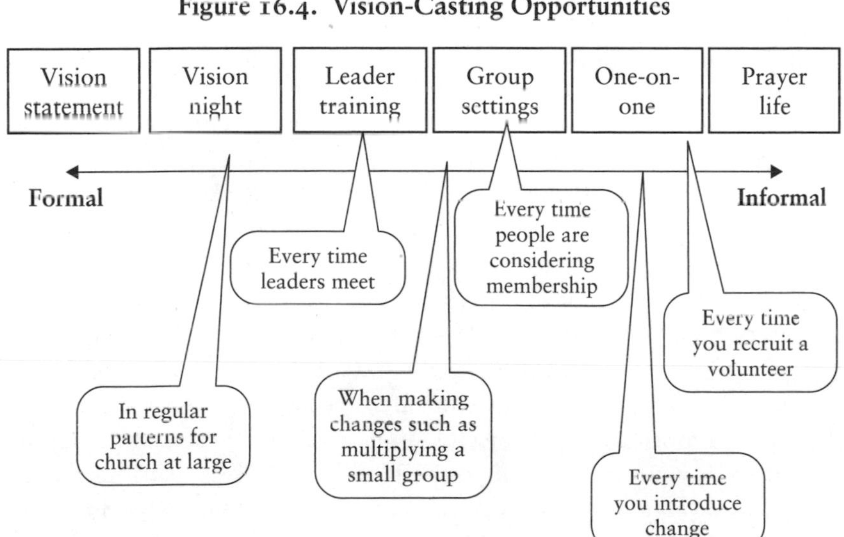

But the work doesn't stop there. Because missional leaders carry a value for team and kingdom multiplication, skilled vision casting each day is even more critical. The more decentralized the structure, and the more leaders who are released, the greater the opportunity for the vision to be diluted and polluted as it moves forward. The multiplication itself necessitates daily rhythm. Missional leaders must excel beyond their mentors at developing teams that cast and carry vision daily. I believe we are still waiting for what this could really look like in the church of North America. Leonard Sweet reminds us that the first words spoken on the moon were in English. But it wasn't the British who got there first; it was people from one of their colonies that became the heroic pioneers.[6] So too, missional leaders will push the envelope of Christendom as they demonstrate new levels of shared vision, taking them further than the generation before.

Blue Jean Visionaries

There is an important relationship among the separate components of the Vision Frame. Specifically, the first four components have been bundled as the four edges of the frame (from the prior four chapters) in contrast to the vision inside the frame—Vision Proper. To explain the benefits of this model, we first explored how most vision statements fall into two ruts: the compelling page dump and the lofty one-liner. To establish an alternative approach, I presented a new definition of vision with a correctional twist: Vision Proper is *the church's living language that anticipates and illustrates God's better intermediate future*. This definition, in concert with the surrounding frame of mission, values, strategy, and measures, takes communicating a vision to a new level, one with an appropriate missional calling. It does this in three ways. First, it injects a dynamic tension that allows the leader to be grounded on the one hand and radical on the other. Second, it enables the leader to make vision casting a team sport. Third, it promotes daily use of vision as something that happens in blue jeans, not in coat and tie.

We turn our attention next to articulating Vision Proper. Up to now, we have offered only a tease as to how to deliver vision, with the introduction of Vision Proper as ^{m}*Mountaintop + Milestones*. The great jazz musician Duke Ellington said, "Music of course is what I hear and something I more or less live by. It's not an occupation or profession, it's a compulsion." The next step is to introduce you to how you can compose the Vision Proper of your Church Unique so that it becomes a compulsion for you, your leaders, and your church. Figure 16.5 is a Vision Path Summary for Faithbridge UMC. This summary represents the simple clarity of the Vision Frame that guides the leadership of their Church Unique.

Figure 16.5. Faithbridge Vision Frame

Mission

To make more and stronger disciples of Jesus Christ by being a bridge of faith to people every day

Values

Fervent prayer
Realizing that apart from God we can do nothing

Ministry excellence
Giving our best to honor God and inspire people

Life-changing community
Becoming more like Christ through close relationships

Authentic Leadership
Exercising Godly influence to advance the Kingdom of God

Generational relevance
Making God real to people in their everyday lives

Intentional loyalty
Working to protect the unity that Christ sought for His followers

Strategy

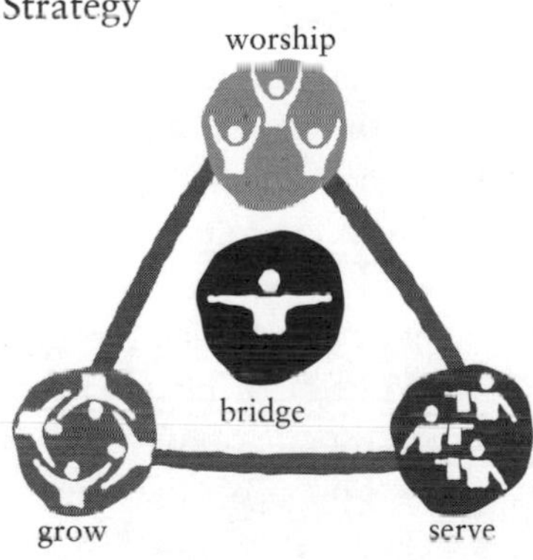

Mission measure

Worship
- Living with Godly priorities and obedience
- Daily attentiveness to the Lord
- Active, regular participation at weekend worship

Grow
- Applying Scripture to life through personal Bible study and spiritual disciplines
- Authentic relationships and accountability
- Active, regular participation in a Grow Group

Serve
- Using your spiritual gifts within the church
- Serving with humility, joy, and sacrifice
- Active, regular participation on a Serve Team

Care
- Meeting physical, emotional, and spiritual needs of the body
- Practicing the ministry of presence
- Protecting the "gossip-free zone"

Give
- Biblical stewardship (tithe, offering, resources)
- Generous giving of time and talents to the body
- Living a financially responsible lifestyle

Pray
- Personal and daily prayer, confession, and praise
- Continual dependence on God for decision making
- Praying with and for others

Bridge
- Local and global outreach to the last, the least, and the lost through Bridging Initiatives
- Sharing faith and inviting others into the church body
- Showing love with people in a practical way

Real people. Real life.

17

SPEAK WITH NEW TONGUES

ARTICULATING VISION PROPER

If you want to build a ship, don't drum up men to gather wood, divide the word, and give orders. Instead, teach them to yearn for the vast and endless sea.

—Antoine de Saint Exupèry

IMAGINE FOR A MOMENT that you are on the deck of a ship headed to the Caribbean, but all you can see is open water and open sky. As you are standing there, the captain of the ship walks over, pulls out a compass, and motions for your attention. You walk over and look at the needle. The captain then acknowledges that your ship is indeed heading in the right direction. At that moment, do you get excited? Probably not. Though you might be reassured that the captain knows how to steer the ship, your pulse does not change. But if the captain brings over a full-color travel brochure, you might have a different response. When you see the exclusive beach, you might start feeling the warm sand between your toes. You turn the page to island adventures and you feel the refreshing clear blue water and see the rainbow delight of exotic fish darting through the coral reef. When you look at the brochure, your heart beats faster; there is a visceral response. The illustration brings anticipation; the compass does not. Think of Vision Proper as your travel brochure that builds anticipation and excitement.

Having established the benefits of developing the Vision Frame, we now turn to *articulating* Vision Proper. How do you actually create the living language that anticipates and illustrates your future? While we begin answering this question, keep in mind that, as Kenn Ash says of music, "Your skill is proportionate to your interest." Duke Ellington reiterated the point another way: "There is no art without intention." These simple observations from these great musicians are true of visionaries; they are artists whose skill progresses on the basis of interest and intentionality.

This chapter offers you tools to improve your skills. But you have to bring the interest. The previous chapter showed us that vision can be a team sport each day. You will have no lack of opportunity to practice your art of vision casting.

Mission and Vision: Clarifying the Difference

So far I have created some new terms for you in the category of vision. Let's take a moment to make a massive clarification. In fact, it is the most common question I hear as a vision consultant. As we turn toward the topic of crafting vision, how do we understand the difference between mission (^{m}*Mandate*) and Vision Proper? In a nutshell, mission is like a compass and Vision Proper is like a developing Polaroid picture of the adventure. One gives direction, and the other gives stimulation.

A classic illustration of this from Scripture relates to the exodus. At the burning bush moment in Exodus 3, we see God giving Moses a mission. He wants Moses to be His point leader in the deliverance from Egypt to the Land of Promise. Moses, in essence, receives a compass. But no less than fourteen times, we see reference to this place as a "land flowing with milk and honey." It is one of the most memorable phrases in the Old Testament. It is a beautiful and picturesque snapshot—a travel brochure, if you will. Take a peek at what was in store for the Israelites:

> For the Lord your God is bringing you into a good land, a land of brooks and water, of fountains and springs, flowing out in the valleys and hills, a land of wheat and barley, of vines and fig trees and pomegranates, a land of olive trees and honey, a land in which you will eat bread without scarcity, in which you will lack nothing, a land whose stones are iron, and out of whose hills you can dig copper. And you shall eat and be full, and you shall bless the Lord your God for the good land he has given to you.
>
> **Deuteronomy 8:7–10**

Here we see that God Himself supplied *living language* that illustrated and anticipated His better intermediate future for Israel. God gave Moses not only a compass but a travel brochure as well. Here is a chart summarizing some of the differences between the two. When you boil it all down, a clear mission never creates heroic sacrifice in and of itself. It is vision that moves the heart on a deep level and engages the imagination with God-sized dreams.

Mission	**Vision**
Compass	Travel brochure
Defines the direction	Describes the future
Informs	Inspires
Doing	Seeing
State in one breath	State of breathlessness
Directs energy	Creates energy
Integrates activity	Encourages risk taking

Vision as Missional Mountaintop + Milestones

The first step toward articulating Vision Proper is the breakdown of your living language into two types: qualitative vision and quantitative vision. The former speaks to the nature, or character, of the future state being described; the latter speaks to a numerical or measurable aspect of the better future. When these ideas collide with a missional reorientation, a journey metaphor is useful. Have you ever been on an exhausting hike, only to be surprisingly refreshed by a breathtaking view? The sudden break in the trees reveals a mind-blowing panoramic view of where you are heading. That's the qualitative view of the missional mountaintop. But on that same journey, the leader might propose to cover five miles by 3:00 P.M. Any journey can be marked with quantitative checkpoints. Vision that sets numerical goals like this speaks to a missional milestone. So the two points of Vision Proper are expressed as ᵐ*Mountaintop + Milestones*. Missional Vision is a double-barreled gun, a combination of inspiration that speaks to head and heart. Table 17.1 shows ᵐ*Mountaintop + Milestones* side by side, with a snippet of vision casting for creating community.

Over the years, as I've worked with leaders I am amazed at the diverse perspectives regarding numerical goals and metrics. Some leaders are repelled by any quantitative vision whatsoever (perhaps burned by the growth idolatry discussed earlier in the book). The ᵐ*Mountaintop + Milestones* perspective allows this diversity as God directs the leader's life.

Table 17.1. Mission Mountaintop and Milestones

Qualitative Vision = Missional Mountaintop	Quantitative Vision = Missional Milestones
Example: "We are a place where no one stands alone . . . where people are elbow-deep in each other's lives. May I ask you, Who is your 2:00 A.M. friend?"	*Example:* "By this time next year, we will have 100 small groups, and 70 percent of them will have apprentice leaders."

More often than not, however, an effective leader will use milestones in an attempt to motivate, challenge, and focus people toward results. The key principle in using both is that *Mountaintop* should always precede *Milestones*. The leader must be careful that the numbers do not become the primary motivator or appear as such. As one CEO said, "Quantitative goals can't invest purpose in a process that has none. The quest for simply more of anything is inherently unsatisfying."[1]

Leading with a View from the Mountaintop

God has a long history of calling leaders—Noah, Abraham, Moses, Deborah, Joshua, Esther, David, Peter, Paul, and the list continues. At some point, each leader has a burning bush experience, a Damascus road light. In those moments, God illuminates a picture of a better intermediate future. When God wants change, He affects the heart of the leader first. When God wants to move a nation, He gives the vision to an individual first. It's as if the leader is standing on top of the mountain, with others below. He or she sees something awesome, something more beautiful, better, and within reach. But the climb up the mountain is hard work—very hard work. How does the leader motivate the team for a strenuous climb? The leader sees the view; the vision feels so worthwhile. It is not close yet, but it is tangible; most important, it is God revealed. But when the leader wakes up in the morning and looks in the mirror, he realizes that no one sees what he sees. The moment of truth comes and the leader decides to paint a picture of the route ahead—to illustrate it so others can anticipate it. He is compelled to show it and walk toward it with everything he has, hoping others will follow. Because he is committed to rallying people toward a better future,[2] the quintessential question is, How to go about it? How does one move others by showing them what one sees?

Communicating to Move People

To help people see the invisible, the leader must understand how to unlock the imagination. The very act of imagination is deeply connected to faith. The author of Hebrews writes, "Now faith is the assurance of things hoped for and the conviction of things not seen" (Heb. 11:1). When a leader activates, or provokes, a follower's imagination, he or she is serving both God and the individual by exercising the muscle of faith. Understanding and engaging the mind's eye is an amazingly powerful practice; even Einstein said that imagination is more important than knowledge. C. S. Lewis stated this idea eloquently when he wrote, "For me, reason is the natural organ of truth; but imagination is the organ of meaning."[3]

Metaphors as Software of Thought

So how does the leader influence the imagination? The answer is through metaphors, blended with the art of storytelling and question asking. Metaphors are the software of thought. Aristotle said that the soul never thinks without a picture. Therefore, the leader who uses metaphors turns the listener's ears into eyes. I was recently with a leader whose organization is growing fast and adding so many excellent staff people that he had a mini-identity crisis. He asked, "What is the most important thing that I should be doing?" The answer was simple: take on the role of chief story officer. The most powerful position in the organization is the role that can choose the metaphors and tell the stories. Leonard Sweet comments on this powerful role:

> Metaphors do more than add to the cognitive impact of language. Metaphors are the stuff of which our mind is made to begin with. In our mental encyclopedia, concepts like "chair" are not based on abstract sets of necessary and sufficient conditions, but on prototypes, best examples, and images. Ezra Pound called an image "that which presents an intellectual and emotional complex in an instant of time." Images do the same as dreams, which in Emily Brontë's words, "go through one's life like wine through water." When someone is in the position to choose metaphors, that someone is in a position to mess with your mind, to change your perspectives, to generate new dreams.[4]

The reality of using images and metaphors to guide thinking and create new realities lies at the heart of Jesus' ministry. In his work *Metaphors for Ministry*, David Bennett reveals that Jesus' primary tool for developing leaders was the everyday images He used to shape the disciples' thinking. The language of family relationships, wedding parties, and shepherding anchor the importance of community with His followers. The stories of servants, harvesters, apostles, fisherman, and images of soil, wheat, salt, and light explode the realities of a movement orientation; Jesus expected his followers to have a penetrating influence on those around them. He fused the deepest pictures of community and cause together with stunning balance and embedded them into his disciples as the epicenter of his worldwide movement.

Jesus did the same with his teaching on kingdom. With the primary message that "The kingdom is at hand," how would Jesus cast vision to a new kind of living? John Adair comments:

> Consequently the "kingdom of God" in parables told by Jesus sounds as if he were talking about an actual place, not some abstract ideal. . . . In seven parables, the kingdom of God is compared to a *house*, while in six others the focus in on a great festive *feast* that takes place in a house. The "kingdom" can be *entered* or not entered (Mark 9:47); one can *sit down* in it; people can *eat and drink* in it (Luke 22:30). A man may be not far from the "kingdom of God" (Mark 12:34). It has a *door or gate* on which one can knock and which may be locked (Matthew 25:1–12). Thus it is like a *house* or *walled city*, a mirror image of Satan's domain (Mark 3:23–25, Matthew 12:25). Men are said to *take it by force* (Matthew 11:12, Luke 16:16). The Greek word used here is *biazesthai* which described attackers storming a city.[5]

Jesus' skill as a masterful storyteller and metaphor handler points the way for the aspiring visionary today. If the leader has any hope of painting a memorable picture of the future, it will be with the vivid and compelling language of metaphor—living language—that penetrates the soul as much as it illuminates the mind.

For example, consider the difference in these two sentences, both designed to motivate a person to join a small group:

> *Appeal number one:* "We have found that people really need and benefit from the opportunity to develop deeper relationships."

Appeal number two: "Have you ever considered who will be at your funeral and not looking at their watch?"

Both of these appeals use sixteen words. The first is bland and the second is a bombshell. One goes in one ear and out the other. The second lodges into the heart and delivers meaning like an IV drip over time. The first one uses descriptive words only. The second puts you somewhere; you can imagine the atmosphere of a funeral, relive the moment, see the anguish of someone who has passed away without meaningful friendships. You can picture the apathy of people looking at their watches; you know what that is like. But most powerful of all is that you can see the expression on their faces; they're ready to go, tapping their toes. The image this scene creates is heart-wrenching; it challenges you to define the quality of the best relationships in your life. The first appeal tells you what to do; the second unlocks what we know people really ultimately want. Finally, the second appeal asks a question. Once you hear it, you can't escape it, whether you want to or not. I love what musician Robbie Robertson said about music: "It should never be harmless." The same is true of a well-cast vision.

So how will you use your sixteen words when you share the [m]*Mountaintop* with your people? "Those who have apprenticed themselves to Jesus learn of an undying life with a future as good and large as God himself,"[6] wrote Dallas Willard. Your role as vision caster is the key connector to how clearly they see this life, the next intermediate future to get there. As an exercise to reflect on metaphor, consider two more vision-casting segments. One is from a great vision moment in the twentieth century. The other is from Jesus.

> *I have a dream that one day this nation will rise to the true meaning of its creed: "We hold these truths to be self evident: that all men are created equal." I have a dream that one day on the red hills of Georgia the sons of former slaves and the sons of former slave owners will be able to sit down together at the table of brotherhood. I have a dream that one day even in the state of Mississippi, a desert state, sweltering with the heat of injustice and oppression, will be transformed into an oasis of freedom and justice. I have a dream that my four children will one day live in a nation where they will not be judged by the color of their skin, but by the content of their character. I have a dream today.*
>
> Martin Luther King Jr., "I Have a Dream" speech, March on Washington, August 28, 1963

> *You are the light of the world. A city set on a hill cannot be hidden. Nor do people light a lamp and put it under a basket, but on a stand, and it gives light to the whole house. In the same way, let your light shine before others, so that they may see your good works and give glory to your Father who is in heaven.*
>
> Jesus Christ, Sermon on the Mount, Matt. 5:14–16

The Six Essentials of Vision as the Missional Mountaintop

Having established that the leader must paint a vivid picture with story and metaphor, let's turn our attention to what must be said in the qualitative vision. There are six essential ingredients. Even the best vision casters get stuck in a groove and may include only three or four of the six.

As I walk you through each essential, refer to the "spider diagram" as an evaluative tool (Figure 17.1). I regularly use this tool with teams as we listen to great vision-casting segments together, and as we evaluate each other on the staff. For each essential, the tool has a line to score on a scale of one to five (one being poor, toward the center; and five being excellent, near the outer edge). At the end of a vision-casting exercise, connecting the scores can plot the vision effectiveness. The ideal is that the vision makes a "wheel" that can roll smoothly. Or to quote another one of our musicians, Eddie Condon, "As it enters the ear, does it come in like broken glass, or does it come in like honey?"

ESSENTIAL ONE: COMMON DENOMINATOR—DO I BUILD AN EMOTIONAL CONNECTION BASED ON SHARED HISTORY? Great vision-casting moments start by looking back momentarily before looking forward. It is critical that you draw attention to shared connections and experiences. You have to remind people why they would want to listen to you. Who are you to them, anyway? Many times the leader is relationally close to the people and doesn't feel the need to retell the stories. But this is shortsighted. Other times, the leader is vision casting in a larger environment and is anxious to get to the meat. But you cannot deliver the meat of your vision without connecting first. My favorite quote from John Maxwell is that "leaders touch a heart before they ask for a hand."[7]

Figure 17.1. Vision-Casting Spider Diagram

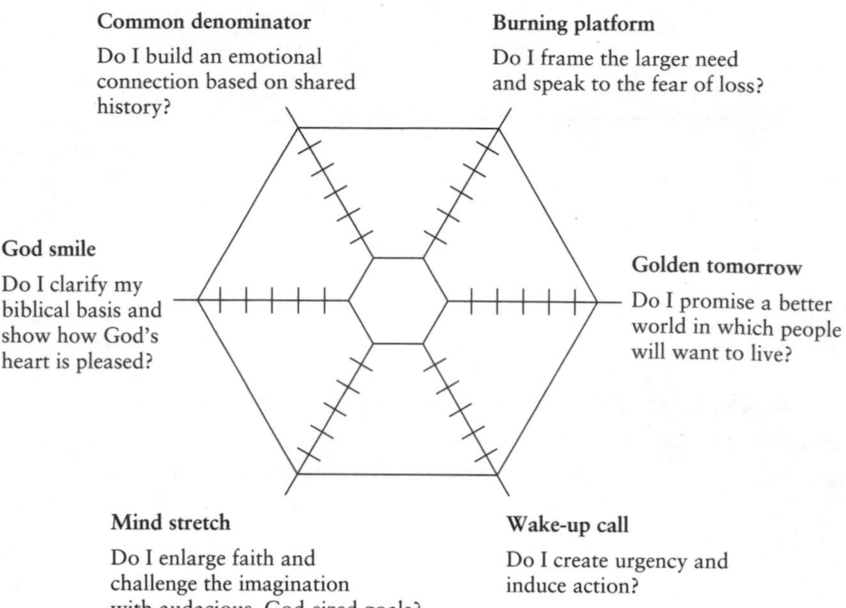
Common denominator
Do I build an emotional connection based on shared history?
Burning platform
Do I frame the larger need and speak to the fear of loss?
God smile
Do I clarify my biblical basis and show how God's heart is pleased?
Golden tomorrow
Do I promise a better world in which people will want to live?
Mind stretch
Do I enlarge faith and challenge the imagination with audacious, God-sized goals?
Wake-up call
Do I create urgency and induce action?

A real example illustrates how this can be incorporated at every level of communication. One church I was working with was recruiting neighborhood captains to do a decentralized neighborhood Easter egg hunt as a "building relationships" event. The children's pastor started her appeal with a common denominator: she asked the adults to think of their own Easter egg hunt experiences growing up.

ESSENTIAL TWO: BURNING PLATFORM—DO I FRAME THE LARGER NEED AND SPEAK TO THE FEAR OF LOSS? The greatest mistake in vision casting is not recognizing that vision is always a solution to a prior problem. The impact of the vision is therefore not tied just to the clarity of the problem but to the deep awareness of the problem and its consequences "for me" if the problem goes unaddressed. In other words, the vision caster must speak to and build up "the fear of loss." Is this manipulation? Absolutely not—if the vision is in accordance with God's truth. If it is a matter of the gospel being heard, then eternity is at stake and the leader cannot shy away from driving home the horror of hell. In other words, speaking to fear of loss is aligning people's emotions with what is really real, and what we may not see or prefer not to look at.

In an effort to show team consensus on a vision night, one pastor brought his team up to the stage. Each took a turn casting a vision for their ministry area. The experience was amazingly flat. Why? Because the team members were so anxious to share their own ideas that *no one presented the compelling need first.* Like the old adage for using illustrations in a sermon, if you want to show off the diamond you have to roll out the black velvet behind it.

ESSENTIAL THREE: GOLDEN TOMORROW—DO I PROMISE A BETTER WORLD IN WHICH PEOPLE WILL WANT TO LIVE? The third essential is a tricky one for church leaders. It may seem straightforward on the surface, but it is very difficult in reality. Why? Because most pastors paint the better future from their personal vantage point of reality. The pastor thinks that a full worship service is a better world to live in. But only he thinks so, and he is deluded if he doesn't step into the mind's eye of the receiver who does not want to deal with a crowd on Sunday morning. In other words, stop vision casting to making the church better and show people how the *church* makes *life* better.

ESSENTIAL FOUR: WAKE-UP CALL—DO I CREATE URGENCY AND INDUCE ACTION? The vision casting moment must remind people why action is required today. "Now is the time" is the mantra of the leader. This essential is closely connected to the notions of burning platform and the golden tomorrow. If the leader successfully shows the better way and establishes what's lost if we wait, then the vision-casting moment must be the alarm clock that awakens action, the starting gun that opens the gates.

I recently attended a training event held for about seventy new leaders. Several were chomping at the bit to get started after the training. Unfortunately, they had to wait for three months before they could take a next step. The effectiveness of the pastor's vision-casting was seriously hampered by the inability to take immediate action.

ESSENTIAL FIVE: MIND STRETCH—DO I ENLARGE FAITH AND CHALLENGE THE IMAGINATION WITH AUDACIOUS, GOD-SIZED GOALS? The mind stretch is a critical component in forging the future and building anticipation. Without a mind-blowing goal in front of them, your people will never have a reason for risk taking, collaboration, and heroic sacrifice. As representatives of God's better intermediate future, God's people should be aware that they are able to do far more abundantly than all we can ask or think. The leader who doesn't champion this spirit of expectation is committing pastoral malpractice.

When Caz McCaslin started Upward, someone stretched his mind by telling him that he needed to put the program in a thousand gyms. Ten years later he had two thousand gyms running Upward leagues through the local church. With the first mind stretch well behind them, Caz observed that they seemed to reach kids in giant-step magnitudes of four: four thousand to forty thousand to four hundred thousand. Seeing the progression, Caz issued the next mind stretch and announced to his international volunteer movement, "I believe God wants us to reach four million children, one million at a time." I can still remember the sighs of the people next to me when Caz shared that vision at one of their training conferences.

ESSENTIAL SIX: GOD SMILE—DO I CLARIFY MY BIBLICAL BASIS AND SHOW HOW GOD'S HEART IS PLEASED? Ultimately the leader is accountable to God and will stand before Jesus with all of his previous "vision-casting reels" in hand. Just as important, the leader must place his appeal clearly on the shoulders of God and not himself. The vision will stay sourced in his persona and charisma if he fails to intentionally show how God's heart is pleased. The vision should be dripping with allusions to Scripture and the unquestionable history of God's work among the local community.

So far we have said two primary things about the vision as the ^{m}*Mountaintop*. First, the leader must employ the art of metaphorical language. A picture is worth a thousand words, but a thousand right words—ones dripping with imagery and the story of a better future can elevate people to a place not yet known. Supplying the right metaphor is like placing a conch shell to your ear; it continues speaking and is always echoing a reality, the truth of its ocean home. Second, I have asserted that there are six essential ingredients for moving people to the mountaintop. Like the periodic table that lists the elements of matter, these six elements make vision: common denominator, burning platform, golden tomorrow, wake-up call, mind stretch, and God smile. The spider diagram is here because your skill will be proportionate to your interest in development; I heartily recommend that before important vision-casting moments you use this evaluation tool on yourself, or better yet give it to someone else to evaluate *you*.

Making Missional Milestones

As you the leader paint future images in the mind's eye of your followers, sometimes you do more than show it; you mark it. Therefore, we define vision as ᵐ*Mountaintop + Milestones*. It is as if the leader reaches forward in time and places a stake or a flag in the ground—a milestone—and attaches a numerical value to it. Think of it as an organizational odometer that tracks distance with regard to some specific expectation. This may be attendance in worship, or it may be much different and subtler. For example, a leader might measure the percentage of people who have at least five individuals outside the kingdom whom they are praying for regularly. Or a pastor might set a numerical goal for how many people a church takes on a cross-cultural mission trip. Or a children's pastor might monitor the percentage of families that have a meaningful devotion in their home at least once a week. The details of what you can measure are endless. A leader placing a time expectation with a measurable goal creates a milestone. A milestone represents a point of progress that will be definitively reached or not.

Until now, I have talked about goals at two different points. The first was in Part One, where we explored the problems associated with strategic planning and the myth that setting more goals leads to more accountability. In this context, the goals were organizational. The uncontrolled population growth of organizational goals within the strategic plan actually fogs clarity and creates silos. Part Three introduced the idea of mission measures as ᵐ*Marks* (missional life marks). In this case, the goal is about the individual not the organization. The church must have a portrait of a disciple as a bull's-eye so it doesn't slip into "assessment drift," measuring hard assets only. In other words, the church needs a common language about the outcomes of life change and discipleship for which it exists.

As important as ᵐ*Marks* are, they are not intended to furnish an organizational goal or metric in and of themselves. Rather, they establish that any goal or metric must be rooted in the life marks of missional living. In other words, the ᵐ*Marks* show us the target, but they don't tell us how many people we are shooting at it or what our percentage of hits is.

Within ᵐ*Mountaintop + Milestones*, the milestones give us the opportunity to put down measurable goals or metrics as a collective group. It is the place where we can embrace goals again, but with some important differences from the strategic planning goals I have critiqued. In the rest of this chapter, I outline a simple process and offer a basic tool to equip your conversations and decision making with ᵐ*Milestones*.

The Guiding Principle of Simplicity—Again!

The principle that guides our development of ^{m}*Milestones* is to have no more than one milestone at a given time. In this case, the leader uses his or her role to manage people's attention carefully. In today's short-attention-span world generally, and in overworked ministry environments specifically, the leader is wise yet again to embrace the less-is-more concept. Again, a musician's perspective adds value to our discussion. Dizzy Gillespie said, "It's taken me all my life to learn what not to play." The church can learn from his words. With milestones, more is rarely better. A few recent voices from the business world have championed this concept with large audiences applauding. One is Marcus Buckingham. Read his exhortation to leaders:

> Don't give us a scorecard with five or ten or twenty metrics on it. Don't take all the many metrics that your organization can generate and present [them] as a "balanced scorecard." Balancing your scorecard might make you happy because you, the analytical leader, have succeeded in imposing some order on your complex world. But we, your followers, don't really care how balanced your scorecard is. It may be balanced or it may be not. Either way it is still too complex. It contains too many scores. And as such it tells us that we should look here and here and here and here to gauge our journey. This complexity confuses us and makes us anxious. It saps our strength and undermines our confidence. . . . If you want us to follow you into the future you must cut through its complexity and give us one metric, one number to track our progress.[8]

His definition of *scorecard* is the same as our milestone, so his words translate directly to what we are saying. Another voice is Patrick Lencioni, who wrote the popular book *Silos, Turf Wars, and Politics.* What is his antidote for too many goals? He calls it a "thematic goal" and defines it as "a single temporary and qualitative rallying cry shared by all members of the team."[9] The purpose of his approach is to bring about real synergy by connecting departments with a cross-functional focus. Again, his thinking supports what we want to accomplish by having only one milestone at a time. This focused dynamic is why so many churches use boxed programs such as "Forty Days of Community," or experience some success with a typical capital campaign approach. For once in the life of the church, everyone is on the same page, working with a shared and concrete perspective of where the

Figure 17.2. Using the Vision Frame to Determine Your [m]*Milestones*

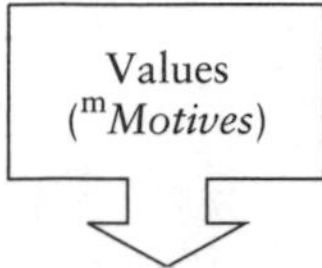

The milestone emphasizes a shift in culture or dramatic cultural awareness.

Example: the value of "sanity" is squelched from overactivity. The pastoral team asks volunteers not to serve in more than two ministry areas. The milestone is 0 percent overcommitment in twelve months.

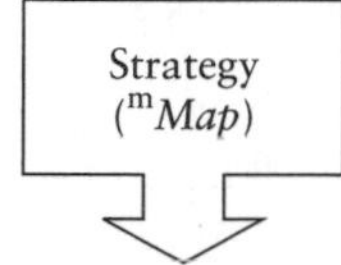

The milestone emphasizes movement of people through assimilation into the church or release out of the church.

Example: increasing the percentage of people in identifiable areas of service from 23 percent to 40 percent in twelve months.

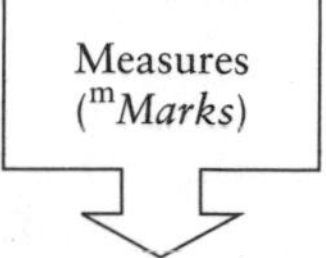

The milestone emphasizes the development of a life change or spiritual formation outcome.

Example: the church decides to help people be more intentional for Christ in their sphere of influence. They decide to measure how many people spend one hour a week in a setting pursued for for *conversation with* and *outreach to* the lost. The milestone is 60 percent in six months.

church is headed. Our desire with the [m]*Milestones* is to make seasons of focus that build synergy and momentum for your Church Unique. This type of focus is systematic and rooted in the Kingdom Concept and Vision Frame rather than being randomly driven by the latest conference or spark of creativity.

Determining Your Milestone

To determine your milestone, you must first identify the most important need or opportunity *at this time* in your church and run it through your articulated frame. (Now you will benefit from the outside edges of our Vision Frame.) Each frame nuances how you look at the organization and what kind of milestone you get. Values emphasize culture, strategy connects to assimilation, and measures point to spiritual formation (see Figure 17.2). For example, one church may identify the need to have more people serving. This connects with the strategy or [m]*Map*, which translates into an assimilation milestone. Another church may be planning for an influx of summer move-ins in their suburban context. To leverage the opportunity, they emphasize the measure or [m]*Mark* articulated as "dedicated to reaching others." Spiritual formation becomes the desired outcome of the metric.

Milestone Trouble Shooting

Several questions pop up in dealing with milestones. Here are three common ones.

How do we determine a single milestone? This important question should flow out of team leadership. Take time to discuss and listen well to one another. If there are two competing ideas, I would recommend having the two ideas presented as passionately as possible to a designated leadership group who will decide. Being unclear is not always bad; it may force you to get clearer feedback from within the organization. Remember that as the leader you can always solicit feedback from as wide a group as possible. If you want, you can conduct a congregational survey to better or more objectively read the pulse of the community. I am not suggesting the community as a whole decide; be careful how you word your questions, should you do a survey. In the end, the importance of which idea you choose isn't as important as having just one. Don't let indecisiveness be your decision. Even if you must arbitrarily choose one, go for it!

How do we measure a milestone once it's determined? Did someone just mention surveys? There are always ways to measure, so long as you are willing to ask. The measurement may involve some creativity. The bottom line is that people are always glad you care and are being intentional (in the local church context). I have never seen a survey or an intentional meeting for listening do anything but enhance leadership credibility. Don't be afraid to design the tools and takes the steps to solicit feedback and measure your milestone progress.

What if we want more than one milestone? I know that reducing it to one can be very difficult for some leaders. If you have to have more than one, I recommend doing it as an executive team or as paid staff only. Don't put the complexity of multiple milestones on your people's shoulders, thereby turning them into millstones. Set your people up for success and lead them to win with one clear score on your card.

Feel the Future

Earl Crepes coins the term "assessment drift" to more precisely show how mission drift begins. It happens because we have no real way to feel as though we are on track. This is why milestones are so important. I encourage you to creatively mix ᵐ*Mountaintop + Milestones* as you hammer out your own Vision Proper. Give your people bold and solid milestones so they can feel the progress and know they are not drifting but instead striding toward God's better future. But it's not all about numbers. Work hard to discover and uncover the metaphors that implant a time-released capsule of meaning and beauty in people's souls. Push yourself by using the spider diagram, and ask for honest input from your closest cadre. Your skill is proportionate to your interest. As you make yourself better, you will not just tell your people about the future; you will *show* it to them and make their heart beat out of their chest. Teach them not just to build the boat, but to yearn for vast and endless seas.

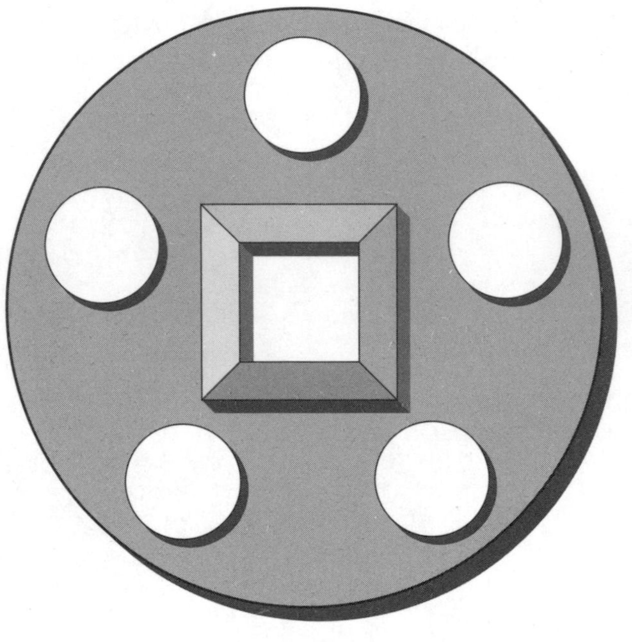

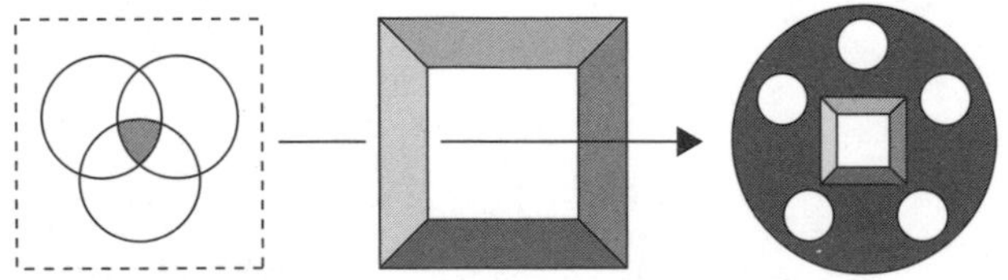

PART FOUR

ADVANCING VISION

IMAGINE SITTING DOWN WITH YOUR FAMILY to design a house. You invest months in the designing process. There are so many decisions and so much to think about. You work hard to accommodate the wishes of everyone in the family. The kids want their rooms a certain way, and as far away from each other as possible. The size of their room is considered, the traffic flow throughout the house, where and how guests will be entertained, the back porch, the bathtub, the placement of the island in the kitchen . . . after months of wrestling with the blueprints, you finally have a clear design.

Then you plan how the project will move, how it will progress. You work with the general contractor to set up the schedule of subcontractors who will come to work. Next you align your resources and people to the plan. You ensure that everyone knows the process and where he or she fits. The project begins.

A few weeks into it, your daughter decides she does not like the location of her room. It is too close to the garage, and the garage door opening will wake her in the morning when you leave for work. She wants her room to be on the back of the house.

Your son is thinking of playing the drums. He was not into drums before the plans emerged, but he is now. At least he thinks he is. His room is far too small

> for a drum set, and your spouse informs you that there is no way the drums are going in the living room.
>
> The project is in jeopardy. Everyone at the time signed off, but now other things are stealing the focus. Drums, garage doors, life. It all happens.[1]

The fourth part of our journey is about "life happening" at church. Once you have clarified and articulated your vision, the messy and complicated work of advancing it begins. The hardest part of the journey is that those who sign off on the vision initially will get distracted, perhaps lose focus, or even want to redesign the blueprints. Your role is to keep the vision alive—to deliver vision daily in order to build momentum for your movement. As you do, you will be constantly aligning, attuning, and integrating the vision into the minds and hearts, actions and passions, and role descriptions and organization charts of your Church Unique.

18

WAGE WAR AGAINST THE STATUS QUO

FROM ARTICULATION TO TRACTION

It may be that the day of judgment will dawn tomorrow; in that case we will gladly stop working toward a better future. But not before.

—Dietrich Bonhoeffer

PAUL'S WORDS FROM ROMANS 7:15 are both haunting and comforting: "I do not understand my own actions. For I do not do what I want, but I do the very thing I hate." The words speak to the tension of being a new creation in Christ and having the residual power of the flesh at work in our bodies. They haunt us because they speak to our own experience. The words comfort us because we know we are not alone in our soul struggle and our war within.

I am convinced that if the body of Christ could speak with a unified voice, that part of her legacy would be, "I do not understand my own actions." There is no greater time to acknowledge this than when a stunningly unique, movement-oriented vision is championed. When the leader and the surrounding team have new clarity, they inevitably face the force of yesterday's inertia. Status quo is not static; it's like a car and driver going sixty miles per hour down the ministry highway. The driver has tense muscles, stiff arms, and focused determination to stay on course, even when the course is tangential to the mission.

Bookshelves are filled with volumes on the topic of change management. I really don't want to talk about change management per se, but vision advancement as integration. Part Four is the shortest part of this book. I want to present some simple direction on the topic of "getting traction" with clarity. What happens in the next six, eighteen, and thirty-six months after a vision is fully articulated? That's what the next three chapters are about.

Alignment: Pre-Traction Action

The ironic part of advancing vision is that the most difficult and most defining work happens pre-movement. Through seminary I drove an old beater, a Toyota Cressida that I bought from another poor seminarian. He was going overseas and had to offload his ride. Around town the car was fine. But on the first trip from Dallas to Houston, when I got that thing over sixty-five, the car wobbled violently. The alignment issues would have torn the car to bits if I had kept pressing on the gas pedal. Eventually, I got a front-end alignment and the problem was resolved. Naturally, while the car was being repaired, it wasn't moving. The parallel for the church is this: *alignment* is the critical work that must be done early in the rollout of vision. You don't just hit the gas pedal when you see where God wants you to drive. You must work on the front end before you put the pedal to the metal. Unfortunately, some leaders don't have the patience. But consider the alternative; for my Cressida being out of alignment meant limiting my top speed. For the church, being out of alignment means severe limitations to missional effectiveness and efficiency.

Kingdom Horsepower That Gets Nowhere

It is helpful to get a picture of alignment as we proceed. My favorite illustration came from the team at Castle Hills First Baptist Church in San Antonio. As we were talking about the concept, Donnie, the student minister at the time, interrupted the process to share a picture he had in his mind: "When you talk about alignment I picture a huge metal ring in the center of the room. It has seven or eight ropes tied to it, the thick kind you use in a tug-of-war. Each rope has a powerful horse harnessed on the other end. Then someone sounds the gun, and the horses start pulling with thousands of pounds of force. The problem is that the ring goes nowhere. All of the horsepower dissipates because of the canceling effect of the horses misaligned across the ring." The sum effect of this picture is zero movement.

I can't tell you how many teams resonate (sadly) with the picture of zero movement. (Donny's picture was so good we now make our own "alignment rings"—rings with little leather strings attached—to allow teams to interact with the idea.) The strings represent staff people, ministry areas, volunteer leaders, programs, you name it. Every activity in your church has a vector. Now, let's take a look at where we want to go. Once you have the Vision Frame in place, the potential dynamic of alignment is huge. As we have noted previously, time and time again it is not until the staff works through the Vision Pathway that they see what strategic clarity and team really look like. The ideal is somewhat obvious, but there are benefits that are hard to imagine.

Four stages of alignment can be identified (Figure 18.1).

The stages vary with *established churches* (more than fifteen years of history) and *entrepreneurial churches* (less than fifteen years of history). Each category faces challenges that can pull it out of alignment, but the dynamics in each context are very different. Let's look first at the established church.

ALIGNMENT IN THE ESTABLISHED CHURCH. For the established church, stage zero alignment is "confusion." Ultimately, to be exceedingly effective the church must move all of the horses to the same side of the alignment ring to achieve stage three alignment: collaboration. Imagine how these vectors multiply energy when they pull together. Two horses that can individually pull 1,000 pounds pull 2,600 pounds together; there is a 30 percent increase in efficiency. Thus the math is more like one plus one equals three. Notice that to achieve alignment, a clear mission is required and added to the diagram. Most of the time, the obstacle to achieving the level of alignment that is seen in stage three is the problem of not having clarity first, especially with your ᵐ*Map*.

The question we then need to ask is how to move from stage zero: confusion to stage three: collaboration. Collaboration is the point where individual ministries and leaders have checked their ego at the door and are actively trying to serve the mission by serving one another. In an established church environment, it takes some time to readjust understanding and expectations. As the process of attaining alignment succeeds, the team does not jump right from confusion into collaboration but learns collaboration from two prior and successive stages. The first is stage one alignment: communication. In the communication stage, leaders and ministry areas learn the value of sharing information and keeping dialogue open. Ministries are friendly with one another. Direct opposition to the mission is easily removed (unless there is someone present with ill intentions). There may be a rogue ministry or two, or simply a misfit program that clearly doesn't contribute. The very process it took to articulate the Vision

Figure 18.1. Stages of Alignment

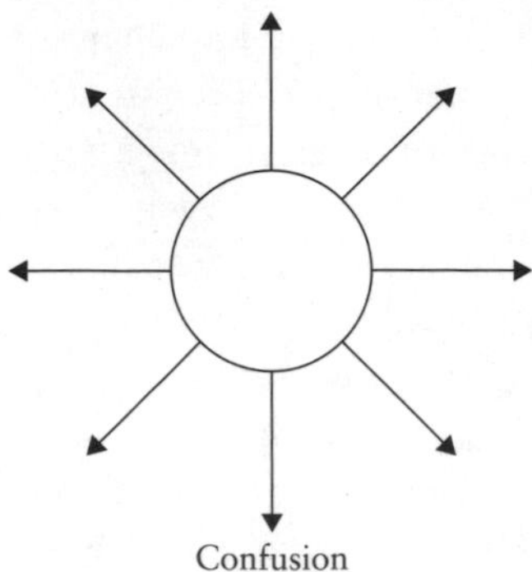

Confusion

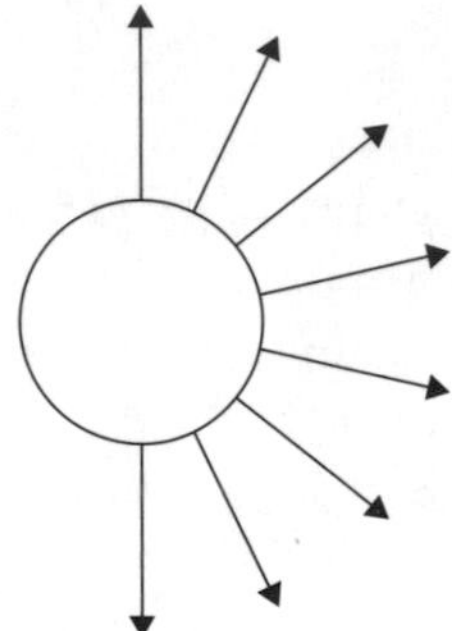

Communication

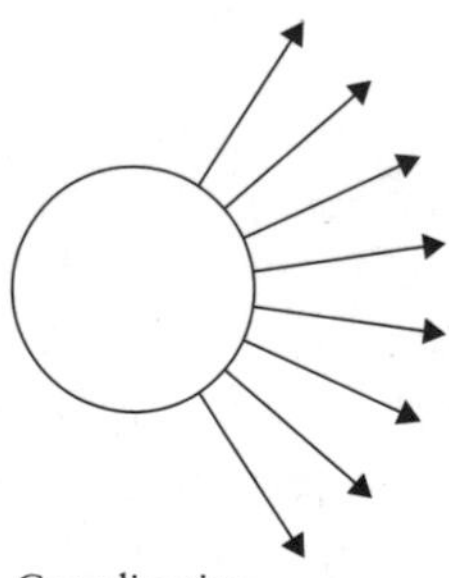

Coordination

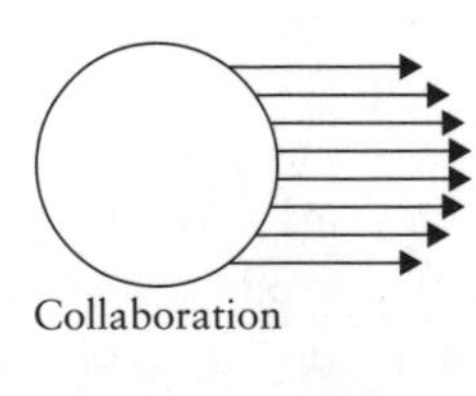

Collaboration

Mission

Frame itself usually generates enough dialogue that stage one can easily be achieved. But communication alone is not enough to remove the raw "sideways energy." Although the picture is much better than with zero movement, there is incredible energy loss and resource inefficiency. Ministries can have vectors that are ninety degrees off mission.

If the leaders in the church hunker down enough to coordinate their efforts better, they will achieve stage two alignment: coordination. Bill Donahue defines coordination as when "two or more ministries sequence and leverage individual activities for collective gains."[1] In this stage, there is hard conversation about what do with programs, ministry initiatives, and people. It is the equivalent to spring cleaning as a church, walking through the cluttered program closets and revisiting the ministry cobwebs. It means talking with crusty Mr. Smith, who has been leading the same class for twenty years under the radar. There is no way to reach the coordination stage without everyone in the church being aware of some changes. At this point, various aspects of the Vision Frame become clearer to people. It is important to acknowledge that even with coordination there are ministries tugging a little off course, albeit generally in the same direction.

The final step from coordination to stage three, collaboration, takes time and new skill development. It means a paradigm shift for your team to begin leading from your missional vision and your Vision Pathway rather than individual goals.

It means leaders' thoughts and actions are guided by the belief that together they can accomplish far more than anyone can individually. The win-wins don't just happen; they are developed from commitment to diligent creativity and dialogue. This transition is a process. If the church is generally successful and more than twenty years old, achieving collaboration can't be done in less than three years.

ALIGNMENT IN THE ENTREPRENEURIAL CHURCH. A note to young leaders and fast-growing churches: the previous section addressed achieving alignment in established congregations, those past the adolescent stage. For them, the starting point is often confusion and not focus. At the other end of the spectrum are an increasing number of growing megachurches that have been built on a simplified approach and a clear vision. About a third of my client churches are less than fifteen years old and growing fast within the eight-hundred-to-three-thousand-attendance range. If you are there, listen closely! The alignment stages work in reverse for you, and the key principle is that you are at best always twelve months away from the next *lower* stage. Here is how it progresses, assuming you started a church in the last fifteen years. Entrepreneurial churches begin at stage three not because they have mastered collaboration, but because they started small. In other words, you were focused by necessity as an entrepreneurial initiative. We would draw one arrow or string on your alignment ring. Congratulations, because anywhere you go, you are in alignment! Here we relabel stage three as "acceleration." (Refer back to Figure 18.1.) By the time the church reaches eight hundred in attendance, stage two has set in. You are considered a growing successful church. You have more resources and consequently more options. We relabel stage two not as coordination but as "expansion." In this stage, everything feels great. But in reality the resources you are adding are a little less focused than in the acceleration stage. Unless there is incredible attention to create collaboration as you add staff, you will keep experiencing the law of diminishing returns as you add infrastructure and ride your success. As you continue adding ministry initiatives, you glide into stage one, this time relabeled as "oscillation." Oscillation is the point where your growth hits the proverbial glass ceiling. Like a wave, the growth curve goes down a little and then shoots up again, only to hit the same invisible barrier. In most cases, this dynamic is related to a critical mass of opposing forces across the alignment ring. The growth dynamic yo-yos back and forth until the practices of coordination and collaboration are engaged to abort the pattern. These dynamics are possible at any size, but it is common to see oscillation occur at the twelve hundred, eighteen hundred, and three thousand attendance marks. If the church keeps adding initiatives, it enters stage zero, or "dissipation." In dissipation, the focus that created the acceleration is no longer discernible and the organization plateaus, in risk of stagnation.

Table 18.1 summarizes the four stages of alignment and interprets each stage depending on which vantage point your church is coming from—an established church or an entrepreneurial one.

Table 18.1. Summary of the Stages of Alignment

	Established Church (More Than 15 Years)	**Entrepreneurial Church (Under 15 Years)**
Alignment Pain	Trying to refocus scattered ministry initiatives	Not realizing that misalignment is occurring through "success"
Desired Dynamic	Refocus by moving from stage zero to stage three	Stay focused at stage three as ministry is multiplied
Stage zero	Confusion	Dissipation
Stage one	Communication	Oscillation
Stage two	Coordination	Expansion
Stage three	Collaboration	Acceleration

Aligning Your ^{m}Map

Doing a front-end alignment on your church requires focusing your attention on a specific component of the Vision Frame: strategy or ^{m}*Map*. There are many reasons strategy draws more attention for initial alignment work. First, strategy involves the moving parts of the church: the programs offered each week, weekend worship, service opportunities, children's ministry, the last missions trip, and so on. It naturally receives the constant attention of your staff and volunteer leadership. Second, it is through communication and implementation of your ^{m}*Map* that most people in the church are introduced to the entire Vision Frame and underlying Kingdom Concept. Think of it this way: if we introduce a change in values, the church calendar probably won't change next week. But when strategy is introduced, how ministries are promoted certainly could. The third reason to focus attention on your ^{m}*Map* is that most churches don't have one. So as you grow more intentional—whether you are an established church or an entrepreneurial church—introducing an ^{m}*Map* or strategy is an immediate opportunity for application. Fourth, having an ^{m}*Map* is the clearest way to explain the concept of focus, the single greatest organizational need in our churches today.

Persistent Modification

Once your ^{m}*Map* is developed, you need a process for doing the work of *persistent modification*, to align existing and new ministry initiatives to both the ^{m}*Mandate* and the ^{m}*Map*. Persistent modification, the unrelenting and continuous adaptation of your ministry to your Vision Pathway, is a discipline that must be engaged by leadership communities that understand the Vision Frame. In working with churches, we have developed a fivefold approach in asking the question, "How does this ministry or program fit?" This approach helps you assess if ministries are in alignment with your Vision Frame with multiple solutions when they are not.

CATAPULT THE MINISTRY. Catapulting the ministry means lifting it up as high as you can to capture the attention of your congregation. It means firing a flare and putting the ministry on the equivalent of your church's largest "billboard," whether that be a Web site, a worship guide, or a note from the pastor. In essence, development of the strategy icon serves the purpose of catapulting. (Refer back to Chapter Fourteen for a review of strategy icons.) So catapulting applies only to the ministries that directly fit on the ^{m}*Map*. For example, if working in children's ministry is a weekly volunteer opportunity, it may show up in the ᵐ*Map* as a "serve" step, as it did in several of our examples. This means the volunteer opportunity is already at the top level within the strategy; it can't go any higher. Keep in mind that promotion for volunteering in children's ministry should not eclipse or overpower the ᵐ*Map* in your internal communications. Rather, it should be communicated as a service option after an individual digests the ᵐ*Map*.

COMBINE THE MINISTRY. Some ministries do not fit the ᵐ*Map*. But after clearly defining the strategy they could fit. Persistent modification often involves tweaking ministries to fit your ᵐ*Map*. Rather than plugging and playing a boxed program, you can add and subtract your own features just the way you want. For example, let's say that your church's ᵐ*Map* has a step for connecting relationally in a small group. But some ladies in your church are very excited about their Beth Moore bible study. When you explore what you want to happen in your ᵐ*Map* component defined as "connect" and compare it to what is happening in the Beth Moore study, you discover that they don't align. Let's say the format is too large and lecture-driven. The "combine" approach considers how the study could meaningfully be adapted to be considered a legitimate connect offering within the ᵐ*Map*. Maybe they hit pause on the DVD lecture to build in more discussion, and instead of the series lasting ten weeks it lasts twenty weeks. If a ministry like this is combined into the ᵐ*Map*, it streamlines how the ministry is communicated because it becomes a legitimate offering within the ᵐ*Map*, not a separate time slot or add-on ministry to the church as a whole.

One church I worked with had a famous men's ministry speaker who spoke on Wednesday nights. The leadership realized that their ministry offerings were overbuilt (promoting the four-step "feed me" strategy) and needed to streamline the men's ministry somehow. Another problem they had was creating room for Adult Bible Fellowships (ABF) on Sunday morning. So they decided to make the Wednesday night a men's ABF, thereby combining it and making it an ᵐ*Map* component. The hard work of adaptation meant reducing the lecture time and building in more time for prayer and accountability. Many leaders don't realize how easy changes like these are to make. With the Vision Frame communicated as a part of the change process, you will be pleasantly surprised by how people embrace the intentional modifications.

CONTRIBUTIZE THE MINISTRY. The idea with "contributize" is to adapt a ministry initiative so that it becomes a contributor, or feeder, to one of the key components of the ᵐ*Map*. Let's say there is a men's morning Bible study that doesn't fit strategically into the ᵐ*Map*. It is also determined that it won't be easy to combine it with anything in the strategy. One alternative is to tweak the ministry to be a permanent feeder to a more strategic ᵐ*Map* component. In other words, it exists as a strategy entry point. For example, if more men are needed in the service part of the ᵐ*Map*, the monthly morning Bible study could end before its usual time for a special testimony and appeal for an immediate opportunity for service involvement. Or the study content could focus on developing an attitude of servanthood.

A Baptist church I work with was trying to make its Sunday evening worship a more strategic step in the ᵐ*Map*. They decided to convert Sunday evening worship into a "contributary" for service and evangelism. In advance, they created six workstations that would facilitate engaging people to work on community development projects or on personal evangelism. On Sunday night, they divided up the congregation by last name into four groups and ceremonially sent one-fourth of the congregation out of the sanctuary to the workstation of their choice. This became the weekly pattern. For the first several weeks, there was some vocal kickback to the plan. But six months later, people were praising the leadership for boldness in getting people out of the pews.

CAGE THE MINISTRY. It is clear that some programs are not strategic and never will be. The leadership decides that they are not worth combining or contributizing. But still, something in the leadership gut says it's not wise to shut the ministry down. Maybe there is a critical mass of influential people who are too emotionally tied to the ministry. Maybe people have not had time to really grasp the less-is-more concept of focus. This is a tough call, but one that has to be made over and over again by ministry leaders. One option is to cage it—that is, cut it off from new resourcing and ministry promotion. You intentionally relegate the ministry to its own little corner of the world, knowing that someday it will die gracefully. The strategic perspective of caging is one of minimizing attention and resources. While the ministry is caged, it does not siphon resources that need to be channeled elsewhere. Nor does it distract from the clear communication of the ᵐ*Map* to those coming in for the first time. The caged ministry does not contribute to ministry clutter, and sideways energy is minimized.

CUT THE MINISTRY. The final option in aligning your ᵐ*Map* is to cut or close down the ministry that does not fit and is no longer effective. For many pastors, the process of thinking about this feels like death.

Immediately, the thought of approaching an influential contributor causes them to wimp out. In the end, continuing the ministry that should be cut hurts the mission of the whole. The leader must revisit the truth that good is enemy to the best and must learn to communicate *no* with wisdom and grace. As the old saying goes, "If the horse is dead, dismount."

It is noteworthy that effective missional churches have cultures where stopping and starting ministries is expected. Remember the chapter on lost congregations? In it, we asserted that in the absence of a Vision Frame people resort to place, personality, programs, and people to derive their membership identity, rather than the unique vision of the church. Imagine for a moment a culture where people are so dialed into your mission, values, and strategy that they could care less about stopping a particular program. They are willing because the program no longer nourishes their identity.

The five C's of persistent modification can be a powerful approach for the leader who understands alignment. For the established leader, it is a guide for creatively reinventing ministries. For the entrepreneurial leader, it is a corrective for not letting expansion override the ability of the organization to stay focused. *Don't add what you can align.*

Use the two sets of vocabulary introduced in this chapter to guide team conversations—the four stages of alignment and the five C's of persistent modification. They are tools to keep you advancing your vision as "life happens" in the ever-changing work of ministry.

19

MEET LONG IN THE UPPER ROOM

THE SECRET OF ATTUNEMENT

Change invokes simultaneous personal feelings of fear and hope, anxiety and relief, pressure and stimulation, threats to self-esteem, and challenges to master new situations. The task of transformational leaders is to recognize these mixed feelings, act to help people move from negative to positive emotions, and mobilize the energy needed for individual renewal.

—Noel Tichy and Mary Anne Devanna

DURING A FAMILY VACATION on the coast of South Carolina, my eight-year-old daughter, Abigail, made a radical decision one evening on the beach boardwalk. Out of nowhere, she decided to step out of her shell and jump into the karaoke line! I couldn't believe she was ready to do it. Feigning my concern for her nervousness, I could hardly control my own. After all, we had not practiced, and she has never really sung at all. As she stepped up to the front of the stage and her little hands grasped the wireless mike, I almost broke out in hives.

When she opened her mouth, I couldn't believe it. She sounded awesome! But not because *she sounded awesome.* In a stroke of luck, her uncalculated song choice was "Sweet Home Alabama." This song was so well loved and well known that people on the boardwalk couldn't keep their mouths shut. My little Abby beamed like Hannah Montana, as a symphony of voices filled the party night atmosphere, with her at center stage.

I like the alignment word a lot. But the mental picture of horses pulling a metal ring in the same direction is not complete if the leader wants to touch the soul of shared vision. We need another picture: a snapshot of spontaneous singing that joins many together in sweet harmony. The leader must understand "attunement." Think of attunement as the kissin' cousin standing right next to alignment. What alignment is to structure and communication (the hard stuff of the organization) attunement is to human emotion (the soft stuff of the organization). We could talk about alignment all day and not have leaders' hearts oriented toward the vision. Such a reality would be tragic. We define attunement as the attraction and emotional connection in the heart of the follower to a given organizational direction. It speaks to the part of the follower's being that makes him or her want to sing when the leader shares the picture of a better future. We can align many things in the organization, but in the final analysis you don't align hearts; you attune them.

The key in advancing the vision is not to see alignment and attunement as two separate, unrelated dynamics. Rather, they work powerfully together. I see them working like a sandwich: in between specific action steps to align (bread on top and bottom) you put the meat in the middle with attunement.

Let's look again at the church's strategy as ^{m}*Map*. In the last chapter, we focused on this component of the Vision Frame from an alignment standpoint. Let's do the same thing from an attunement perspective.

Through the process of walking the Vision Pathway, your leadership will reach a moment of decision. When it is time to communicate the strategy as ^{m}*Map*, the first step is communication. Communication is something that can be aligned. We can, in one day, 100 percent align how we talk about the church's ministry. In one day, we can print the ^{m}*Map* on a worship guide, for example. At that moment, it would appear to a guest that the ministries are aligned and always have been, even though the church is still in the process of persistent modification. Therefore, we build our attunement sandwich with a slice of bread on bottom as communication alignment (see Figure 19.1). In the process of making real ministry decisions such as change in roles and structures or allocation of resources, the leadership begins to align other organizational hard stuff. Even though communication alignment can happen quickly, other aspects of alignment may require years. This is the top slice of bread on our attunement sandwich, which I refer to generally as "structural alignment."

Figure 19.1. The Attunement Sandwich

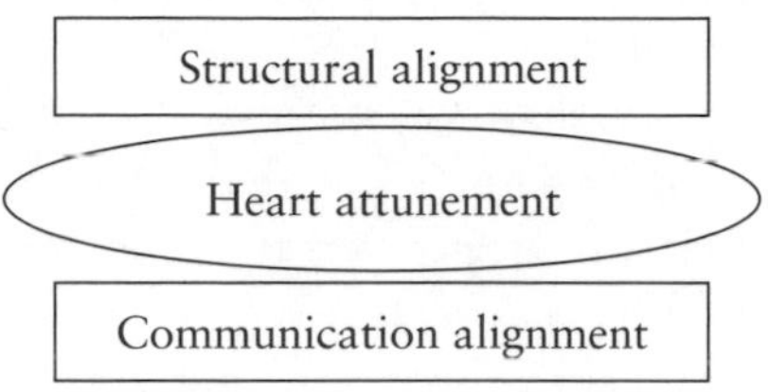

Are you ready to eat your sandwich? Go ahead and take a bite! The sandwich with no meat in the middle is not very satisfying. It is the same kind of turn-off if you are following a leader who cares nothing for attunement. Attunement is the meat in the middle that must be stacked between successive steps of organizational alignment. Mark Lipton reminds leaders: "Alignment on its own is not sufficient because it is a managerial artifact. While some people may change some behaviors by management fiat, change won't last unless they are emotionally integrated with the new direction."[1]

Practices That Harmonize Hearts

So the question becomes, How does a leader accomplish the work of attunement? How do you help people *want* to go and not *have* to go? The real answer is that you cannot, ultimately. But you can create a climate as a leader that produces real, dynamic, emotional resonance for your vision.

There are two specific practices that I want to share with you. Obviously, there are many complexities in achieving attunement that are a function of an individual's make-up both as leader and as follower. But if you master these practices, you will be well on your way to creating harmony with those you lead.

Creating Real Dialogue

The first practice is dialogue. The leader must engage people with appreciative inquiry and enter into the point of view of others. I say create "real" dialogue because it is not uncommon for leaders to be listening with their ears wide shut. When it comes to paying attention, many leaders fake it, or listen so as to react rather than listen to really hear. Instead, they embrace the image of listening with your eyes.

Creating real dialogue for the leader is sometimes difficult because of spiritual formation work going on in the leader's heart. The question then arises as to whether the leader really wants attunement to begin with or is more interested in a command-and-control dynamic. With regard to this problem, I commend the model of Jesus. Even though he created followers, they became more than followers—they became partners. That's why the movement survived his bodily departure. Paul, taking his lead from Jesus, refers at least thirteen times to "fellow-workers" in his writings. The Greek word here is *synergos*. It conveys the picture we painted in the last chapter, of a team of horses pulling together in the same direction. The apostolic model is one of pursuing teamwork. Peter even led the early team to replace their twelfth teammate after Judas' betrayal. This type of teamwork assumes dialogue and demonstrates the repulsion of the lone ranger approach or authoritarian tactics. To the extent that dialogue does not happen because of the leader's maturity, no amount of skill training will create an atmosphere of attunement.

DISCUSSION VS. DIALOGUE. Real dialogue differs from discussion. A discussion creates winners and losers, but in a dialogue everybody wins. The term *dialogue* comes from the Greek *dialogos. Dia* means through and *logos* means word or meaning. (These are two of the most recognized Greek words for us preachers.) The idea of dialogue is that of "meaning passing or moving through" two people.[2] It's an exchange and experience that brings both individuals to a higher level of understanding of one another's perspectives. Why is this distinction critical? Because attunement is not about everyone getting her own way. It is about everyone having the opportunity to be listened to and truly understood in order to move ahead enthusiastically. Therein lies the great irony of dialogue: if the leader does not force his position first, he creates a shared understanding that make force and authoritative posturing unnecessary.

LISTEN UP AND LISTEN IN. The first key to attunement is listening. Create real dialogue by scheduling the time to do so. Know that you are speeding up the mission by slowing down to have the conversation. But as the leader, you want to maximize efficiency, right? In this case, don't turn your listening ears off. Listen in on the organization, and to other leaders, all of the time. If you are working at it, you might be surprised how much you learn without having to ask.

Unwilling Contributors vs. Misdirected Contributors

The practice of dialogue is important for everyone. But there are times when the leader must do more. The second practice I want to mention,

Figure 19.2. The Attunement Grid

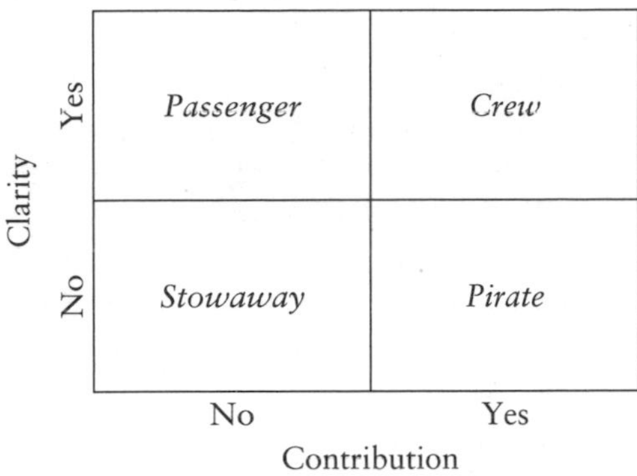

however, requires a nuanced understanding of the kind of attunement we are attempting to achieve. This understanding places people in one of two categories: *unwilling contributors* or *misdirected contributors*. A simple grid illustration helps to clarify. Imagine that everyone in your church is on a cruise ship with a clear vision. The people on your boat can be put into one of four categories created by a quadrant. One side of the grid asks the simple question of whether they are clear on the vision (yes or no). The other side asks if they want to be a contributor to the vision (yes or no). The quadrant creates an attunement grid (Figure 19.2) and puts everyone in your organization in one of four categories:

Stowaways: people who don't know the vision and don't want to contribute

Passengers: people who do know the vision and don't want to contribute

Crew: people who do know the vision and do want to contribute

Pirates: people who don't know the vision and do want to contribute

Does the reference to "piracy" seem a little strong? I think it is an important concept for the leader to grasp and sets up the second practice I want to talk about. The first push-back when I use the word is due to pirates having such ill intent. For the church leader, these people are clearly around, but so are a lot of people without harmful desires. There are many good people who do not get the vision and still want to contribute. Therein lies the challenge. To want to contribute and to not agree with the vision is an act of piracy, whether the person has harmful intentions or not. Our perspective polarizes the reality around the vision.

So the pirate fits the category of the misdirected contributor, while the passenger fits the category of the unwilling contributor.

The Power of the Positive "No"

Throughout this book we have talked about focus, alignment, clarity, and related ideas. These ideas are rooted in understanding what God is up to and not what we want to create for ourselves. For the leader who understands the church's unique vision—the Kingdom Concept expressed through the Vision Frame—the practice of the positive no becomes the most important discipline for achieving the vision. Someone once said that we cannot do anything great until we know what we cannot do. This is the second practice of attunement: articulation of the positive no.

Where does this leave us with the pirates on our boat? To use a musical analogy, they must either start to harmonize or join another choir. Your church cannot move toward God's vision if people are trying to steer the ship in a different direction or are trying to poison the crew as to the vision's integrity.

These are the next important questions for the leader:

- How do I talk to someone in my congregation with wisdom and grace even though she disagrees with the vision?
- Have I allowed enough time for adequate dialogue with this person?
- When is enough, enough, and I have to ask the person to leave?

Only you can answer these questions for your situation. In my experience, the most helpful practice in discerning these questions, especially the final one, is related to articulating the positive no.

William Ury is a negotiator who coined the term "positive no." In an earlier coauthored book, he chose the title *Getting to Yes*. But after years of negotiating, he argues that the most important skill is knowing how to say no. Hence the title of his recent book, *The Power of a Positive No*.

For the leader, application of this idea is twofold. First, the leader must appreciate that the vision is the deepest yes, and as such the integrity of the vision requires a thousand nos. This can only happen through reflection that brings deep resolve. To stimulate some thoughts about your vision being the deepest yes, here are some quotes from Ury's book:

- I slowly came to appreciate that the main stumbling block is often not the inability to get to Yes but a prior inability to get to No.
- All good No's are in service to a higher Yes.
- The right No is not the opposite of love but comes from love and grows toward love.
- Saying No has always been important, but perhaps never as essential a skill as it is today.
- There are three "A's" that trap us from getting to the positive No: Accommodating, which is saying Yes when we want to say No; Attacking, which is saying No poorly; and Avoiding, which is saying nothing at all.
- Anytime you have to say No make sure you root it in a deeper Yes.
- It's easier to say No with a deeper Yes burning inside.[3]

Second, the leader must pull the trigger and articulate the positive no. In many cases, the skill in getting to the no can enable attunement. The other person finally catches the vision, or slowly begins to willfully submit. I see this all the time. At other times, if the person still does not emotionally tune in with the vision, the person will most likely leave voluntarily. The hardest spot for the leader is when the pirate does not want to go. Once adequate dialogue has occurred, and multiple opportunities to articulate the positive no have transpired, the difficult decision remains: live without harmony, or remove the source of dissonance. If the leader brings this kind of attunement, as hard as it is, the church's mission will experience a "blessed subtraction" and may enjoy new acceleration.

A recent conversation with Brian Tome of Crossroads Community Church in Cincinnati illustrates the positive no. After a message series clearly articulating the identity and direction of the church, Brian actually listed other churches in the area on the screen during the service. He invited people to check out other churches if they were not excited about the direction of Crossroads. Through a conviction that most leaders find difficult to muster, Brian has learned the benefits of the positive no. The focus at Crossroads expands. Year after year, they reach thousands more people, not *in spite* of the positive no but *because* of it.

Missional Love

Once the Vision Frame is articulated, advancing the vision requires the premotion work of alignment, similar to aligning the front end of your car before a journey. But this is only a start. As the car begins to move, people will have questions. The conversation after the first steps of alignment in the church creates the need for attunement—helping people emotionally connect to the unique and newly clarified vision. The leader must make an attunement sandwich while aligning the nuts and bolts of things, being careful to create real dialogue and practice the power of a positive no.

As the leader forges the future through the difficult decisions of alignment and attunement, a new reality of love will unfold: "love does not consist in gazing at each other, but in looking together in the same direction."[4] If most churches don't achieve a stunning point of clarity or movement, it is because the leadership settles for "pseudocommunity"—an appearance of love for one another. This appearance of love prevents two breakthroughs. The first is having difficult conversations to get the leadership community on the same page. The second is making sure that the same page is a true page in the storybook of God's redemptive history. Ultimately, being attuned reflects not just our effectiveness together but the essence of looking together in the same direction as Christ, toward the men and women, boys and girls that he misses most. Real community lives with a clearly defined cause that all members pursue with reckless abandon.

20

TRANSFORM THE FUTURE

DELIVERING VISION DAILY

Spiritual leaders are the carriers of God's DNA in the church, the shapers of a church's vision and core values. They are influencers of what the church embodies. . . . The key to radical discipleship is the development of trainer-coaches that carry the DNA to the edges of the movement.

—Michael Slaughter

ON OCTOBER 15, 1981, one man initiated an act that would change the stadium experience of professional sports for all time. It was the third game of the American League play-off series between the Oakland Athletics and the New York Yankees. On that day, Krazy George Henderson knew he wanted to do something extraordinary. He saw it before anyone else in the stadium. With a drum in his hand, he worked hard to rally the attention of those in the sections around him. He started to generate enthusiasm for what he imagined: "a gesture that would start in his section and sweep successfully through the crowd in a giant, continuous wave of connected enthusiasm."[1] This transformative event later proved historic because on that day Krazy George invented "the Wave." Dov Seidman comments on the phenomenon: "The Wave is an extraordinary act. All those people spread out over a vast stadium, with limited ability to connect and communicate, somehow come together in a giant cooperative act inspired by a common goal: to help the home team win. It defied language and culture, occurring regularly throughout the world at Tower of Babel events as diverse as the Olympics. . . . It transverses gender, income and societal status. It is a pure expression of collective passion released."[2]

Making Waves

As we come to this culminating chapter in this Church Unique journey, I am aroused by thought that your stunningly unique, movement-oriented vision might behave like a Wave in your community. Not a sport-crazed crowd swinging their arms in the air, but a gospel revolution, marked by waves of life change and the unmistakable presence of God's Spirit. Imagine your unique vision as a "pure expression of collective passion released."

In the Introduction, I uncovered a driving assumption of this book: that the success of advancing vision is directly proportional to the degree to which the vision is first aligned and integrated. For the wave to sweep across the stadium that October day, Krazy George had to persevere through many failed attempts. One try after another and the wave would die early, putter out, and inspire only boos from whole sections of fans. But finally, with a critical mass of supporters around him, he enabled his message to reach and saturate the entire stadium. Eventually, thousands of people whom George would never know caught his vision. Twenty-five years later, his silly little stadiumwide pep rally religiously engages millions of sports fans across the world. Similarly, the church leader must summon the enthusiasm of those closest to him. As the leader builds consensus and enthusiasm he or she must deliver vision daily. One section at a time, one leader at time, one ministry at a time, the church will begin to see the big picture. Eventually the vision will reach thousands of people who the leader personally never knew.

During my career as a vision architect, I have been consumed by the question, What is the best way for any church to understand how its vision can penetrate and influence the culture of the church? This chapter presents the answer: the Integration Model. My primary motive is to give you and your team a simple tool to have conversation that will release a collective passion. I mean no disrespect to Rick Warren in saying that the Integration Model is a way to start being "purposeful for your church" rather than "purpose driven."

Approaching the topic of integration is a daunting task. After all, the church is a living organism of complex systems. In the **Integration Model,** I am not introducing a systems theory, but *a conversation starting point*. It is built by looking at the church through five perspectives: leadership, communication, process, environment, and culture (Figure 20.1). For each perspective, I present three principles for weaving vision into the life of the church. The result is no less than fifteen integration principles that

Figure 20.1. The Integration Model

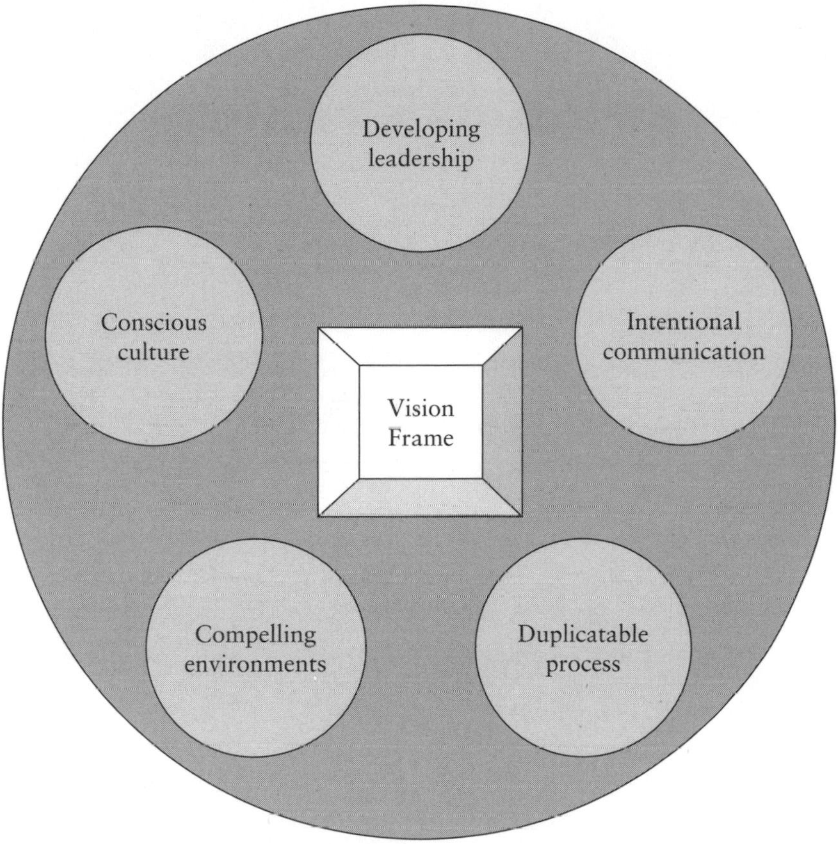

will fuel your team conversations for months to come. Through the model, we hope to achieve redemptive waves that harness the full participation of the congregation. The epicenter is your unique vision expressing God's specific work and call for your community.

Developing Leadership

The first of the five circles in the Integration Model is *leadership* (Figure 20.2). How will you use vision to recruit leaders, develop leaders, structure people, and divide your attention among the right leaders? Take leaders out of the equation and the visionary is a daydreamer. Take the stadium away from Krazy George and he is just another guy waving his hands in the air.

Figure 20.2. Integration Model: Developing Leadership

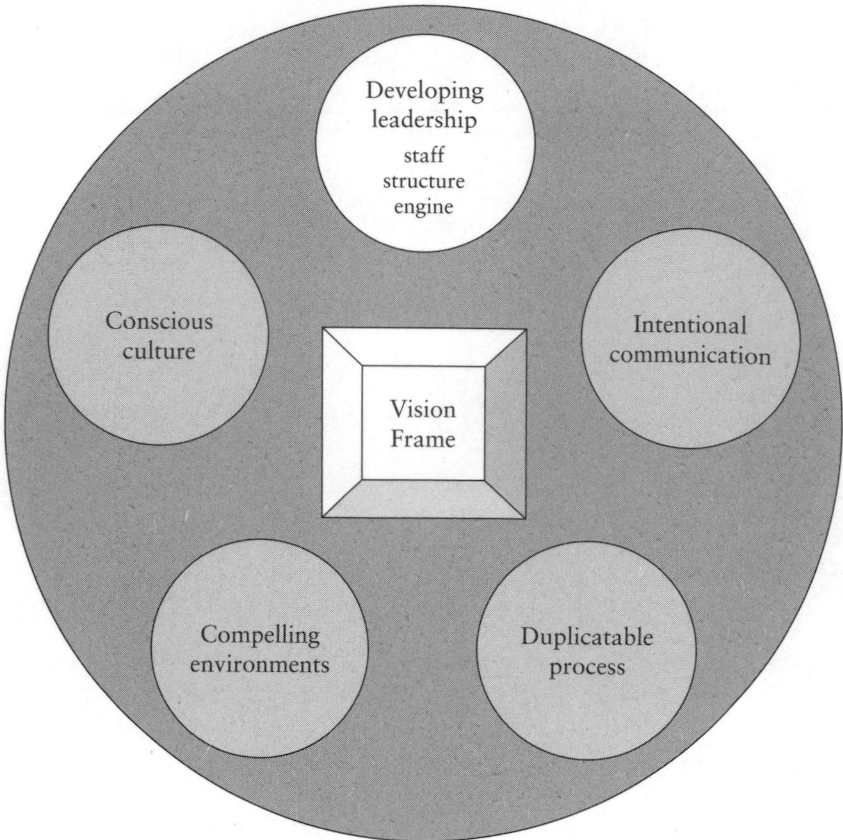

STAFF: GET PEOPLE WHO GET THE VISION. Hiring good staff is more difficult than ever. As an example, I was recently asked to help hire a pastor. Ads were placed at two seminaries and on churchstaffing.com. Within two weeks, I had more than fifty resumes, of which I talked to eight candidates, of which I was only interested in one. To complicate matters, you may be working through a committee that is also reviewing resumes.

Remember that once you have your Vision Frame in place, the individuals who make up your team can profoundly accelerate—or aggravate—your ability to deliver vision daily. There are some key questions to ask.

Do their personal values line up with the organization's? You can't ask, by the way; you have to discern this creatively.

Do they demonstrate the egoless clarity required to collaborate on a team?

Does their own apostolic esprit mesh with that of others on your leadership team? In addition to character and competence, what is their team chemistry?

Do they have experience leading in an organization with clarity? Ask them about the vision of where they are coming from.

Do they resonate with your vision articulation in general? Do they lean in and get excited about it, or do they remain distant and indifferent? If they aren't noticeably interested, strongly consider striking them as candidates.

Are you hiring to create progress or order for the vision within the organization? Every person on your leadership team contributes in some amount to creating one or the other. I recommend striving for an equation of "progress before order"; that is, making sure that the team is weighted toward progress. How do I define a progress orientation? Generally, it is the gifts, personality, and strengths that attract and connect people, rather than those that train and sustain people. Look for motivation in the apostle, evangelist, and prophetic range of APEPT (recall mention in Chapter Nine and the discussion in Chapter Sixteen); "D" and "i" orientations on the DiSC Profile personality assessment; Extroverted and Intuitive emphases on the Myers-Briggs Type Indicator; or red and yellow colors on the Insights Discovery Personal Profile. In contrast, order on the team may be more important if there are already too many entrepreneurial, apostolic, and progress-oriented types. Too much progress without order and the progress will undo itself. Look for the pastors and teachers from the APEPT range, "S" and "C" wirings on the DiSC, Introverted and Sensing on the Myers-Briggs, and blue and green colors on the Insights profile.

If your church is more than four hundred people, I would caution against hiring a person without the demonstrated spiritual gift of leadership (Rom. 12:8). Particularly if the person is going to oversee a large number of volunteer leaders, it is absolutely critical that this person be a delegator rather than a doer. To assist you in discerning this gift, look for the traits identified by Russ Robinson and Bill Donahue: (1) a strategic orientation, (2) conceptual thinking, (3) intellectual curiosity, and (4) others-focused mind-set.[3]

STRUCTURE: LET STRATEGY DETERMINE STRUCTURE. I was working with a church that completed the Vision Pathway and developed a wonderfully clear ^{m}*Map*. Six months later, the pastor called me when he was about to hire an "adult ministries pastor." I asked him a simple question about what this guy was supposed to do. The pastor paused. I realized that he had no good answer, and he certainly had no answer that was based on strategy. Why? Adult ministries pastor was the default expectation of the denominational system. It was the inertia of yesterday holding back the system! There are three cardinal rules for integrating your Vision Frame into your structure. The first is to communicate the vision in how you name the position. You cannot transform the future if your people are locked into the mental models of a previous structure. By the way, titles may be cheap, but resist the temptation to give someone a title he likes because it sounds better to him. The second is to clarify the top three key responsibility areas, including accountability for ᵐ*Map* components. The staff cannot drive the strategy if people do not have clear lines of responsibility and authority based on the ᵐ*Map*. The third rule is to structure for strategy over affinity, not affinity over strategy. In the absence of a vision and strategy, churches have defaulted toward hiring affinity groups, like "young adults pastor" or "men's minister," or program areas. If your staff is first organized around the ᵐ*Map*, then you may hire additional staff for affinity or programming depending on your size. The problem with structuring for affinity over strategy is that the affinity-based staff person cannot easily be held accountable for a component of the strategy.

ENGINE: LEAD LEADERS! The engine for your vision is your leadership. Period. Neglect it and you neglect your vision; lead your leaders well and everything else will take care of itself. The church today demonstrates a profound, disproportionate emphasis on crowds over core—I call it "crowd fixation." We have completely forgotten the model of Jesus as he spent a majority of his time with twelve men in order to release a worldwide movement. In fact, whenever the largest crowds were gathered in the gospels, Jesus had an agenda for training the twelve more than he did for teaching the crowd. We do the opposite today. We build everything around the crowds coming to worship, and we're lucky if we get all of our leaders together once or twice a year. Other than a clear Vision Frame, the greatest need in the church today is recovery of a centralized leadership development process. (Aubrey Malphurs and I wrote *Building Leaders* to address this need.)

With your Vision Frame developed, you now have a new basis for leadership development. It's not about giving them more "Maxwellisms" alone, it's about developing their appreciation, understanding, and skill around the Kingdom Concept and Vision Frame. They become the trainer-coaches who take the DNA to the edges of the movement.

Intentional Communication

Every day, your church stewards thousands of moments of truth. Every time a member talks to a neighbor, someone drives by the church facility,

Figure 20.3. Integration Model: Intentional Communication

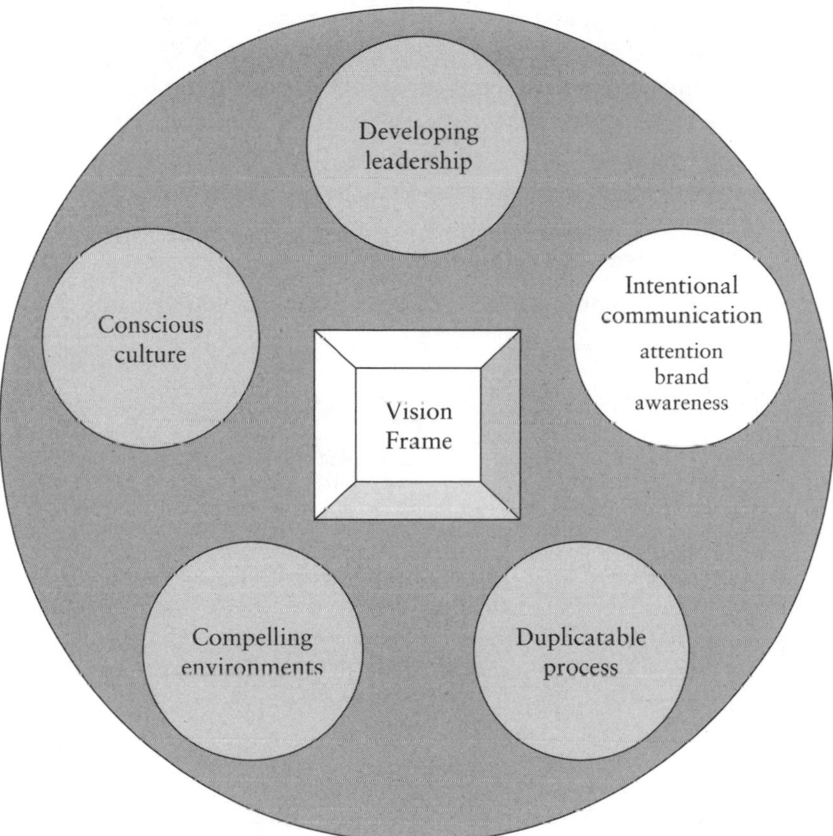

a ministry e-mail goes out, a pastor's business card is left on a desk, some interaction on behalf of the church has transpired. Every time these events happen, the church's vision glows brighter or dims in the tiniest little increments. The leader's role is to crank up the wattage. The visionary cares too much about the message to let it just blow in the wind, unattended. Rather, he grabs his message and affixes it to a kite for all to see. This can happen only with a tremendous amount of intentionality in the complex discipline of church communications (Figure 20.3).

ATTENTION: GRAB ATTENTION OR HOLD NOTHING. When Thomas Davenport and John Beck wrote the book *The Attention Economy,* they brought a very important message to church leaders. The book argues that information and talent are no longer your most important resource, but rather attention itself. People cannot hear the vision unless we cut through the clutter. When Krazy George invented the Wave, he beat a drum endlessly to capture and hold people's attention. What drum are you going to hold as a leader?

The principle of attention requires church leaders to be bold and relevant as they integrate vision into the internal communication of the church. According to Davenport and Beck, these are the most important characteristics to get attention:

- The communication is personalized.
- The communication comes from a trustworthy source.
- The communication is brief.
- The communication is emotional.

Imagine the implications of these attributes for your church's communications. Are you sending targeted, HTML e-mails to supplement snail mail and print communication? Are you delivering your most important sound bites via podcast?

Finally, it is important to keep good communications people close to the core leadership. They shouldn't have to guess about your church's DNA. Rather, allow them to be privy to all the conversations and dialogue that surround development and articulation of your Vision Frame.

BRAND: COMMUNICATE VISION VISUALLY. We live in a media-savvy, graphics-saturated world that bombards our minds with brand promises and visual stimulation all day long. Then we go to church, where gifted leaders attempt to cast a life-changing, revolutionary vision for following the God of the universe. The problem? Churches pump out communications all day long and miss the opportunity to constantly reflect and reinforce the vision. Yes, your church needs to brand—it's not a four-letter word imported from the corporate world. Branding is about taking your Kingdom Concept and Vision Frame, and communicating them with *consistent* consistency across all communication platforms. The baseline of your visual brand contains three components:

Logo: a distinct mark that identifies your name in the local community

Tagline: a short compelling phrase that positions your Church Unique and delivers a promise according to your strengths as a church (See appendixes for examples.)

Graphic identity: the styles, shapes, and colors that carry and define the look and feel of all your visual communication

With these three components of your brand, you can integrate your messaging across all ministries and levels in your organization: guests, attenders, members, and core leadership. The key is that these visual elements must tie into and leverage the Vision Frame articulation. I recommend that you bring in outside help from a ministry marketing company or a local ad agency to help you do this. But don't choose a company that uses predesigned approaches. That violates the whole basis of this book; your church represents something unique and you must intentionally communicate your uniqueness. (Because of the limitation of black and white on these pages, we have set up some color examples of vision-driven branding at www.churchunique.com; check it out.)

AWARENESS: BROADCAST YOUR POSITION. John 15 tells us that the Spirit of God is sovereignly convicting people of sin and righteousness and judgment. In other words, God is wooing men, women, boys, and girls to Him in your community. The question is, When they are ready to act on it, where will they go? Even though the primary mode of awareness happens through word-of-mouth advertising, the North American culture supplies other media to help broadcast your position. By broadcasting your position, I mean two things. First, think like a retailer and let people know *that* you exist and *where* you exist. Second, position yourself in the sense of differentiating yourself among other churches in your community. In the kingdom economy, other churches are not competitors but collaborators. The best thing you can do is broadcast a clear, crisp message of what makes your Church Unique.

Remember that there are competitors to your mission—that is, anything else that distracts people from being the church under the Lordship of Jesus. These competitors, whether Home Depot, the local sports league, Old Navy, or 24 Hour Fitness, are doing everything to broadcast their position. Shall we stand by as nonparticipants in the game of PR, marketing, and advertising and let them take the day?

Use of marketing should never replace the essence of a missional heartbeat: a life-oriented, conversation-driven, love-lavished pursuit of those whom Jesus misses most. Jesus' famous sermon was not "in the valley" but "on the mount." Jesus positioned himself to broadcast his message. If we propose to advance the gospel in and through the culture, we can't afford to see the cultural use of communication as an enemy but as an ally. Use of marketing tools can be a powerful support to personal evangelism. These are exciting times to steward the most important message to be heard.

Duplicatable Process

For a leader, the maxim is true: it's not about what you can do, but what you can duplicate (Figure 20.4). At some point your vision must transcend your skills and be deposited into the basic reproducible habits of the entire congregation. There are three processes to start thinking about: (1) How do people move other people through your ^{m}*Map*? (2) How do your people do the work of evangelism? (3) How does your church body multiply itself?

Figure 20.4. Integration Model: Duplicatable Process

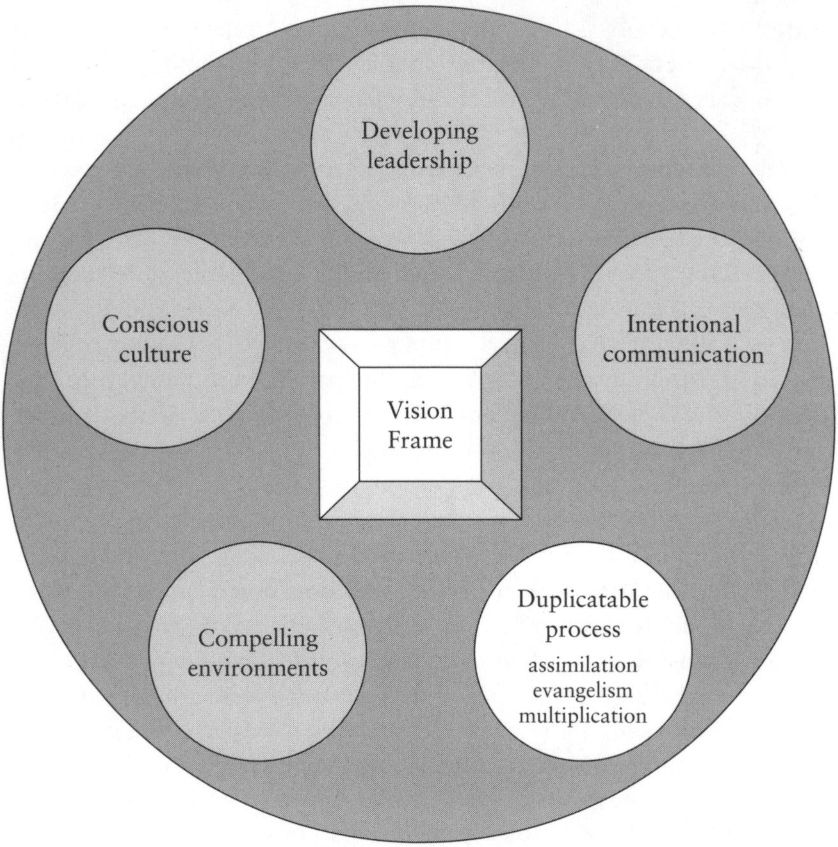

ASSIMILATION: HELP PEOPLE ATTRACT PEOPLE. We have already presented our golden rule that programs don't attract people; people do. As the leader you want to lubricate the gears of this process. This means motivating people to do whatever it takes to help others move through the ᵐ*Map*. It's like building a customer service impulse into every heart and hand that calls your church home. Put down these steps, these words, these ideas, and teach them to your people. Grow them from your vision, and make them simple and reproducible enough that people can step in at any time. At Sagemont Church, members are prepared to offer "a word, a look, or a touch" as gestures of hospitality to guests. At another church, leaders are encouraged to engage in the "ten-minute mingle" just after the service in order to invite people into groups. At Faithbridge, unpaid servants turn on their headlights so they can be directed to park *further* away than those not serving. At North Coast, those who ride the parking shuttle bus receive a silly little fluorescent sticker that says "I rode the bus" as a mini "reward" for parking remotely. Churches talk all the time about assimilation as an important function. Don't miss the opportunity to leverage your vision generally, and your ᵐ*Map* specifically, to make assimilation a function of culture through microsteps that everyone can take.

EVANGELISM: ACCESSORIZE THE MISSION. When people think of evangelism at your church, what reproducible steps, skills, tools, or processes do they think of? When I say *accessorize the mission,* I mean two related ideas. The first is a pretty forced pun (the idea of making mission accessible); that is, how do you concretely encourage the practice of missional living? The second is to give people the tools and processes for them to be evangelists. Someone with the spiritual gift of evangelism may not need these helps, but most of us do. Studies show that when a leader casts vision, the most common question that followers ask is, "What support and tools are available to us?"[4] So when you stand up and remind people of your ᵐ*Mandate*, you will want to know there is the necessary follow-through to equip them. There is no right way to be an evangelist; some of the best processes may arise out of a church's Kingdom Concept. When Bruce Wesley, senior pastor at Clear Creek Community Church, shares his mission to lead unchurched people to be fully devoted followers of Christ, his people know that he has a "top five" card in his wallet—the unchurched people for whom he is praying. Another pastor encourages his people to prayer-walk through their neighborhood. My father led a new member of his small group to Christ several months ago. At lunch he drew a simple bridge illustration, a basic gospel sharing process that has been duplicated in his life for years. Another church asks each member to write out a three-minute testimony in preparation for sharing it on a moment's notice. As a beach head for spiritual conversations, the people of Bandera Road Community Church rally around the idea of sharing a meal.

Keep in mind that we are not talking about formulaic approaches. What we are talking about is more in line with the eloquent plea of Frost and Hirsch: "We yearn for something richer and more complex, more daring, and dangerous. As we have already noted the one-size-fits-all to church mission and evangelism must be abandoned. This wouldn't seem to be such a radical statement, but churches throughout the West seem to be more eager than ever to embrace formularized, 'successful' prepackaged models of evangelism. Fewer and fewer churches, from our experience, seem to be developing evangelistic ministries specifically contextualized to the geographic area or subculture in which they are living."[5] These words are apt, reminding us that knowing our local predicament is essential in creatively, yet thoughtfully, engaging our culture.

MULTIPLICATION: DECIDE HOW YOU DUPLICATE. One of the values of the missional church is healthy orientation toward kingdom growth over the necessary growth of one local church. On the basis of your Kingdom Concept and your Vision Frame, you must decide what size is best, what timing is best, and what kind of multiplication is best. An elephant reproduces according to the biomass of an elephant, and a mouse reproduces according to the biomass of a mouse. Are you planning to grow to six hundred before you plant, or sixteen hundred? Are you reproducing multisites, church plants, house churches, or organic faith communities, or adding multiple services and venues to one location? Are you planting a church in your city, in your state, or in unreached people groups? Will you play an active role or a passive role in the planting process? As you can see, there are many questions to ask about the process. So this process must be tied to the vision. Hope Baptist Church in Las Vegas has a unique vision for city transformation. To accomplish it, they have decided to plant one church a year for five years in their community and ask each church they plant to do the same. They envision playing an active role that includes bringing the planting pastor onto Hope's staff a year prior to the launch. This reproducible process is how they plan to tackle the rapid growth in their local area.

Compelling Environments

Having designed hundreds of strategies during the last decade, I find that there are three dominant environments that every local church is attempting to create: worship environments, connecting environments, and serving environments. Each one plays a significant role in transmitting and realizing the vision. Most important, amid a missional reorientation we must acknowledge that our environments have tended to be an end and not a means to Christian mission. The missional leader must constantly show that the church gathered is actually a time of preparation for "being the church" outside of its walls (Figure 20.5).

Figure 20.5. Integration Model: Compelling Environments

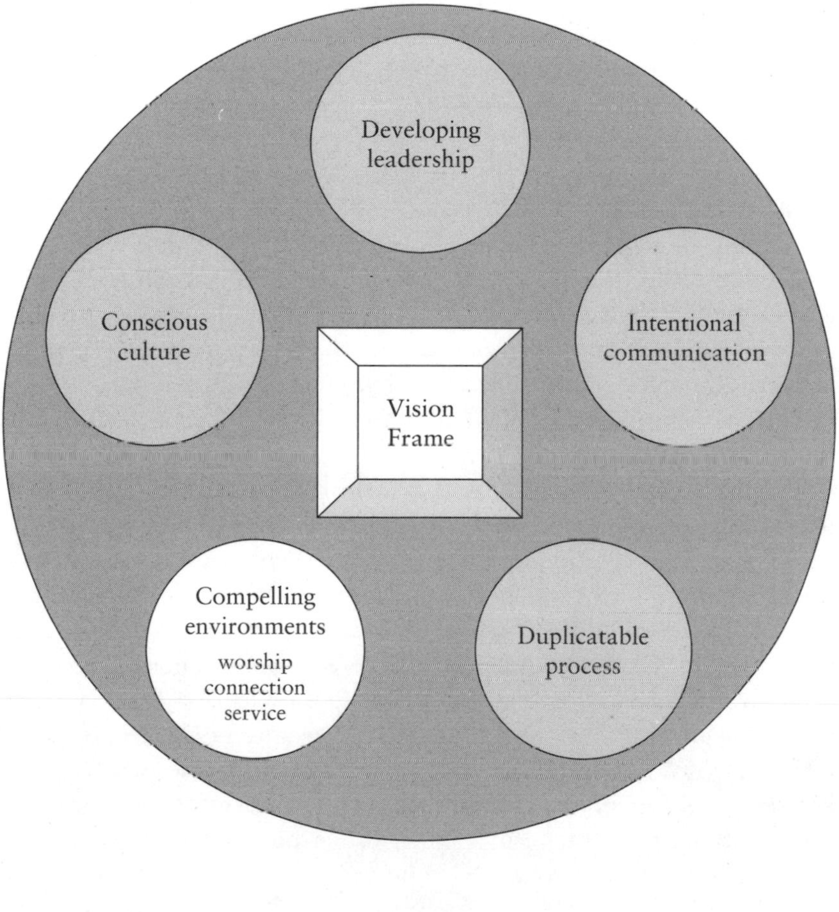

WORSHIP: REFOCUS JESUS, TOGETHER. The pattern of weekly worship and Sabbath was embedded into the fabric of early church culture. Every church has some environment for worship. The question is, How does your vision integrate into your worship? What aspects of the vision are communicated during the worship experience? How do the elements and order of worship communicate values? How does the vision itself affect the design of the worship space? The vision of raw simplicity in a Quaker meetinghouse is a stark contrast to a large downtown stained-glass sanctuary.

The Latin phrase *lex orandi, lex credendi,* used in the Roman Catholic Church, refers to the relationship between how we worship and how we believe. It implies that we learn about values and beliefs by how worship takes place, even before we are taught. Experience precedes thought. In other words, before you think you are casting vision you already are, by how you worship.

The other role of worship is to keep the community so God-centered that the euphoria of being used by God doesn't replace intimacy with God Himself. Jesus had to tell his disciples after a successful mission to rejoice not that they have authority over demons but that their names are written in heaven (Luke 10:20). Worship keeps our grandest visions God-centered and Jesus-focused.

CONNECT: INTEGRATE EVERYTHING RELATIONALLY. What would church be without relationships? Every church draws people into some kind of setting where the "one anothers" of Scripture are applied. The groups may be tight-knit, gender accountability groups of three to six, or they may be thirty to forty people in an on-campus adult Bible fellowship. Your Kingdom Concept and your Vision Frame reflect some basic unit of community through which relationships can form and thrive.

Perhaps the most important principle of integration is that for discipleship to happen in a church of more than four hundred people, the relational point of integration for the Vision Frame necessarily moves from a staff pastor to a lay leader in the church's connecting environment. For example, in a medium-sized church of groups, the DNA of the church is likely to be transmitted through the volunteer small-group leader. There is simply not enough time and relational exposure for a staff pastor to do it. (This again reinforces our principle of "Engine: Lead leaders!")

This makes the connecting environment, in most cases, the locus of both spiritual formation and vision discovery. For example, in the small group I lead, I carry the responsibility of teaching and shepherding the members toward our church's "G7 Guide," which is our way of defining the ᵐ*Marks* as fully devoted followers of Christ. Yes, the group members hear about the vision in other church venues, but the rubber must meet the road in the most time-relationship-intensive environment. If they don't get the vision in the connecting environment, the vision won't stick. The Wave will not go very far around the stadium.

SERVE: SERVE INSIDE OUT. Because God has given spiritual gifts for the edification of the body (Eph. 4), the church is incomplete and immature unless individual members are serving one another. Every church has environments of service: leading in worship, instructing children, or welcoming guests, to name a few. The Vision Frame should guide how the church builds its serving environments.

The missional mind-set pushes the envelope on how we think about service. Do we serve people only after we somehow convince them to come onto our holy turf, or do we push out into the community and demonstrate the love of Jesus in their midst? There has been growing emphasis on two dynamics related to service. One is shared projects with other community participants. Hope Baptist Church recently launched a nonprofit organization called Surgance, whose mission is to "channel waves of servanthood for community transformation." The whole idea behind the organization is to connect churches and volunteers with nonchurch entities in working for community impact. Another dynamic is what Frost and Hirsch call "proximity spaces," which they define as "places or events where Christians and not-yet-Christians can interact meaningfully with one another."[6] The bottom line is this: we have to get out of our church boxes if we are going to effectively model the lifestyle of Jesus, who engaged and served people who were deeply embedded in *their* spaces.

Conscious Culture

The missional visionary is also a cultural architect. We started the book with the assertion that each church has a unique culture. While walking through the Vision Pathway, we emphasized the importance of close observation and listening in order to better understand the surrounding culture, and of unlocking the past in order to unleash the future. But now we speak generatively about the church's culture (Figure 20.6). The leader shapes the culture with the Vision Frame, informed by the Kingdom Concept. Transforming the future is made possible because the cultural perspective is held in conscious view.

SCRIPTURE: REVEAL GOD'S SIGNATURE. Whatever the leader draws attention to and rallies support for, he must show the signature of God

Figure 20.6. Integration Model: Conscious Culture

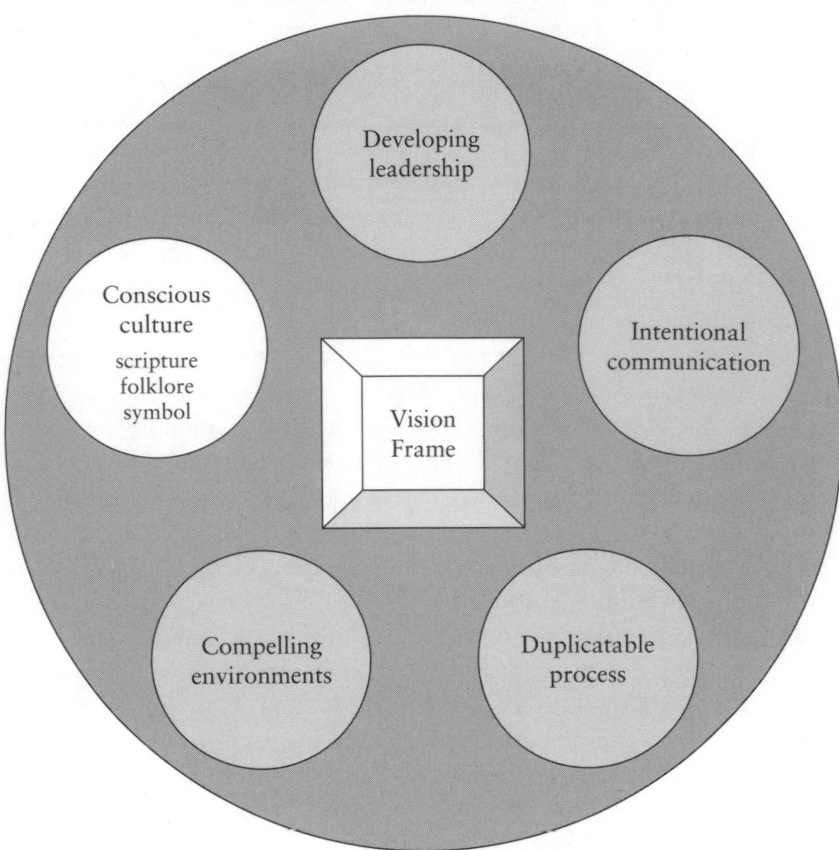

behind the appeal. The Vision Frame must be squarely and repeatedly illuminated with God's Word. The visionary must always point back to the Original Visioneer.

Specifically, the leader must own the texts that mark his own apostolic esprit. Look for the passages that fuel your passion, enlarge your own vision, inform your [m]*Motives*, and distinguish your strength as a church. Master the exposition of these texts. Then look for opportunities to ooze the vision through the pages of Scripture everywhere you go. Whenever and wherever the vision speaks, your job is to make sure God's voice is heard.

FOLKLORE: RETELL THE STORY. The leader who shapes culture understands that not all stories are created equal. Folklore is a special class of story—stories that speak so fundamentally and clearly to the church's vision that they have to be told, retold, and told again. Aubrey Malphurs and I discuss the importance of creating culture with story in *Building Leaders*:

> Life is narrative. As humans, we are hardwired to live from and respond to the stories of our lives. Imagine, for example, trying to foster intimacy with another person without being able to share a story. It is entirely possible to share facts and data about a person's life all day without really getting to know them. Or, imagine trying to communicate "the way things are" in an organization without telling stories to make it clear. Story is an indispensable tool for communicating on a heart-to-heart level; for communicating things like values, passion, convictions, history, and vision. Keep in mind that when God chose to reveal himself through Scripture, he chose the primary form of narrative. And when Jesus instructed the multitudes, he told story after story in the form of parables. Therefore, pastors who want to impact church leaders on the cultural level must become proficient with the tool of story.
>
> All preachers are familiar with story as either an illustrative tool or message construct for the preaching event. But it is also important to view storytelling on a broader level as a tool for creating culture. Creating culture requires the identification and development of special stories or folklore that serve as foundational, identity shaping stories within the leadership culture. The texture and color of the culture is then painted artistically by the telling and retelling of these stories. For example, every Marine knows the story of the Battle of Chapultepec, which occurred on September 13 of 1847 in the Mexican-American War. In the Corps, the story is retold of the courage and self-sacrifice of the NCO Corps who stormed the Chapultepec Castle outside of Mexico City. There, they shouldered the weight of large casualties as 90 percent of them died taking the Mexican stronghold. To be a Marine means to know this story and to reflect the values of self-sacrifice exemplified in the story.[7]

I was listening to my home church pastor and dear friend Bruce Wesley preach several months ago. He made a simple statement I will never forget: "Religious people have preferences; missional people have stories." As you lead, stories will emerge in the most unlikely places. Be sure to play the role of story collector; through them you will cultivate the missional imagination of your people, and reorient them back to God's vision.

SYMBOL: MARK DEFINING MOMENTS. A symbol is a visible sign of something invisible. The term literally contains the idea of "throwing together"—associating something intangible with something concrete. A lion for example, is a concrete and visible way of representing the invisible, intangible idea of courage. For the leader, expression of old familiar symbols and creation of new ones can shape a culture. Erwin McManus writes: "In every culture you will find essential metaphors that define and shape its ethos. Your symbols hold your secret stories. The metaphor causes an eruption of images, ideas, dreams, beliefs, and convictions all at one time."[8] For McManus, the term *mosaic* eventually became the name of the church, to reflect its identity and vision. The metaphor reflects at least three components of their culture: (1) vibrant expression of a multiethnic congregation, (2) emphasis on personal brokenness lived out in community, and (3) awareness of a sovereign God who works as the master artist. Using this beautiful and compelling symbol, McManus took a giant leap in creating culture in his church.

One of the reasons new symbols are so important is that they cultivate a shared memory. Alan Roxburgh writes, "The key to innovating missional community is the formation of a people within a specific memory and narrative"[9] As your vision unfolds and you see God's work, let use of symbols mark the moments and foster a shared memory. This memory glues the community together and multiplies the values defined by the memory. This is why tattoos hold meaning for emerging generations of our culture. They are body symbols that mark defining moments and recall the most important stories in shaping personal identity.

In some cases, the symbol may take the form of a symbolic act. For example, in Luke chapter 9 Jesus beats the drum three times; the disciples' job is to *proclaim* the kingdom of God. Then in verse 27, he changes the verb from "proclaim" to "see": "I tell you truly there are some standing here who will not taste death until they see the kingdom of God." Eight days later, Peter, James, and John have the experience of a lifetime. On top of a mountain, they get a glimpse of kingdom glory as Jesus "transfigures" and Moses and Elijah enter the heavenly scene. For some reason, in the middle of boot camp for proclaiming the kingdom Jesus creates a shared experience: the disciples see the kingdom. Jesus marks the moment in a way only he could: with a supernatural symbolic act.

As the leader lives the vision and speaks into the church's culture, symbols—visual signs and symbolic acts—become powerful tools. What is the most important symbol? It is your church logo as described in the principle "Brand: Communicate Vision Visually." Does the identifying mark of your church open a door to tell a story? In addition to your logo, there are many opportunities to use symbols to communicate other aspects of your Kingdom Concept and Vision Frame as we have illustrated specifically with your ^{m}*Map* in this book.

Pulling It All Together

To integrate means to join two or more objects so they can become part of a larger whole. We started the book talking about the problem of photocopied vision. The more you photocopy, the more you fragment. Churches in North America are some of the most fragmented communities I see.

The purpose of reviewing this Integration Model is to give you and your team a working vocabulary for pulling your unique vision together. The vision will not move forward unless it ties into and brings together leadership, communication, processes, environments, and culture. If it does, your Church Unique will capture your culture and build a movement that flows into your community with contagious redemptive passion (Figure 20.7).

Figure 20.7. The Integration Model's Fifteen Principles

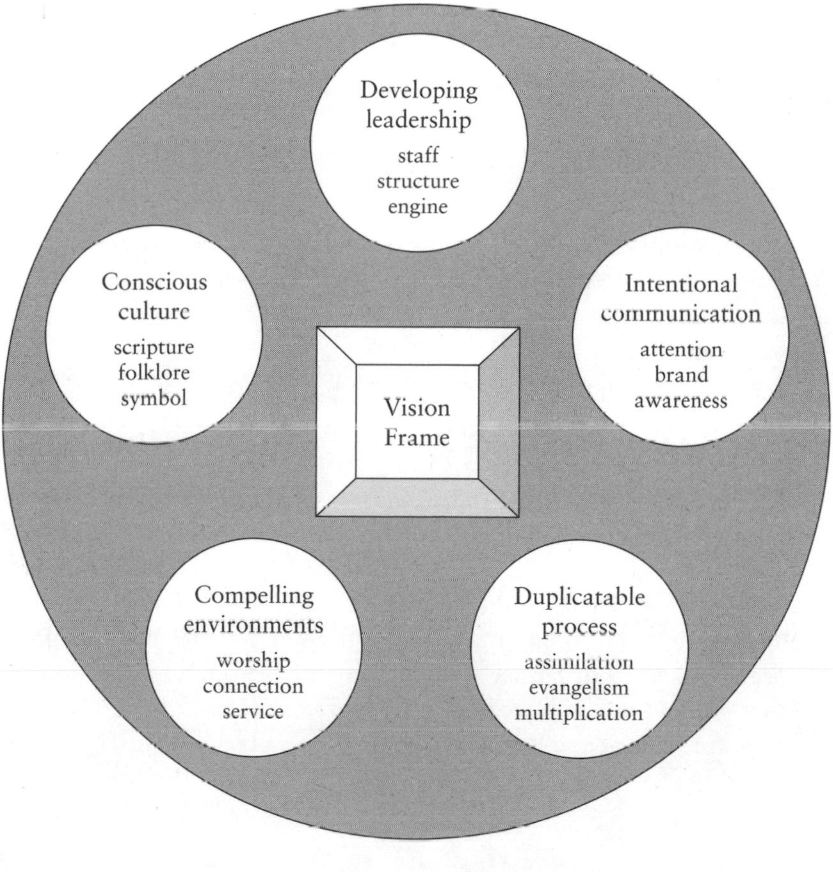

PARTING THOUGHTS

21

RESURRECT YOUR UNIQUENESS

IF YOU COPY SOMEONE ELSE'S VISION, WHO WILL ACCOMPLISH YOURS?

All is I want is a simple, purpose-driven, organic, and externally focused church on one hundred acres.

—The pastor's unspoken desire

WHAT IF OUR LIVES were marked with a deep peace, a thorough wellbeing that ran deep within our souls?

What if prayer and reflection were our true diet, and moments with God were palpable, and the Spirit really did whisper?

What if we slowed down enough to see the world and ourselves as if for the first time? What would we see?

What if we had nothing to prove and nothing to lose? And like little children we knew our Father's joy did not come from what we do, but who we are? Who would we be?

Whoever you are and wherever God has placed you, therein is uniqueness.

Whoever co-labors with you, in front of you, behind you, all around you, therein is uniqueness.

God is calling you today to an incomparable journey with Christ. Where will yours take you?

My incomparable journey has taken me to a place of hurricane-force unrest. I did not choose this burden; God chose it for me when He put it in me. This book is a wind gust from that storm. I would describe my burden as eyes that see unoriginal tragedy. But I fear that this is just a symptom of something deeper. Who doesn't want to be original? It is not our desire that is blocked but our state of being, our state of nearness, our state of stillness, and consequently our ability to ascertain. I ask again, What would you see? Who would you be? What better intermediate future were you created to bring?

Do you remember the dire straits of the race of men, toward the end of J.R.R. Tolkien's trilogy, in *The Return of the King*? In the 2003 film directed by Peter Jackson, when it appeared that Sauron's evil masses would win the day, Elrond, the leader of the elves, comes with a special gift: the sword of Elendil. It is fragmented from a battle long ago, but Elrond secretly forges the sword back into one piece, from useless bits to an integrated whole. The sword holds untold power that can change the fate of the hour. Elrond knows he must give it to Aragorn, the rightful heir. As Elrond shows Aragorn the sword, Aragorn is struck with disbelief. A defining point of the trilogy occurs at this moment when the Elf King offers the sword to Aragorn. He proclaims that the man who is able to wield the power of the sword can gather and command the most deadly army that has ever been formed. He exhorts Aragorn to take the sword, leave behind his life as a ranger, and become the man he was born to be.

Lord, show us Yourself as we have never seen You before. We know Your peace, so show us our piece, our place behind You as we follow Your lead. How can we serve You, how can we incarnate Your presence to *those You miss the most all* around us? Show us Yourself, Lord, that we might be free to become who we were born to be. In doing so, may Your church be unleashed.

APPENDIX A

LOGOS AND STRATEGY ICON EXAMPLES

THE FOLLOWING EXAMPLES FROM DIFFERENT churches illustrate the principle of communicating vision visually from Chapter Twenty. The examples have three key elements: logo, strategy icon, and tagline. Each of these churches developed their branding with Auxano after walking the Vision Pathway. Note how their logos represent distinct images and stylization in order to reflect the unique vision and culture of the organization. Their icons not only visualize the content of the strategy but also relate to the design of the logo and become an important internal communication tool. Their taglines are simple, short phrases that play a significant role in positioning their church and making a promise to people both inside and outside the congregation, highlighting their strengths.

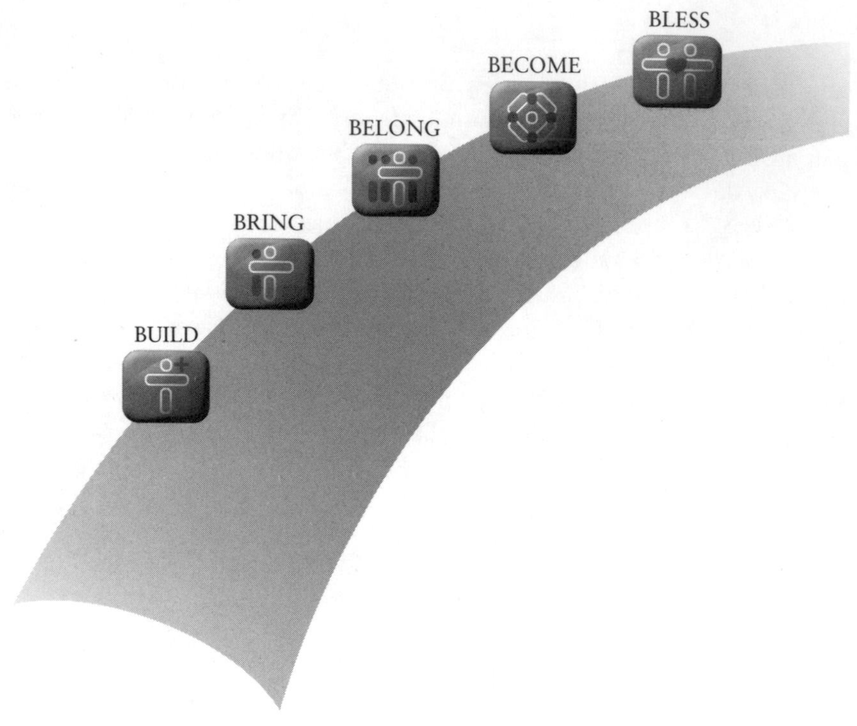

for life's journey

there's more.

Real people. Real life.

Where lives change for Good

Reach for life.

APPENDIX B

VISION PATH EXAMPLES

IN ADDITION TO THE FAITHBRIDGE example in Chapter Sixteen, I am including three Vision Path examples from ministries that have completed the four sides of their Vision Frame. The first is from Discovery Church in Orlando, which employs the metaphor of home. Note that the mission, strategy, and mission measure all relate to this dominant metaphor. The second example is from First Presbyterian Church in San Antonio. The third example is from Upward Sports, an international evangelical ministry. I included Upward as a nonchurch ministry to show that the Vision Frame can answer the irreducible questions of leadership in any context.

Mission (^{m}*Mandate*)

Leading people to discover all of their home in Christ

Discovery Difference (^{m}*Motives*)

Passionate discovery
We are believers passionate about discovering all that Christ and His Word offers and seizing opportunities to share Him with others.

Community transformation
We intentionally reach out to others by serving their needs and sharing the gospel in relevant ways so that they can access the life of Christ.

Authentic relationship
We engage in loving, authentic relationship with God and others.

Compelling environments
We create compelling environments that are conducive for the Holy Spirit to work in the hearts of people.

S2 leadership
We develop effective leaders who are "Spirit-led" and then "strategically focused."

Growth Markers (^{m}*Marks*)

Pursue, relate, serve, give, invite

Discovery Process (^{m}*Map*)

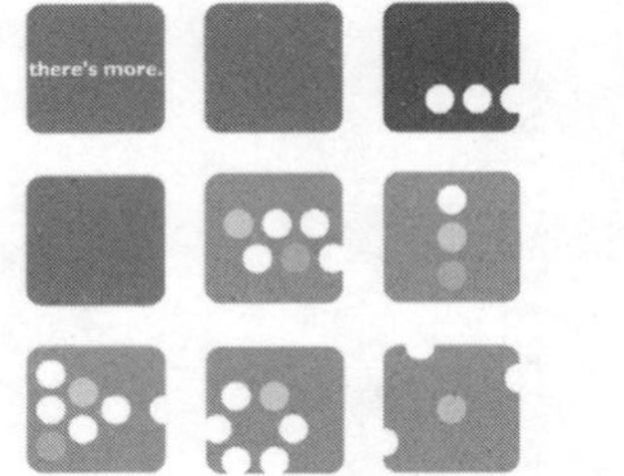

Mission (^m^*Mandate*)

Renewing minds and redeeming lives
with the steadfast love of Jesus Christ.

Values (^m^*Motives*)

City transformation
Demonstrated by an unwavering commitment to redeeming the heart of the city for Jesus Christ.

Gospel integration
Demonstrated by the merging of the Biblical with the social.

Spontaneous compassion
Demonstrated by the incredible and natural outpouring of love for others.

Gracious dedication
Demonstrated by the selfless devotion of leadership within the church.

Hands-on mission
Demonstrated by the philosophy that lives are changed by experiential learning.

Family education
Demonstrated by the reality that family is God's primary vehicle for discipleship.

Strategy (^m^*Map*)

worship

Mission Measure (^m^*Marks*)

Heart for God
Mind for truth
Knees for prayer
Mouth for encouraging
Hands for caring
Feet for going

Imagine life differently

Mission ([m]*Mandate*)

To introduce children to Jesus Christ by creating opportunities to serve through sports.

Values ([m]*Motives*)

The priority of children: We believe that every child is a winner.

The expectation of God-moments: We believe that God is a work all around us.

The discipline of excellence: We believe in serving that exceeds expectations.

The life of integrity: We believe that how we live is more important than what we say.

Leagues on Mission: Questions for Church Partners ([m]*Marks*)

U plifting their league in prayer?

P resenting the Gospel and scripture?

W anting every child to know Christ?

A ctively developing leadership?

R einforcing Christ as the character model for coaches and referees?

D elivering a fun experience to every participant?

Strategy ([m]*Map*)

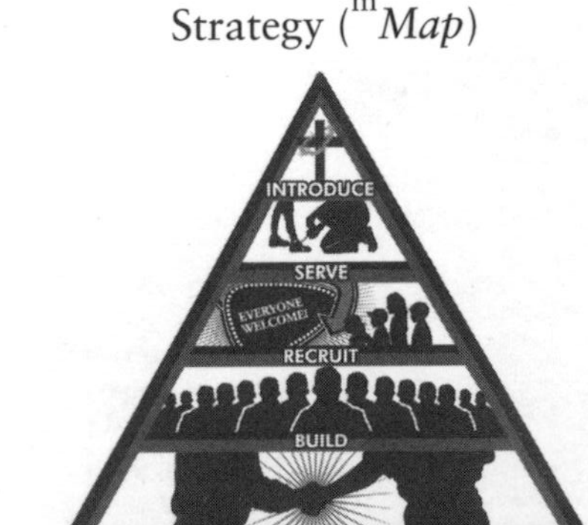

Every child is a winner

NOTES

INTRODUCTION

1. Schaller, Lyle E. *The Interventionist.* Nashville, Tenn.: Abingdon Press, 1997, p. 144.

PART ONE

CHAPTER 1

1. Libbrecht, Kenneth G. "Is It Really True That No Two Snowflakes Are Alike?" [www.its.caltech.edu/~atomic/snowcrystals/alike]. 2006.
2. Barna, George. *A Fish out of Water.* Nashville, Tenn.: Integrity, 2002, p. 119.
3. Lewis, Robert, and Cordeiro, Wayne. *Culture Shift: Transforming Your Church from the Inside Out.* San Francisco: Jossey-Bass, 2005, p. 3.
4. Lewis and Cordeiro, 2005, p. 2.
5. Lewis, Allyson. *The Seven Minute Difference: Small Steps to Big Changes.* Chicago: Kaplan, 2006, p. 57.
6. Barna, George. *The Power of Vision.* Ventura, Calif.: Regal Books, 2003, p. 11.
7. For a useful explanation of how changes in technology and communication affect culture, see Miller, M. Rex. *The Millennium Matrix: Reclaiming the Past, Reframing the Future of the Church.* San Francisco: Jossey-Bass, 2004.
8. Schaller, 1997, p. 13.

CHAPTER 2

1. Adapted from Stanley, Andy, and Jones, L. *Communicating for a Change: Seven Keys to Irresistible Communication.* Sisters, Ore.: Multnomah, 2006, pp. 93–94.

2. Stanley, A., Joiner, R., and Jones, L. *Seven Practices of Effective Ministry.* Sisters, Ore.: Multnomah, 2004, p. 130.

3. Gladwell, Malcolm. *The Tipping Point: How Little Things Can Make a Big Difference.* New York: Little, Brown, 2002, p. 99.

4. Collins, Jim. *Good to Great.* New York: HarperBusiness, 2001, pp. 90–91.

5. "The Masters of Business Imagination Manifesto." [http://www.jimcarroll.com/10s/10MBI.htm]. 2006. Used by permission.

6. McNeal, Reggie. *The Present Future: Six Tough Questions for the Church.* San Francisco: Jossey-Bass, 2003, pp. 92–96.

CHAPTER 3

1. Engle, Paul, and McIntosh, Gary. *Evaluating the Church Growth Movement: Five Views.* Grand Rapids, Mich.: Zondervan, 2004, pp. 20–21.

2. Engle and McIntosh, 2004, p. 12.

3. Engle and McIntosh, 2004, p. 9.

4. Engle and McIntosh, 2004, p. 21.

5. Stetzer, Ed, and Putman, David. *Breaking the Missional Code: Your Church Can Become a Missionary in your Community.* Nashville, Tenn.: Broadman and Holman, 2006, p. 46.

6. Warren, Rick. *The Purpose Driven Church.* Grand Rapids, Mich.: Zondervan, 1995, front cover flap.

7. Stetzer and Putman, 2006, p. 49.

8. Barna, George. *Growing True Disciples.* Ventura, Calif.: Regal, 2002, pp. 31–48.

9. Guder, Darrell, and Barrett, Lois. *The Missional Church: A Vision for the Sending of the Church in North America.* Grand Rapids, Mich.: Eerdmans, 1998, p. 6.

10. Guder and Barrett, 1998, p. 5.

11. Frost, Michael, and Hirsch, Alan. *The Shaping of Things to Come: Innovation and Mission for the 21st Century Church.* Peabody, Mass.: Hendrickson, 2003, p. 12.

12. Henderson, Jim, and Casper, Matt. *Jim & Casper Go to Church: Frank Conversation About Faith, Churches, and Well-Meaning Christians.* Ventura, Calif.: Barna Group, 2007, p. xvii.

13. Guder and Barrett, 1998, p. 3.
14. McNeal, 2003, p. 23.

CHAPTER 4

1. Barker, Joel Arthur. *Future Edge: Discovering the new Paradigms of Success*. New York: W. Morrow, 1992, p. 140.
2. Collins, 2001, p. 82.

PART TWO

CHAPTER 5

1. Buckingham, Marcus. *The One Thing You Need to Know.* New York: Free Press, 2005, p. 145.
2. Stanley, Joiner, and Jones, 2004, pp. 69–84.

CHAPTER 6

1. Willard, Dallas. *The Divine Conspiracy.* New York: HarperCollins, 1997, p. 11.
2. Adair, John. *The Leadership of Jesus and Its Legacy Today.* Cleveland: Pilgrim Press, 2002, p. 117.
3. Blanchard, Ken. *High Five: The Magic of Working Together.* New York: HarperCollins, 2001, p. 184.
4. Deming, Edwards. "A System of Profound Knowledge." In Neff, Dale, and Cefola, Jacquelyn. *The Economic Impact of Knowledge.* Woburn, Mass.: Butterworth-Heinemann, 1998, p. 161.

CHAPTER 7

1. Coleman, Robert. "The Master's Plan." In Winter, Ralph, and others. *Perspectives on the World Christian Movement.* Pasadena, Calif.: William Carey Library, 1999, p. 101.
2. Smith, Dwight. "Identifying People of Vision: God's Design for Antioch, Apostolic, Visionary Kinds of Leaders." [http://www.scpi.org/index.php?page=peopleofvision]. 2001.

CHAPTER 9

1. Colson, Charles. *The Body: Being Light in the Darkness*. Dallas: Word, 1992, p. 65.
2. Cannistraci, David. *God's Vision for Your Church*. Ventura, Calif.: Regal Books, 1999, pp. 276–277.
3. Spaugh, Herbert. "A Short Introduction to the History, Customs, and Practices of the Moravian Church." [http://www.everydaycounselor.com/archives/sh/shistory.htm]. December 16, 1999.
4. http://en.wikipedia.org/wiki/Facing_the_Giants.
5. James, William. *The Varieties of Religious Experience: A Study in Human Nature*. New York: Modern Library, 1936, p. 9.
6. Tichy, Noel. *The Leadership Engine: How Winning Companies Build Leaders at Every Level*. New York: HarperBusiness, 1997, p. 3.

CHAPTER 10

1. [http://www.southwest.com/about_swa/airborne.html], 2007.
2. Collins, Jim. *Good to Great and the Social Sectors: Why Business Thinking Is Not the Answer: A Monograph to Accompany* Good to Great: Why Some Companies Make the Leap—and Others Don't. Boulder, Colo.: J. Collins, 2005, p. 27.
3. Rainer, Thom S., and Eric Geiger. *Simple Church: Returning to God's Process for Making Disciples*. Nashville, Tenn.: Broadman Press, 2006, p. 76.

PART THREE

CHAPTER 11

1. http://www.37signals.com/svn/archives/001074.php, 2005.

CHAPTER 12

1. Jones, Laurie Beth. *The Path: Creating Your Mission Statement for Work and for Life*. New York: Hyperion, 1996, p. ix.
2. Cole, Neil. *Organic Church: Growing Faith where Life Happens*. San Francisco: Jossey-Bass, 2005, p. xxvii.
3. Minatrea, Milfred. *Shaped by God's Heart: The Passion and Practices of Missional Churches*. San Francisco: Jossey-Bass, 2004, p. 11.

CHAPTER 14

1. Dahle, Cheryl. "Can This Off-site Be Saved?" *Fast Company,* September 2001, p. 118.
2. Laermer, Richard, and Mark Simmons. *Punk Marketing: Get Off Your Ass and Join the Revolution.* New York: HarperCollins, 2007, p. 123.
3. Stanley, Joiner, and Jones, 2004, p. 87.
4. Hawkins, Greg L., Cally Parkinson, and Eric Arnson. *Reveal.* Willow Creek Resources, p. 33.
5. Hawkins, Parkinson, and Arnson, p. 65.
6. Rainer and Geiger, 2006, p. 67.

CHAPTER 15

1. Pope, Randy. *The Prevailing Church: An Alternative Approach to Ministry Design.* Chicago: Moody Press, 2002, p. 84.
2. Frazee, Randy. *The Connecting Church: Beyond Small Groups to Authentic Community.* Grand Rapids, Mich.: Zondervan, 2001, p. 69.
3. McNeal, 2003, p. 106.
4. Barna, George. *Growing True Disciples: New Strategies for Producing Genuine Followers of Christ.* Colorado Springs, Colo.: WaterBrook Press, 2001, pp. 74–76.
5. Barna, 2001, pp. 75–76.

CHAPTER 16

1. Warren Bennis. *On Becoming a Leader.* New York: Perseus, 1989, p. 31.
2. Barna, George. [http://www.barna.org/FlexPage.aspx?Page=Excerpt&ProductID=57]. Excerpt from Barna, George. *The Power of Team Leadership: Achieving Success Through Shared Responsibility.* Colorado Springs, Colo.: WaterBrook Press, 2001.
3. Regele, Mike, and Mark Schulz. *Death of the Church.* Grand Rapids, Mich.: Zondervan, 1995, p. 229.
4. www.philvischer.com/index.php/?p38, 2007.
5. Frost and Hirsch, 2003, pp. 170–171.
6. Sweet, Leonard. *SoulTsunami.* Grand Rapids, Mich.: Zondervan, 1999, p. 57.

CHAPTER 17

1. Lipton, Mark (quoting Tom Chappell). *Guiding Growth: How Vision Keeps Companies on Course.* Boston: Harvard Business School Press, 2003, p. 100.
2. Buckingham, 2005, p. 132.
3. Weems, Lovett H. (quoting C. S. Lewis). *Church Leadership: Vision, Team, Culture, and Integrity.* Nashville, Tenn.: Abingdon Press, 1993, p. 59.
4. Sweet, 1999, p. 201.
5. Adair, 2002, pp. 125–126.
6. Willard, Dallas. *The Divine Conspiracy.* New York: HarperCollins, 1997, p. 375.
7. Maxwell, John C. *The Irrefutable Laws of Leadership: Follow Them and People Will Follow You.* Nashville, Tenn.: Thomas Nelson Publishers, 1998, p. 111.
8. Buckingham, Marcus. 2005, p. 177.
9. Lencioni, Patrick. *Silos, Politics, and Turf Wars: A Leadership Fable About Destroying the Barriers That Turn Colleagues into Competitors.* San Francisco: Jossey-Bass, 2006, p. 179.

PART FOUR

INTRODUCTION

1. Rainer and Geiger, 2006, pp. 202–203.

CHAPTER 18

1. Donahue, Bill, and Russ Robinson. *The Seven Deadly Sins of Small Group Ministry: A Troubleshooting Guide for Church Leaders.* Grand Rapids, Mich.: Zondervan, 2002, p. 45. (Here I adapt their use of the terms *collaboration, coordination,* and *communication.*)

CHAPTER 19

1. Lipton, 2003, p. 109.
2. Senge, Peter (quoting David Bohm). *The Fifth Discipline: The Art and Practice of the Learning Organization.* New York: Doubleday, 1990, p. 240.

3. Ury, William. *The Power of a Positive No: How to Say No and Still Get to Yes*. New York: Bantam Books, 2007, pp. 1–28.
4. Adair (quoting Antoine de Saint Exupery), 2002, p. 151.

CHAPTER 20

1. Seidman, Dov. *How: Why HOW We Do Anything Means Everything . . . in Business (and in Life)*. Hoboken, N.J.: Wiley, 2007, p. 1.
2. Seidman, 2007, p. 3.
3. Donahue and Robinson, 2002, p. 68.
4. Jensen, Bill. *Simplicity: The New Competitive Advantage in a World of More, Better, Faster.* Cambridge, Mass.: Perseus Books, 2000, pp. 72–73.
5. Frost and Hirsch, 2003, p. 84.
6. Frost and Hirsch, 2003, p. 24.
7. Malphurs, Aubrey, and Will Mancini. *Building Leaders: Blueprints for Developing Leadership at Every Level of Your Church*. Grand Rapids, Mich.: Baker Books, 2004, p. 217.
8. McManus, Erwin Raphael. *An Unstoppable Force: Daring to Become the Church God Had in Mind*. Loveland, Colo.: Group, 2001, p. 113.
9. Roxburgh, Alan J., and Fred Romanuk. *The Missional Leader: Equipping Your Church to Reach a Changing World*. San Francisco: Jossey-Bass, 2006, p. 71.

BIBLIOGRAPHY

Bailey, Mark. *To Follow Him: The Seven Marks of a Disciple*. Sisters, Ore.: Multnomah, 1997.

Barna, George. *Growing True Disciples: New Strategies for Producing Genuine Followers of Christ*. Colorado Springs, Colo.: WaterBrook Press, 2001.

Bennett, David W. *Metaphors of Ministry: Biblical Images for Leaders and Followers*. Grand Rapids, Mich.: Baker Book House, 1993.

Cole, Neil. *Organic Church: Growing Faith Where Life Happens*. San Francisco: Jossey-Bass, 2005.

Collins, Jim. *Good to Great and the Social Sectors: Why Business Thinking Is Not the Answer: A Monograph to Accompany Good to Great: Why Some Companies Make the Leap—and Others Don't*. Boulder, Colo.: J. Collins, 2005.

Creps, Earl G. *Off-Road Disciplines: Spiritual Adventures of Missional Leaders*. San Francisco: Jossey-Bass, 2006.

Davenport, Thomas H., and John C. Beck. *The Attention Economy: Understanding the New Currency of Business*. Boston: Harvard Business School Press, 2001.

Driscoll, Mark. *Confessions of a Reformission Rev.: Hard Lessons from an Emerging Missional Church*. Leadership Network Innovation Series. Grand Rapids, Mich.: Zondervan, 2006.

Faber, R. "The Apostle and the Poet: Paul and Aratus." [http://www.spindleworks.com/library/rfaber/aratus.htm]. 2001.

Frost, Michael, and Hirsch, Alan. *The Shaping of Things to Come: Innovation and Mission for the 21st Century Church*. Peabody, Mass.: Hendrickson, 2003.

Gibbs, Eddie, and Ryan K. Bolger. *Emerging Churches: Creating Christian Community in Postmodern Cultures*. Grand Rapids, Mich.: Baker Academic, 2005.

Gladwell, Malcolm. *The Tipping Point: How Little Things Can Make a Big Difference*. Boston: Little, Brown, 2000.

Guder, Darrell, and Lois Barrett. *The Missional Church: A Vision for the Sending of the Church in North America*. Grand Rapids, Mich.: Eerdmans, 1998.

Lewis, Robert, and Rob Wilkins. *The Church of Irresistible Influence*. Grand Rapids, Mich.: Zondervan, 2001.

Lucado, Max. *Cure for the Common Life: Living in Your Sweet Spot*. Nashville, Tenn.: W Publishing Group, 2005.

Malphurs, Aubrey. *Advanced Strategic Planning: A New Model for Church and Ministry Leaders*. Grand Rapids, Mich.: Baker Books, 1999.

Maxwell, John C. *Thinking for a Change: Eleven Ways Highly Successful People Approach Life and Work*. New York: Warner Books, 2003.

McGavran, Donald. *The Bridges of God: A Study in the Strategy of Missions*. New York: Friendship Press (distributor), 1955.

McGavran, Donald. *Understanding Church Growth*. Grand Rapids, Mich.: Eerdmans, 1970.

McGrath, Alister. *Beyond the Quiet Time: Practical Evangelical Spirituality*. Grand Rapids, Mich.: Baker Books, 1995.

McNeal, Reggie. *Practicing Greatness: Seven Disciplines of Extraordinary Spiritual Leaders*. San Francisco: Jossey-Bass, 2006.

Mintzberg, Henry. *The Rise and Fall of Strategic Planning: Reconceiving Roles for Planning, Plans, Planners*. New York: Free Press, 1994.

Newbigin, Lesslie. *The Other Side of 1984: Questions for the Churches*. Risk Book Series, no. 18. Geneva: World Council of Churches, 1983.

Peterson, Eugene H., and Janice Stubbs Peterson. *Living the Message: Daily Help for Living the God-Centered Life*. San Francisco: HarperCollins, 2003.

Peterson, Eugene H. *Run with the Horses: The Quest for Life at Its Best*. Downers Grove, Ill.: InterVarsity Press, 1983.

Peterson, Eugene H. *Under the Unpredictable Plant: An Exploration in Vocational Holiness*. Grand Rapids, Mich.: Eerdmans, 1992.

Quinn, Robert E. *Building the Bridge As You Walk on It: A Guide for Leading Change*. San Francisco: Jossey-Bass, 2004.

Ries, Al, and Jack Trout. *Positioning: The Battle for Your Mind*. New York: McGraw-Hill, 1986.

Rusaw, Rick, and Eric Swanson. *The Externally Focused Church*. Loveland, Colo.: Group, 2004.

Schaller, Lyle E. *The Very Large Church*. Nashville, Tenn.: Abingdon Press, 2000.

Senge, Peter M. *The Fifth Discipline: The Art and Practice of the Learning Organization*. New York: Doubleday/Currency, 1990.

Slaughter, Michael, and Warren Bird. *Unlearning Church: Just When You Thought You Had Leadership All Figured Out!* Loveland, Colo.: Group, 2002.

Southern, Richard, and Robert Norton. *Cracking Your Congregation's Code: Mapping Your Spiritual DNA to Create Your Future*. San Francisco: Jossey-Bass, 2001.

Stanley, Andy. *Visioneering*. Sisters, Ore.: Multnomah, 1999.

Stetzer, Ed, and David Putman. *Breaking the Missional Code: Your Church Can Become a Missionary in Your Community*. Nashville, Tenn.: Broadman and Holman, 2006.

Stone Yamashita Partners. *Chemistry (and the Catalysts for Seismic Change)*. San Francisco: Stone Yamashita Partners, 2001.

Sweet, Leonard. *SoulTsunami: Sink or Swim in New Millennium Culture*. Grand Rapids, Mich.: Zondervan, 1999.

Taylor, Steve. *The Out of Bounds Church?: Learning to Create a Community of Faith in a Culture of Change*. El Cajon, Calif.: Emergent YS, 2005.

Ury, William. *The Power of a Positive No: How to Say No and Still Get to Yes*. New York: Bantam Books, 2007.

Warren, Rick. *The Purpose Driven Church: Growth Without Compromising Your Message and Mission*. Grand Rapids, Mich.: Zondervan, 1995.

Wiersbe, Warren W. *Developing a Christian Imagination: An Interpretive Anthology*. Wheaton, Ill.: Victor Books/SP, 1995.

Willard, Dallas. *Renovation of the Heart: Putting on the Character of Christ*. Colorado Springs, Colo.: NavPress, 2002.

Winseman, Albert L., Donald O. Clifton, and Curt Liesveld. *Living Your Strengths: Discover Your God-Given Talents and Inspire Your Community*. New York: Gallup Press, 2004.

ACKNOWLEDGMENTS

I SEE THE PEOPLE who contribute to my life's work as being like a ride on a Ferris wheel. Some take one loop around the ride and make an unmistakable impact. Others travel with you for years, providing support and sharing the view of the adventure over and over.

My ministry as a consultant-navigator would not have been possible without countless people who have taken short trips with me. I especially want to thank all of the ministry leaders who have opened up their lives and their organizations to me as a trusted co-laborer. Each time you do, I learn a great deal, which I hope will in turn help others.

The words of this book flow from the collective voice of the Auxano team, those with whom I have enjoyed years of riding with some breathtaking views. I am most grateful to Jim Randall and Cheryl Marting, who were co-pioneers in starting our ministry. Many have followed and added invaluable contributions to our approach. Specifically, I want to thank James Bethany, Auxano's creative director; Justin Johnson, Crull Chambless, Jeff Harris, Rich Kannwischer, Dave Saathoff, and Christopher Willard.

The daily wind in my sails during the season of the book's preparation has come from seven people. First, my mother and father, Bill and Lee Mancini, have been consummate encouragers and models of kingdom living. Then my incredible trio, Jacob, Joel, and Abigail, have been more than great children; they have been inquisitive and joyful participants who inspire me constantly. Our frequent Jamba stops and Halo breaks have marked the journey with many laughs. Sixth, their mom, Katrina, still captivates me with her smile, which hardly sees a dim moment. The seventh person is Cheryl Marting, Auxano's chief connection officer and my dear friend.

Cheryl has been a "great storm" of skill, support, and inspiration—more than any other. This book is a testimony to her work as a leader and writer in the process of collaboration. To the degree that this book is helpful, it has come through her consistent push and push-back in expressing thoughts. I am overwhelmingly grateful for her support as a co-laborer in bringing vision and clarity to ministry leaders.

ABOUT THE AUTHOR

WILL MANCINI emerged from the trenches of local church leadership to found Auxano, a first-of-its-kind consulting ministry that focuses on vision clarity. As a "clarity evangelist," he has served as vision architect for hundreds of churches across the country, including the leading churches within Baptist, Methodist, Presbyterian, Lutheran, and nondenominational settings, and for the notable pastors Chuck Swindoll and Max Lucado. Will's style blends the best of three worlds: process thinking from the discipline of engineering, communications savvy as an ad agency executive, and practical theology as a pastoral leader. His education includes a Th.M. in pastoral leadership from Dallas Theological Seminary and a B.S. in chemical engineering from Penn State. He is the coauthor with Aubrey Malphurs of *Building Leaders: Blueprints for Developing Leadership at Every Level of Your Church*. Will resides in Houston, where his favorite diversions are mountain biking and playing Halo with his three kids.

INDEX

A

Abendon, L., 80
Abraham, 71–72
Accountability, fallacy of, 23–24, 26
Actionability Rule, 116, 133–134
Acts 13:36, 85
Acts 17, 87–88
Adair, J., 183
Adam and Eve, 71
Advanced Strategic Planning (Malphurs), xvii, 168
Alignment steps, in vision advancement, 198–206
Analysis, function of, 21–22
APEPT Leadership (apostle, prophet, evangelist, pastor, teacher), 174
Apollo 13 (film), 128
Apostolic esprit, and Kingdom Concept, 94–98, 100–102, 103
Assimilation, concept of, 225
The Attention Economy (Davenport and Beck), 58, 221–222
Attention, importance of, 221–222
Attractional model, of church, 34–35, 37
Attunement: and contributor types, 210–212; definition of, 208–209; and dialogue, 209–210; and positive "no", 212–213
Auxano, xv, 134, 149
Awareness, importance of, 223–224

B

Bandera Road Community Church, 8, 88, 125, 226
Bannockburn Baptist, 9, 96, 125
Barker, J., 44–45
Barna, G., 7, 10–11, 31, 155–156
Barna Group, xvii
Baseball diamond concept, of R. Warren, 148
Beck, J., 221–222
Bell, R., 58–59, 61–62
Bennett, D., 183
Bennis, W., 165
Better intermediate future, 72–73, 171, 176
Bible. *See* Scripture
Blanchard, K., 65
Bonhoeffer, D., 122, 197
Bosch, D., 34
Bottger, J. F., 27–28
Bouquet Rule, 116, 120
Brand, concept of, 222–223
The Bridges of God (McGavran), 29
Bridging behaviors, and clarity gaps, 57
Brochures, assessment of, 139–140
Buckingham, M., 51, 61, 190

Buechner, F., 73–74
Building Leaders (Malphurs and Mancini), 231
Built to Last (Collins), 46
Burning platform, and vision casting, 186–187
BuzzChurch, 13–14, 16

C

Caging, of ministry, 205
Calvary Baptist Church, 144–145, 148
Cannistraci, D., 90
Capital campaign consulting industry, 43
Carroll, J., 24–25
Castle Hills First Baptist Church, 96, 198–199
Catapulting, of ministry, 203–204
Catholic Church, 42–43
Center Point Community Church, 95–96
Chambers, O., 74
Christendom, close of, 32–33
Church effectiveness, 31–33
Church growth movement, 28–39
Clarity: as catalyst, 53–55; complexity factors and, 57–60; four imperatives and, 62–68; gaps in, 55–57; and leadership, 52–53; and Scripture, 70–74
Clarity funnel, 59–60
Clear Creek Community Church, 96
Cole, N., 122
Coleman, R., 71
Collaboration, 64–65, 67, 199–201
Collective potential, and Kingdom Concept, 89–94, 100–102, 103
Collins, J., 22, 46, 99, 104–105, 154
Colonial Heights Baptist, 125
Colson, C., 89
Combining, of ministries, 204
Common denominator, and vision casting, 185–186
"Community without a cause" concept, 45–46
Compelling environments, and Integration Model, 227–229
Compelling page dump, 168–169, 176
Competency trap, 11, 16
Complexity: and clarity, 57–60; fallacy of, 21–23, 26; and four imperatives, 62–63
Conference maze, 14–15, 16
Confessions of a Reformission Rev (Driscoll), xviii
Connection, importance of, 228–229
Conscious culture, and Integration Model, 229–232
Contributizing, of ministry, 204–205
Contributors, types of, 210–212
Cordeiro, W., 7
Core ideals, 46–47
1 Corinthians 6:19, 89
2 Corinthians 5:17-18, 72
Creation story, as vision artifact, 79–80
Creativity, exercises for, 160–161
Crepes, E., 192
Cross-firing ministries, 151–152
Crossroads Community Church, 213
Crozet Baptist Church, 125
Cultural whirlpools, 12–14, 16
Culture, 6–9, 132–135, 229–232
Cutting, of ministry, 205–206

D

Davenport, T., 221–222
Deming, W. E., 66
Demographics, and United States, 12–13
Denominational rut, 15–16
Deuteronomy 8:7-10, 179
Devanna, M. A., 207
Discovery Church, 95, 145–146, 148
Donahue, B., 201
Driscoll, M., xviii
Duplicatable process, and Integration Model, 224–226

E

Eden, Garden of, 70, 71
Effectiveness, and ministry, 31–33
Egoless Clarity, 134
Emmons, M., 151
Enduring organizations, and vision, 46–47
Engel, P., 28
Engine, and leading leaders, 220
Entrepreneurial church, alignment in, 201–202
Ephesians 4:11, 174
Established churches, alignment in, 199–201
Evangelism, 9, 35, 225–226
Eve, and Adam, 71
Everett, E., 21
Exodus 3, 179–180
Exodus 18, 67
Experiences, in common, 8
Ezra, 73

F

Facing the Giants (film), 93
Faithbridge United Methodist Church, 125, 137, 141–143, 148, 176–177, 225
Fallacies, of strategic planning, 20–26
Fast food, for soul, 41–47
Fellowship Bible Church, 158
Fellowship Church, 13–14, 15
First Church Pasadena, 9
First Presbyterian Church (Houston, Texas), 146–147, 148, 161–162
First Presbyterian Church (Midland, Texas), 88
First Presbyterian Church (San Antonio, Texas), 125
Five C's, and Vision Frame, 116, 126–127, 162
Five C's, of persistent modification, 203–206
Five G's statement, of Willow Creek Community Church, 157–158
Focus, importance of, 104–105
Folklore, and shaping culture, 230–231
Ford, H., 54
Four imperatives, and clarity, 62–68
Fox and hedgehog fable, 22–23
Framework, 63–64, 67. *See also* Vision Frame
Frazee, R., 153–154
Frost, M., 174, 226, 229

G

Gallup, G., 31
Gallup Research, xvii
Gaps, in clarity, 55–57
Garden of Eden, 70, 71
Gateway Community Church, 9, 134
Genesis 1-2, 70
Gifts, types of, 8

Global positioning system (GPS), 69–70
Goals, confusion and, 23–24
God: and God smile, 188; and relationship, 70; and vision statements, 170–171, 176
Golden tomorrow, and vision casting, 187
Good Samaritan, parable of, 140
Good to Great (Collins), 22–23
Grace, and group, 90–93
Grace Point Church, 125
Grainger Community Church, 15
Graphic identity, 223
Great Commandment, 105
Great Commission, 9, 85, 105, 120–121
Groeshel, C., 14
Group grace, 90–93
Growth idolatry, 36–39
Guder, D., 33–34, 164

H

Hall of Fame memorabilia, as vision artifact, 81–82
Harris, G., 96
Hedgehog concept, 22–23, 99
Henderson, G., 215–216
Henderson, J., 35
Hendricks, H., 59–60, 78–79
Heritage, type of, 8
Hirsch, A., 174, 226, 229
Holmes, O. W., 62
Homogeneous principle, 30
Hope Baptist Church, 88, 96, 106, 162, 226, 229
Humility, and four imperatives, 67
Hus, J., 86, 93
Hybels, B., 15, 35, 95, 123, 148–149

I

Idolatry, of growth, 36–39
Imagination, and Missional Mountaintop, 182–185
Imago Dei, aspects of, 70
Imperatives, and clarity, 62–68
Incarnational model, of church, 34–35
Indulgences, sale of, 42–43
Integration Model: and compelling environments, 227–229; and conscious culture, 229–232; and duplicatable process, 224–226; and intentional communication, 220–224; and leadership development, 217–220
Intentional communication, and Integration Model, 220–224
Intermediate futures, 72–73, 171, 176
Isaiah 40:8, 80
Israel, 72

J

Jacob, 90–91
Jesus: at end of time, 69; and humility, 67; and meeting needs, 12; and red-letter vision, 117–118; redemptive passion and, 122; and sentness, 120–121; and Sermon on the Mount, 185; and use of metaphors, 183; views of, 89–90
John 4:21-23, 42
John 15, 223
John 17:4, 12
John 20:19-22, 120–121
John of the Cross, Saint, 63
Jones, L. B., 119
Junior High Rule, 116

K

Kannwischer, R., 80–81
Keating, J., 75
Kennedy, A., 105–106
King, M. L., Jr., 185
Kingdom Concept: and apostolic esprit, 94–98, 100–102, 103; and collective potential, 89–94, 100–102, 103; and local predicament, 85–89, 100–102, 103; objections to, 102–107
Kingsland Baptist Church, 105–106
Kouzes, J. M., 111
Krazy George, and the "Wave", 215–216

L

Labeling, 133
Leadership: and APEPT, 174; and apostolic esprit, 94–98; and clarity, 52–53; development of, 217–220; examples of, 8; and need for repentance, 62–68; questions for, 113
Leadership Blinders fallacy, 24–26
Lencioni, P., 190
Less-is-more dynamic, 59–60
Lewis, R., 7, 151
Life Church, 14, 88, 125, 134
Lincoln, A., 21
Lipton, M., 209
Listening, 64, 67, 93, 210
Living language, importance of, 170, 176
Local predicament, and Kingdom Concept, 85–89, 100–102, 103
Lofty one-liner, 169, 176
Logo, 222
Love, missional, 213–214
Loveless, D., 95
Lucado, M., 44, 81, 96, 132
Luke 10, 140–141
Luther, M., 42–43

M

MacDonald, G., 38
Malphurs, A., xvii, 128, 154–155, 168, 231
Mancini, W., 231
Mark, book of, 117–118
Mars Hill Community, xviii
Martha and Mary, story of, 140–141
Maxwell, J., 185
McCaslin, C., 80, 188
McFarland, L., 79
McGavran, D., 27, 28, 29–30, 36
McIntosh, G., 28, 31
McManus, E., 232
McNeal, R., 25, 38, 120, 155
Meant to Live (Switchfoot), 61
Measures. *See* Missional life marks
Megachurches, 14–15
Membership identity, 41–46
Metaphors for Ministry (Bennett), 183
Metaphors, use of, 182–185
Michener, J., 63
Milestones. *See* Missional Milestones
Minatrea, M., 126
Mind stretch, and vision casting, 187–188
Ministry: assessment of, 203–206; and cross-firing, 151–152; effectiveness of, 31–33; options for, 139–141; treadmills in, 10–11, 16

Mintzberg, H., 17
Missio Dei, doctrine of, 34
Mission. *See* Missional mandate
Mission man exercise, 160
Mission statements, 123–125
The Missional Church (Guder), 33–34
Missional church reorientation, 33–35
Missional interviews exercise, 160–161
Missional life marks: benefits of, 153–154; definition of, 152–153; development of, 159–163; examples of, 157–159; practice of, 154–157
Missional love, 213–214
Missional mandate: definition of, 120–121; mission statements and, 123–125; and mission vs. vision, 179–180; redemptive passion and, 122–123; tips for developing, 125–127
Missional map: alignment of, 203; benefits of, 141–147, 150; developmental checkpoints of, 147–149; as different from Missional marks, 159–160; examples of, 144–149; strategy as, 137–141
Missional Milestones: definition of, 189; as quantitative vision, 180–181; questions about, 192; rule of simplicity for, 190; and Vision Frame, 191
Missional motives: benefits of, 129–130; discovery of, 130–132; guidelines for, 132–135
Missional Mountaintop: and essentials of vision casting, 185–188; and imagination, 182–185; as qualitative vision, 180–181; view from, 181
Modeling, 133
Modernity, end of, 32–33
Moravian Church, 93
Morgan Hill Bible Church, 123
Moses, 179–180
Motivation, 9
Multiplication, and kingdom growth, 226

N

Natural Church Development, 32
Navigator's Wheel, 157–158
Needs-based slippery slope, 11–12, 16
Nehemiah, 41, 72–73, 78
New Jerusalem, 70, 71, 73
Newbigin, L., 36
Nite, J., 95–96
Noah, 71–72
North Coast Church, 37, 225
North Point Church, 15, 149

O

Oak Hills Church, 81, 96
Objectivity, and imperative four, 66, 67
One Breath Rule, 116
Osborne, L., 37
The Other Side of 1984: Questions for the Church (Newbigin), 36
Overinformation, flood of, 58

P

Pantego Bible Church, 154, 158
Paradigm shifts, 44–45
Park Place Methodist Church, 96
Pastors, and church identity, 43–44

Paul, Apostle: and collective potential, 89, 90; epistles of, 91; and locality, 87–88; and rescuing role, 72
People, and membership identity, 45–46
People groups, 30
Perimeter Church, 153–154
Persistent modification, and alignment, 203–206
Personality: assessment tools for, 65, 95; of church, 9; and membership identity, 43–44
Peterson, E., 5, 168
Pitman, V., 96, 106
Place, and membership identity, 41–43
Pope, R., 153–154, 156
Post-Christian era, rise of, 32–33, 36
Postmodernity, dawn of, 32–33
The Power of a Positive No (Ury), 212–213
The Power of Vision (Barna), 10–11
Predictability, fallacy of, 24–26
The Present Future (McNeal), 155
Program: and membership identity, 44–45; options for, 139–141
Proverbs 29:18, 40, 41
Purpose, and core ideals, 46–47
The Purpose Driven Church (Warren), 32, 105–106, 148, 168
Purpose-driven emphasis, 105–106
Putnam, D., 31, 32

Q

Qualitative vision, 180–181
Quantitative vision, 180–181

R

Rainer, T., 105, 136, 149
Recovery, from sin patterns, 9
Red-letter maturity exercise, 160
Red-letter strategy, 117–118
Redemption, metaphor of, xxii
Redemptive history, 70–74
Redemptive passion, and missional mandate, 122–123
Relationship, and God, 70
Reorientation, and missional church, 33–35
Repentance, and leadership, 62–68
Resonance Rule, 116, 126
The Return of the King (Tolkien), 235
Revelation 2, 91
Revelation 21:11, 73
Revelation 22:13, 69
Revelation, last chapters in, 70
Rice, W., 66
Romans 1:11, 90
Romans 7:15, 197
Romans 10, 58
Roxburgh, A., 232
Rush, R., 96

S

Saathoff, D., 8
Saddleback Community Church, 14
Sagemont Church, 225
Saint Exupèry, A. de, 178
Schaller, L., xv, xxi, 16, 78–79
Schwartz, C., 32
Scripture: and clarity, 70–74; and group grace, 90–91; role of, 229–230. *See also specific books*

Seidman, D., 215
Sentness, concept of, 34, 120–121
Sermon on the Mount, 185
Service, concept of, 229
Seven-step strategy, of B. Hybels, 148–149
Sherwood Baptist Church, 93
Shupp, J., 96
Silo Builder fallacy, 23–24, 26
Silos, Turf Wars, and Politics (Lencioni), 190
Simple Church, of T. Rainer, 149
Simplicity, and four imperatives, 62–63
Slaughter, M., 215
Small-group movement, 45
Smith, D., 74
Soul fast food, 41–47
Southern Baptists, and evangelism, 35
Southwest Airlines, 104
Space, and membership identity, 41–43
Spider diagram, 185–188
Spiritual leaders, and church identity, 43–44
Spirtual matters, nebulosity of, 58
Staff, selection of, 218–219
Stanley, A., 22, 58, 143, 149
Starbucks, 149–150
Stetzer, E., 31, 32
Stewardship consulting, 43
Stonebriar Community Church, 9
Strategic planning: assessment of, 18–20; fallacies of, 20–26; vs. Vision Pathway, xix
Strategy. *See* Missional map
Strategy icon, 149
Structure, determination of, 219–220
StuckChurch, 14, 16
Success, opportunity of, 58–59
Sugar Creek Baptist Church, 134
Sunday school, 45, 46–47
Surveys, xvii–xviii, 31
Sweet, L., 176
Swindoll, C., 9, 44, 66
Switchfoot, 61
Symbol, role of, 231–232
Synergy, 23–24
Synthesis, function of, 21–22

T

Tagline, 222
Taylor, H., 77
Taylor, J., 96
Teams, working with, 64–65, 67
Ten words or less exercise, 111–112
Thinkholes, 10–16
Thirty core competencies, of Pantego Bible Church, 158
Three environments of the home concept, of A. Stanley, 149
Tichy, N., 95, 207
Timothy, 88
Titus, 88
Tolkien, J.R.R., 235
Tome, B., 213
Tradition, impact of, 8
Truth spots, 155
Tunnel of chaos, 62–63, 107

U

Understanding Church Growth (McGavran), 29
Uniqueness, culture and, 6–9
United States, demographics and, 12–13
Upward, 80, 188
Ury, W., 212

U.S. Mint, 136–137
Utopia, 70–74

V

Values: decision making and, 8–9; and enduring organizations, 46–47. *See also* Missional motives
Values statements, 131
Vinci, L. da, 63
Vision advancement, alignment stages of, 198–206
Vision, and enduring organizations, 46–47
Vision artifacts, 79–82
Vision casting, 175, 185–188
Vision Deck tool, 160–161
Vision Frame: components of, 113–114, 115; definition of, 115; and five C's, 116, 126–127; success of, 114–115; summary of, 167; and ten words or less exercise, 111–112. *See also* Missional life marks; Missional mandate; Missional map; Missional motives; Vision Proper
Vision Integration Model. *See* Integration Model
Vision Pathway: preview of, xx; vs. strategic planning, xix; summary of, 113, 176–177; and Vision Proper, 165–167
Vision Proper: concept of, 113, 115; definition of, 170–171; and mission vs. vision, 179–180; nature of, 165; and vision advancement, 198–206; and Vision Frame, 171–177; and Vision Pathway, 165–167; and vision statements, 167–169. *See also* Missional Milestones; Missional Mountaintop
Vision Shredder fallacy, 21–23, 26
Vision statements, types of, 167–169
Vision vacuum, 40–47
Vocabulary, as artifact, 80–81

W

Wagner, P., 29
Wake-up call, and vision casting, 187
Wal-Mart, 149–150
Warren, R., 15, 32, 105–106, 148, 168, 216
"The Wave", and Krazy George, 215–216
Wayfarer, 64–65
Werlein, K., 137
Wesley, B., 96, 225, 231
Westlake Hills Presbyterian, 125
Whispering legacies, 77–79
Willard, D., 184
Willow Creek Community Church, 14, 35, 157–158
Winchester Mystery House, 40–41
Wood, S., 96
Worship, assessment of, 223
Wyeth, A., 83–84, 97, 106

Y

You, as plural, 89
Young, E., Jr., 14